TALKING, LISTENING, AND LEARNING IN ELEMENTARY CLASSROOMS

Research on Teaching Monograph Series

(continued on last page of book)

TALKING, LISTENING, AND LEARNING IN ELEMENTARY CLASSROOMS

Greta Morine-Dershimer

SYRACUSE UNIVERSITY

Longman
New York & London

Excerpts on pp. 9–10, 11–12, and 133 are from *Language, Schools, and Classrooms,* by Michael Stubbs (London, England: Methuen & Co., 1976), and are reprinted with permission.

Talking, Listening, and Learning in Elementary Classrooms

Longman Inc., 95 Church Street, White Plains, N.Y. 10601
Associated companies, branches, and representatives
throughout the world.

Copyright © 1985 by Longman Inc.

Developmental Editor: Lane Akers
Editorial and Design Supervisor: Naomi Silverman
Production Supervisor: Karen Lumley/Diane Kleiner

Library of Congress Cataloging in Publication Data

Morine-Dershimer, Greta.
    Talking, listening and learning in elementary
classrooms.

        (Research on teaching monograph series.)
        Bibliography: p.
        Includes index.
        1. Education, Elementary.   2. Children—Language—
Research.   3. Elementary school teaching.   I. Title.
II. Series.
LB1028.M645   1986   372   84-23392
ISBN 0-582-28479-1

Manufactured in the United States of America
Printing: 9 8 7 6 5 4 3 2 1 Year: 93 92 91 90 89 88 87 86 85

To **Mort Tenenberg,** my friend and colleague, who was codirector of the research reported here, and who is in a very real sense coauthor of this book, despite his decision not to compose the actual prose.

Contents

Part II
The Construction of Meaning 37

Foreword

In this research monograph Greta Morine-Dershimer, an author well qualified to write on the topic, explores the social meaning of language in naturalistic classroom settings. The study reported in this monograph was conceptualized in the fall of 1977 and data were collected over the following 2 years. Subsequently the author spent another 2 years of reflection and synthesis. This book presents the first complete synthesis of findings from the entire study.

During the 7-year period in which this research was planned and executed, there had been a great deal of interest in classroom research. The author identifies four major approaches to research on teaching, and describes related recent studies (process–product studies; teacher planning and interactive decision making; sociolinguistic/ethnographic studies; and studies of pupil processes), in addition to presenting results of her own research.

The study reported in this monograph is basically a sociolinguistic study; however, it focuses on pupil processing of sociolinguistic information and examines teacher information processing as well. Also, like process–product studies, it examines relationships between classroom interaction and pupil achievement. Thus, the study is an integrated research effort that represents major characteristics of the four dominant paradigms that guide research on classroom teaching today.

Sociolinguists make important distinctions between the correctness and the appropriateness of language use and between the production and the comprehension of appropriate language. Following this tradition, Greta Morine-Dershimer argues that sociolinguistic concepts and findings help to define the problem of investigating participant perspectives on classroom discourse. The classroom is viewed as one social situation among several in which the child participates. It can be expected that the language appropriate to each of these different situations will vary, and that children will have various degrees of communicative competence in each of these various situations.

It seems reasonable that children from different cultural backgrounds may have different assumptions about what is appropriate linguistic behavior in a given classroom situation and that pupils' assumptions may vary from their teachers' assumptions. This suggests that the process of learning the rules of classroom discourse can be illuminated by comparing pupils' conceptions of these rules to their conceptions of the rules of discourse in the other social situations in which they participate (home, playground, etc.).

In particular, the general problem that guided this study was the identification of possible causes of pupil misunderstanding of the rules and processes of classroom discourse and the identification of possible effects of such misunderstanding on school achievement. The task of understanding the meaning that language has for participants in a conversation in any social setting is a difficult one. Because meaning is never directly observable, researchers may either infer meaning from the behavior of the participants or interview participants directly about the meanings they ascribe to events. In this study, both of these procedures were used. However, the author also used another approach, the *indirect* interview technique. This was an attempt to get information on participants' perceptions through indirect means, as well as through direct observation and questioning.

Descriptions derived from three systems of sociolinguistic analysis were first tested against each other, and then synthesized to produce a comprehensive comparison of language use in the six classrooms under investigation. Teacher and pupil perceptions of classroom language were compared and synthesized to develop an understanding of the meanings that participants in these six classrooms ascribed to classroom discourse. These two sets of data were then coordinated to identify possible relationships between language use and language meaning.

The observational aspects of the study focused on how students develop an understanding of who and what to listen to in a discussion and how this understanding shifts as the social situation or the instructional task varies. In addition to studying communication cycles in the classroom, data were also collected in nonschool situations in order to examine students' use of language in informal social situations. This allowed the investigators to explore the possibility that the peer group is an important linguistic influence on children. Indeed, some of the data indicate that when children were asked who they spoke with most often at home, 57% answered my brother or sister, while only 31% said my mother, and only 12% said my father. Clearly, if students' perceptions are correct, they spend much time in social conversation with siblings, much more than they do in conversation with adults.

The author discusses the implications of the results for classroom practitioners, although she is careful to note that her interpretations are only guidelines for considering and analyzing classroom behavior. Still, the findings provide a great deal of practical information that will stimulate teachers' thinking. Among the many topics included in the discussion of the results for practitioners are (1) how to encourage students to believe that they can learn from classroom discussions by listening to the comments of their classmates; (2) teacher actions in conducting lessons that enable pupils to acquire information and to practice processing information within the same lesson; and (3) abilities teachers need to construct lessons in which they can be "winners" in the classroom communication game because varying opportunities are provided for many pupils to participate.

Greta Morine-Dershimer stresses that the value of her research for teachers depends on teachers testing these findings in their own classrooms. In my opinion, practitioners who seriously consider these results and attempt to apply them to their own classroom teaching will find the book extremely valuable. In addition, researchers interested in this topic will develop an enhanced understanding of the methodological problems and strategies related to doing research in this area. I recommend *Talking, Listening, and Learning in Elementary Classrooms* as a valuable and enjoyable learning experience.

Thomas L. Good

Preface

Planning and conducting a descriptive study is rather like weaving a tapestry. The first threads for this particular tapestry were spun in 1959. It was in the early days of the "Bruner era" of curriculum revision. There was excitement in the air, and the most stimulating ideas for me were those about teaching concepts to children by involving them in thinking processes used by specialists to develop knowledge within the discipline itself. I was teaching a gifted class of fourth, fifth, and sixth graders, in a multiethnic school district on Long Island, and my task was to teach them in ways that encouraged their creativity and sharpened their logical abilities. Materials for teaching the "new math" were emerging, but other areas of the curriculum lacked materials conducive to discovery learning. I appealed to Neil Postman, a good friend from college days and a specialist in English education. I described the inductive discovery strategies I was using, and asked if he had any suggestions to offer for using these procedures in teaching language arts. He introduced me to the inductive strategies Hilda Taba was developing for teaching social studies, and to a college textbook by Paul Roberts on structural linguistics. The lessons that I subsequently developed to teach structural linguistics taught me a great deal about the forms and functions of language and sparked a deep and enduring interest in children's conceptions of linguistic phenomena. This interest formed one of the important threads that were eventually woven into the tapestry of this study.

As I was working to master the skills of teaching by discovery methods, it was my privilege to be supervised by Ray Scheele, an anthropologist-turned-educator, who introduced me to classroom observation techniques by helping me to "see" my own interactive behavior objectively. This experience taught me a great deal about myself as a teacher and sparked a deep and enduring interest in the verbal interaction patterns that could be associated with different instructional strategies. This interest formed another important thread in the tapestry.

Between 1959 and 1978, when the study reported in these pages was "officially" begun, many additional threads were gathered as I wandered along what could appear to be a rather meandering professional path. At Teachers College, Columbia University, in 1963, while working on my dissertation, I learned about developmental research on children's thinking. At Hofstra University, in 1966, I began to develop descriptive category systems while teaching student teachers to examine their own interactive behavior. At California State University, Hayward, in 1970, I experimented with videotaping lessons while supervising student teachers in an environmental education program in the Santa Cruz mountains. At Nueva Day School, in 1972, on leave from Hayward, I renewed my explorations of children's concepts of language, while developing new instructional skills in a team-teaching, open-space, open-education setting. At the Far West Laboratory, in 1975, I learned to use a variety of procedures for investigating teacher and pupil thinking about classroom verbal interaction, while directing two special studies in the Beginning Teacher Evaluation Study. All of these experiences were drawn together in the planning of this sociolinguistic study, forming the warp on which the tapestry was woven.

The easy answer to the question, How did you come to do this study? would be that I responded to a request for proposals to conduct sociolinguistic studies of classrooms, a request issued by the National Institute of Education in the fall of 1977. The truth of the matter is that the interests, skills, and research techniques I had developed over many years enabled me to see some of the unique opportunities that were provided by the request for proposals. Certainly the funding support proffered (NIE G-78-0161) was an important factor, for I never could have attempted this study without such support. But the various educational institutions and the students and teachers who provided me with such valuable learning experiences over a 20-year period were an equally important factor. Ultimately, this study was woven out of those experiences.

Greta Morine-Dershimer

Acknowledgments

A number of people have contributed in a variety of ways to the conduct of this study and the preparation of this book and I am grateful to them all. First and foremost was Mort Tenenberg of the California State University at Hayward, who was codirector of the project and who participated extensively in planning for data collection, as well as in data analysis and initial preparation of technical reports. Without his thoughtful participation this study might never have been started, and it certainly could not have been completed in such detail.

Rosedith Sitgreaves, now retired from Stanford University, gave invaluable advice on questions of statistical analysis. Roger Shuy of Georgetown University was a major consultant on the sociolinguistic analysis of the data and was assisted in his analyses by Steve Cahir. Arnulfo Ramirez of the State University of New York at Albany conducted a substudy that provided a speech act analysis of all 36 lessons. Margaret Lay-Dopyera of Syracuse University conducted a substudy that provided a description of children's communication patterns in play settings.

Research assistants who bravely waded with us through the masses of data, contributing important ideas of their own along the way, included Mary Hamilton at the California State University at Hayward and Gary Galluzzo, Fred Fagal, Patricia Graham, and Heather Tully at Syracuse University. The hardy souls who sat on the floor talking with pupils throughout the school year of 1978–1979, and who enabled us to gather a wide variety of rich and relevant data because they so quickly won the trust and cooperation of those pupils, are Susan Lytle, Kitty Norton, Stephanie Gannon, and Greg Nierman.

Kent Viehoever and Virginia Koehler of the National Institute of Education provided advice and assistance in dealing with administrative idiosyncracies of the project. Harold Shatzen (Research Foundation, California State University at Hayward) and William Wilson (Office of Sponsored Programs at Syracuse University) provided assistance in budget matters.

Questions raised by Judith Green during her preparation of a review of NIE-funded sociolinguistic studies helped me to see this study in a broader perspective. Tom Good provided thoughtful suggestions for improvement of this presentation in reviewing the manuscript for the editorial board of this monograph series. Ruth Norton, an experienced teacher and doctoral student, also reviewed the manuscript to judge the clarity and interest it might have for other teachers, and gave many helpful comments.

Production of the manuscript was speeded by the skillful typing of Linda Wozniak, slowed by periodic breakdowns of my second-hand home computer, and smoothed by the understanding and encouragement of my husband and children.

I am indebted to all of these people, but most of all, I owe thanks to the pupils and teachers who shared with me their thoughts about language in classrooms, to the parents, who welcomed me into their homes to videotape their family conversations, and to the principal of the school where I "lived" for more than a year, who provided the support and resources to make me feel at home. I have learned much from all of them and will not soon forget any of them.

TALKING, LISTENING, AND LEARNING IN ELEMENTARY CLASSROOMS

Part I

The Centrality of Meaning

This book is all about the discovery of meaning, but what is meant by *meaning*? The word can mean different things to different people, depending on their point of reference. In this case, *meaning* refers to the interpretation of classroom language by the classroom participants—pupils and teachers. Part I provides some reference points to clarify the meaning of *meaning*, as investigated in this study. It locates the study at a particular point in the development of the field of research on teaching and within a particular set of research traditions, and it indicates the central position that meaning played in the design of the study.

1

Freezing a Moment in Time

In the ordinary course of events, a report of research begins by placing a study within a theoretical and methodological context, and this is accomplished by reporting upon the procedures and findings of prior and contemporaneous studies dealing with the same general topic. This practice enables the reader to interpret the study more accurately, that is, to understand more fully the meaning that the study may hold for the researcher(s) who conducted it and for the field of research in which it is embedded.

The study described here was conceived in the fall of 1977. Data collection began in the fall of 1978 and continued for one year. Two years of data analysis followed, yielding five separate technical reports, each dealing with a different aspect of the study. Another two years of reflection upon and synthesis of selected pieces of the study resulted in several articles and papers. This book, which was begun seven years after the original conception of the study, represents the first complete synthesis of findings for the full study.

During that seven-year period much has happened in the field of research on teaching. At least four major approaches to research on teaching can now be identified, each of which has been prolific enough to merit careful and extensive reviews in recent years. (See, for example, the May 1983 issue of the *Elementary School Journal*, the Fall 1983 issue of the *Educational Psychologist*, and a December 1983 monograph of the American Association of Colleges of Teacher Education entitled *Essential Knowledge for Beginning Educators*.) Process-product studies have identified teaching behaviors that lead to improved pupil achievement (Brophy

1983a; Brophy, 1983b). Information-processing studies have refined techniques of tracing the mental processes of teachers and probed teacher planning and interactive decision making (Shavelson, 1983; Shavelson & Stern, 1981). Sociolinguistic/ethnographic studies have described the complexities of language and culture in the classroom (Green, 1983a; Green, 1983b; Green & Smith, 1983). Studies of pupil processes have examined the classroom from the pupil's perspective and investigated pupil variables as mediators between instruction and learning (Marx, 1983; Weinstein, 1983).

The study reported here was basically a sociolinguistic study, but it focused on pupil processing of sociolinguistic information and examined teacher information processing as well. Furthermore, like process-product studies, it examined relationships between classroom interaction and pupil-achievement gains. Thus it could be said to have at least one foot in each of the four major approaches to research on teaching (which makes it a strange-looking creature indeed).

At the time this study was begun, however, only the area of process-product research was a well-developed approach to the study of teaching. To present here, in this introductory chapter, a review of the current research that is relevant to the methodology and findings of this study would be to provide an inaccurate impression of the field in which the study was actually grounded at the time of its conception. For this reason, the book contains two chapters that review related research: Chapter 8 places the findings of the study within the context of the present (i.e., 1984) state of knowledge derived from research on teaching and this introductory chapter attempts to relocate the reader at the particular point in the development of the field at which this study was begun. Imagine, then, that it is the summer of 1978, and, as Edward R. Murrow was fond of saying, "You are there."

THE NATIONAL RESEARCH AGENDA

In the summer of 1974 some 100 people sweltered for five days, imprisoned at a motel at Dulles Airport outside Washington, D.C. They were researchers and practitioners selected to provide the National Institute of Education (NIE) with an agenda for research and development related to the improvement of teaching. Gary McDaniels of NIE, at the urging of a small group of nationally prominent researchers called together by Ned Flanders of the Far West Laboratory for Educational Research and Development, had decided that substantial input from the field was essential in designing the direction that NIE would take in supporting and encouraging research on teaching. McDaniels selected a format for obtaining that input in an effective and efficient way. It was a format that had been highly productive when used by the National Institute of Health to design an agenda for research on cancer. McDaniels called on Nate Gage of Stanford University to plan and organize a conference where leading researchers in education and other social sciences would work together with teachers and teacher educators to identify issues and suggest essential programs of research to be undertaken. The Dulles Conference was the result.

Many of the conference participants had high hopes that the formation of the National Institute of Education signaled a new era in which the potential value of research on teaching would be more widely recognized and acknowledged. They worked long and hard to generate ideas that would provide a strong framework on which new research could be built. They took a long-range view, anticipating that their ideas would have an impact on studies that might be designed 5, 10, or 15 years in the future. In many instances they were correct in that belief.

Participants at the Dulles Conference were organized into ten panels and each panel was charged with the task of identifying and briefly describing several viable and potentially productive programs of research on teaching. Each panel focused on a different aspect of teaching or teacher education. Panel 5 was the panel on Teaching as a Linguistic Process in a Cultural Setting. It was chaired by Courtney Cazden of Harvard University. This panel, in its final report (Cazden, 1974), recommended six different "approaches" for sociolinguistic research on teaching and identified some specific research programs within two of these approaches. A brief outline of the approaches and programs recommended by this panel is presented in Figure 1.1.

The recommendations of the panels at the Dulles Conference on Studies in Teaching were submitted to the Teaching and Curriculum division of NIE, with the expectation that some of the recommended programs would eventually be funded. That expectation was initially realized in 1976 with the funding of the Institute for Research on Teaching at Michigan State University, after a competition based on the report of Panel 6, on Teaching as Clinical Information Processing (Shulman, 1974). In 1977 the expectation was further fulfilled with the issuance of an NIE grants announcement requesting proposals for research based on the report of Panel 5.

The NIE request for sociolinguistic/ethnographic proposals presented a model of possible causes and effects of inadequate learning of the processes and rules of classroom discourse. Figure 1.2 presents that model, with certain modifications. In this illustration, double lines around two of the boxes indicate the educational "treatment points" and arrows indicate the expected relationships, as identified by NIE. Double arrows leading from one box to another indicate the aspects of the model that were proposed for consideration in the study under discussion here.

I. Determine the rules governing classroom discourse and the relationship between classroom discourse and frame factors in the institutional setting of the school
   A. Investigate the nature of rules governing classroom discourse
   B. Determine ways in which classroom language varies as a function of frame factors (i.e., subject matter, forms of knowledge, task orientation, student and teacher characteristics, time allocation, materials of instruction, physical facilities, size and structure of interaction groups, and administrative structure) and their interaction, in the institutional setting of the school
II. Study the acquisition by students of rules for school discourse
III. Determine the ways in which differences in dialect, language style, and interactional norms affect learning in the classroom
   A. Compare children's interaction patterns in multiple settings, out of school as well as in school
   B. Determine how two languages or dialects are combined in a classroom and how language and dialect differences are exploited for communicative ends through code and style switching (code switching involves including within a single spoken message elements from two distinct grammatical systems; style switching is a similar phenomenon involving changes in vocabulary, rhythm, or tone)
   C. Explore science as a curriculum context for teaching children to use more context-independent speech
IV. Describe and analyze patterns of student-teacher communication in order to determine the effect of the social identity of the participants on the way in which teachers overtly and covertly present information; and analyze the effect of such differential presentations on the acquisition of knowledge and skill
V. Specify the critical components or characteristics of natural communication situations that are necessary for the acquisition of communicative skills in a second language, and that encourage native-language maintenance
VI. Develop and field test materials and procedures to improve teaching, and thereby learning, on the basis of knowledge about linguistic processes in classrooms

FIGURE 1.1 Outline of the report of the NIE panel on Teaching as a Linguistic Process in a Cultural Setting.

This study, as proposed, was designed to

> investigate participant (pupil and teacher) perspectives of the nature of communication in the classroom, describe pupil conceptions of the differences between discourse in the classroom, at home, and at play, examine the correspondence between pupil and teacher conceptions of the rules of classroom discourse, and compare participant conceptions to those of a sociolinguistic specialist in analysis of classroom discourse. (Morine-Dershimer & Tenenberg, 1977, p. 1)

In addition, the proposal promised to examine "pupil acquisition of the rules of classroom discourse, with particular attention to pupil differences in cultural background, academic ability, and grade level, and to teacher-perceived differences in pupils' communicative behavior in the classroom" (p. 1).

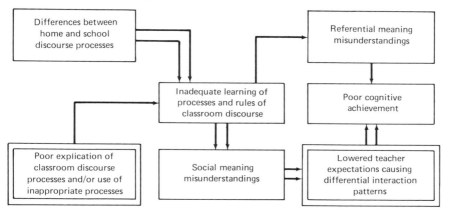

FIGURE 1.2   Model of the causes and effects of inadequate learning of the processes and rules of classroom discourse.

RELEVANT RESEARCH, CIRCA 1977, REVIEWED

In an attempt to preserve historical accuracy and avoid a reinterpretation of the research available in 1977, which would be unavoidably enriched by changes in the knowledge base that have occurred over the past seven years, what is presented here is the actual review of research that was contained within the proposal submitted to NIE. What follows is basically an unedited, unexpurgated, unexpanded version of that review. It is a statement of what knowledge was seen as pertinent by the investigators at the time. (Pertinent research circa 1984 is discussed in Chapter 8.)

The two major areas of research most relevant to the proposed study are classroom research and research on children's language development. Classroom research has expanded within the past several years to include a variety of approaches to collection and analysis of data. At least four different approaches can be identified whose methods and findings have relevance to the design of this study. These are classroom interaction studies, ethnographic studies, sociolinguistic studies, and studies of teacher information processing. Within the field of child development research, both psycholinguistic and sociolinguistic studies of language development have some relevance to this study. Each of these types of studies can provide useful information about communication processes in the classroom, and relevant findings from all of these approaches will be presented here. But special emphasis will be given to sociolinguistic concepts and methods, for it is this approach that responds most directly to the questions that are addressed by this study.

Relevant Sociolinguistic Concepts

The basic question that sociolinguists ask is this: What differences in form, content, and sequence make one sentence different from another with regard to the kind of attitude conveyed, the kind of situation it is (e.g., intimate, formal), the kind of act it is (e.g., request, command), or the kind of person who is talking (e.g., student, teacher)? (Hymes, 1972). Sociolinguists identify the social context as the most powerful determinant of verbal behavior (Labov, 1970; Philips, 1972) and point out that different cultural groups have quite different sociolinguistic assumptions about how and when it is appropriate to talk to different audiences (Boggs, 1972; Dumont, 1972). It has been demonstrated that all speakers are multidialectical or multistylistic (Labov, 1970) and that each adapts his or her style of speaking to the social situation (Bloom & Gumperz, 1972; Cazden, 1970). An understanding of how to use language appropriately in social situations is termed "communicative competence" (Hymes, 1972). It has been suggested that children learn what is socially appropriate linguistic behavior through a process of "cultural transmission" (Bernstein, 1971), in which they acquire "symbolic orders," or ways of organizing experience. Bernstein identifies four critical socializing contexts, which are the regulative (e.g., parental scolding), the instructional (e.g., classroom discussion), the imaginative (e.g., talk during play), and the interpersonal (e.g., conversation between friends).

Sociolinguists make important distinctions between the correctness and the appropriateness of language use, and between the production and the comprehension of appropriate language (Stubbs, 1976). A major problem for speakers of nonstandard dialects in interaction with speakers of standard dialects may be the mutual ignorance of each other's language (Labov, 1970). Dialectical differences may result in social judgments about the speaker (Hammersley, 1974; Shamo, 1970; Wight, 1971, 1975), but they can also function in other ways. Dialects can serve as the focus for powerful feelings of group loyalty (Labov, Cohen, Robins, & Lewis, 1968). Style switching or code switching in the middle of a conversation can serve to signal a change in the situation (Gumperz & Hernandez, 1972; Rainey, 1969).

A problem of concern to some sociolinguists has been the fact that educational failure often appears to result from sociolinguistic differences between teachers and pupils (Stubbs, 1976). There is some evidence that dialectical differences cause educational problems only indirectly (Sinclair, 1973; Wight, 1971, 1975; Wight & Norris, 1970), that is, by affecting the *attitude* of the teacher toward the pupil (Stubbs, 1976). The attitudes that teachers and many other speakers of standard English display toward dialectical differences do not square with the facts. It is not the case that some languages or some dialects within a given language are less complex than others (Labov, 1970, 1972). It is not the case that the linguistic differences among various English dialects are extensive enough to interfere with understanding when speakers of different dialects attempt to communicate (Gumperz, 1971; Labov, 1972). It is not the case that differences in native language imply differences in cognitive ability (Cole & Bruner, 1971; Keddie, 1973).

Taken together, these sociolinguistic concepts and findings help to define the problem of investigating participant perspectives of classroom discourse. The classroom is viewed as one social situation among several in which the child participates. It can be expected that the language appropriate to each of these different situations will vary and that the child will have some measure of communicative competence in each of these varied situations. It is also probable that children from different cultural backgrounds may have different assumptions about what is appropriate linguistic behavior in a given situation and that pupils' assumptions may differ from the teacher's assumptions. This suggests that the process of learning the rules of classroom discourse can be illuminated by comparing pupils' conceptions of these rules to their conceptions of the rules of discourse in the other social situations in which they participate, as well as to teachers' conceptions of classroom discourse rules. In addition, it can be expected that teachers will form judgments about pupils based on their use of language in the classroom, and it is probable that these judgments will affect teacher expectations for pupils. This suggests that teachers' observations and conceptions of pupils' communicative ability need to be examined in more detail.

Relevant Sociolinguistic Methods

Most classroom researchers would agree that "a major problem in studying classroom behavior is that it takes a tremendous effort to really see what *is* happening, rather than simply taking the scene for granted and interpreting it in terms of conventional categories" (Stubbs, 1976, p. 70). Proponents of classroom interaction analysis have dealt with this problem to some extent by having the teacher code the interaction and make his or her own interpretations (Flanders, 1970; Morine, 1975; Parsons, 1968). Ethnographic studies, sociolinguistic studies, and studies of teacher information processing have dealt with it by making a concerted effort to gather data about the participants' interpretations of the behavior, chiefly through a variety of interview techniques. Sociolinguists particularly have emphasized the need to study participant interpretations of the social situations in which language occurs. As Hymes (1972) points out:

> Authority accrues to an investigator from knowledge of a wide range of relevant materials, from mastery of methods of analysis, from experience with a type of problem. But the authority also accrues from mastery of activities and skills, from experience with a variety of language, in a community. An investigator depends upon the abilities of those in the situation, whether it is a question of scientific inquiry or practical application. (p. xv)

Stubbs (1976) argues as follows:

> Research on children and classrooms is usually done by outsiders, but ultimately it is only the participants in a situation who have full access to all its

relevant aspects. Ultimately, a sociolinguistic description of classroom language must come to grips with the values, attitudes, and socially loaded meanings which are conveyed by the language, and only the participants have full access to these values. (p. 76)

In addition to an acknowledgment of the importance of participants' interpretations, two other methodological matters are of concern to sociolinguists engaged in classroom research or studies of language development in children. The first is the problem of studying the "natural situation," a problem for all classroom researchers, for it has frequently been noted that having an observer present in itself creates an unnatural situation. This is particularly true when the *social* setting is what is being studied, for it is the social aspects of the situation that may be most affected by the presence of an outside observer. Pride (1970) underscores this nicely when he points out the difficulties inherent in observing private verbal behavior, for with the presence of an observer, privacy disappears.

Studies differ widely in how closely they sample the natural language setting and in whether they report examples of actual language used. Rather removed from the natural situation are studies where participants' retrospective reports are used as the basic data, supported by observations of a few actual communication events (e.g., Woods, 1975). Children's language in experimental or test situations has been examined in a series of studies (e.g., Brandis & Henderson, 1970; Hawkins, 1969; Heider, Cazden, & Brown, 1968). Mehan (1973) has argued that a child's language ability is not an absolute quality, but rather the outcome of a social encounter, thus suggesting that the test situation itself "constructs" the child's ability and is not a valid measure of his or her actual use of language.

A large preponderance of studies have been conducted through observation of and participation in the natural speech situation. Labov (1970, 1972) in particular has based his work on long-term intensive fieldwork and participant observation in the speech communities he has investigated. He provides detailed analyses of the actual language recorded in these natural settings. A variety of methods are used for recording naturally occurring discourse. Analysis has been based on paper and pencil recordings (Atkinson, 1975; Torode, 1974), transcripts of sound recordings (Bellack, Hyman, Smith, & Kliebard, 1966), the actual sound recordings (Gumperz & Herasimchuk, 1972), and sound recordings supplemented by timed photographic records (Walker & Adelman, 1972, 1975, 1976).

Some investigators observe and report on only one type of social situation, focusing primarily on the classroom or instructional setting (e.g., Atkinson, 1975; Bellack et al., 1966). Gumperz and Herasimchuk (1972) varied the social situation by varying the role relationships when they compared the discourse of an adult teacher with a group of children to a six-year-old teaching a five-year-old child. Several investigators have compared children's language use in two different social situations, thus obtaining further insight into characteristics of classroom discourse. Philips (1972) compared school settings to community settings in her study of Native American children. Boggs (1972) recorded and observed Hawaiian children in lessons, on the playground, and in conversation with an adult observer, and identified different patterns in their speech that corresponded to these different situations. In studying the functions of silence in Sioux and Cherokee classrooms, Dumont (1972) observed children in classrooms and in the community.

Taken in their totality, these studies demonstrate that sociolinguists have made a concerted effort to observe language in natural social situations, to record it as completely and accurately as possible, and to compare classroom language to language used in other social situations in order to better understand the social meaning of classroom discourse.

The second methodological matter of concern has to do with the features of language that ought to comprise the basic data for analysis, and to some extent this appears to be based upon the "whim of the researcher" (Stubbs, 1976, p. 107) as well as upon the problem under study. The selected features have included silence (Dumont, 1972), children's responses to and uses of questions (Boggs, 1972), the topic under discussion (Torode, 1974), talk-about-talk, or "metacommunication" (Atkinson, 1975; Stubbs, 1976), disruptive events (Atkinson, 1975), and instances of miscommunication (Adelman & Walker, 1975). Some studies have used a combination of features, such as words, sentence form, and intonation (Gumperz & Herasimchuk, 1972).

There are relatively few examples where researchers have analyzed classroom language as a *system* rather than focusing on isolated features of the language. Bellack, Hyman, Smith, and Kliebard (1966), Schlegoff (1968), and Turner (1969) are important examples of this approach. Sinclair and Coulthard (1974) have identified a hierarchical structure of classroom discourse in which acts (e.g., elicitation, prompt, nomination) build up into moves (e.g., initiation, response; frame, focus), which combine to form teaching exchanges or boundary exchanges. These exchanges combine to form transactions, and a series of transactions form a lesson.

Stubbs (1975, 1976) has roundly criticized the tendency for researchers to select as evidence any feature of language that strikes them as interesting, and urges the importance of analyzing language as a self-contained system with an inherent organization. In particular, he calls for close attention to language sequences (e.g., sequences of words and sequences of conversational acts) as a critical feature of language organization.

The critical aspects of methodology discussed above have been aptly summarized by Stubbs (1976) in the following statement:

> The demands which one has to make for work on language in education are therefore as follows. The work should be based primarily on naturalistic observations and recording of language in real social situations: mainly in the

classroom itself, but also in the home, and in the peer group, which is the most powerful linguistic influence on children. The work must be based on a linguistically adequate analysis of what is said. This means both being explicit about the relation between language forms and language functions and also analysing the language as linguistic systems. It is not enough, however, for the analysis to be rigorous in a mechanical way: what is required is an analysis of the social meanings conveyed by language and an analysis of people's attitudes to language. Finally, if we are to understand the general principles underlying the sociolinguistic forces at work in schools, the analysis of language in educational settings must be related to what we know of sociolinguistic behavior in other settings.

    These demands are stringent, and . . . no work . . . yet satisfies them on all counts. (p. 112)

These requirements have been echoed in part by Robinson (1968), Hymes (1971), and Adelman and Walker (1975).

    This review of methodology strongly supports the intent of this study to examine the social meanings that pupils and teachers, as important participants in the classroom setting, attach to classroom discourse; to examine teacher judgments about pupils' communicative behavior; to compare pupil conceptions of classroom language to their conceptions of language in other social situations; to engage pupils and teachers as "research assistants" or informants in the analysis of classroom discourse as a linguistic system; and to compare their analyses to that of a specialist in sociolinguistic analysis of classroom discourse.

Relevant Findings from Classroom Research

Although sociolinguistic studies of the classroom are still largely "exploratory work on a relatively narrow range of classrooms" (Stubbs, 1976, p. 90), when the full range of classroom research is considered, a number of important findings can be cited. To begin with, classroom dialogue is asymmetrical, with teachers contributing two-thirds of the language on the average (Flanders, 1970). The question-answer sequence is the most basic pattern of classroom dialogue (Bellack et al., 1966; Sinclair & Coulthard, 1974), and it has been found to be stable over 50 years (Hoetker & Ahlbrandt, 1969) and across different countries (Bellack, 1973). This recitation pattern is one of the characteristics of "direct teaching," and recent studies have provided some evidence of the effectiveness of this strategy (Berliner & Rosenshine, 1976; Rosenshine, 1977).

    However, the question-answer pattern carries different meanings for pupils from different cultural backgrounds (Boggs, 1972; Dumont, 1972; Philips, 1972). Moreover, teachers characteristically use questions that are not genuine requests for information, but are "test questions" (Labov, 1970). The rules of classroom dialogue are quite distinct from those of conversation between social equals (Stubbs, 1976). Such rules may act to inhibit children's use of language by setting up a social situation in which they play a passive role, giving short answers to discrete questions and seldom initiating discussion themselves (Flanders, 1970). There is evidence from several studies that teacher absence can lead to productive and complex discussion among children (Barnes & Todd, 1975; Labov, 1970, 1972; Wight, 1975), and that children follow different rules of discourse in social situations other than the classroom (Boggs, 1972; Dumont, 1972; Philips, 1972). This evidence supports the sociolinguistic thesis that the social situation is the strongest determinant of verbal behavior.

Several distinct functions are served by language in the classroom. Research has explored some of the disciplinary functions (Woods, 1975), language control functions (Atkinson, 1975; Stubbs, 1976), status-definition functions (Torode, 1974), and socialization functions (Jackson, 1968; Snyder, 1971). The effects of pupil language on teacher judgments can be critical. Hammersley (1974) has described how the language of pupils, particularly their responses to questions, can lead to teacher judgments about the intellectual capacity of pupils. Wight (1971, 1975) has demonstrated that children's dialectical differences can also lead to nega-tive teacher judgments about pupil ability (Juskin, 1970; Shamo, 1970). The informal assessments that teachers make as a result of their face-to-face encounters with pupils can lead to decisions that greatly influence the school lives of children (Leiter, 1974; McDermott, 1974; Mehan, 1974; Rist, 1970).

A recent study suggests that several different aspects of the com-municative behavior of pupils may stand out to teachers. Morine-Dershimer (in preparation in 1977; eventually published in 1979a) asked teachers to generate categories that reflected their observations of pupils, and to group pupils on the basis of these categories. At the end of the first day of school, six of the ten teachers studied generated groupings based on pupils' communicative behavior. Almost half of the categories formed by teachers on that occasion related to language use. The behaviors em-phasized, in order of emphasis, were participating in classroom discussion, "talking out of turn," listening attentively, and using nonstandard English. In addition to grouping pupils on the basis of their observations, these teachers were asked to predict pupils' probable success in reading. When teacher predictions made at the end of the first day of school were compared to pupil ranking in reading achievement at the end of the school year, teachers were found to be highly accurate in their predictions at differentiating among "very successful," "successful," and "average" pupils, but not in differentiating "unsuccessful" from "average" pupils. The number of first-day teacher observations with regard to pupils' communicative behavior suggests that teacher expectations for pupils may stem from some of these types of behaviors. It has been demonstrated that teacher expectations are related to patterns of teacher-pupil interaction in the classroom (Brophy & Good, 1969, 1974; Rowe, 1969) and that teacher expectations have an effect on pupil achievement (Beez, 1968; Burnham, 1968; Schrank, 1968).

Teachers' attentiveness to pupils' communicative behavior reflects their general concern with the management of discourse as an important and integral part of the classroom culture. Tikunoff and Ward (1976) studied three teachers intensively in the opening weeks of school. Among them they had established a total of 40 classroom rules by the end of the second week of school. Ten of these, or one-fourth, were rules relating to classroom discourse. All teachers had established rules about listening to the teacher, and about the appropriateness of pupil-pupil talk during instructional activities.

Teachers use language in different ways to establish the classroom culture. One teacher in the Tikunoff and Ward (1976) study stated a rule, then had pupils discuss why it was necessary. Another never stated the rule beforehand, but when pupils violated it, he commented on their violation. Each succeeding infringement drew more extreme language, for example, from "Hey hon, don't move the desk around, please," to, "Blast it, if you move your desks one more time, you're going to see what a temper tantrum is. Have you heard that?"

The research indicates the range of features and functions of classroom discourse that researchers are aware of and concerned about. A few studies have been based on and have utilized the perceptions and concerns of teachers and/or pupils as well. These include Adelman and Walker's (1975) emphasis on miscommunications; Woods's (1975) emphasis on the disciplinary technique of "showing them up," or public embarrassment of pupils; Dumont's (1972) focus on pupil silence; and Boggs's (1972) examination of pupil responses to teacher questions. There have been no studies in which an examination of *pupil* conceptions of classroom discourse has been a major objective.

Teacher beliefs and teacher thinking about children and learning have been studied, under the assumption that these affect teacher behavior and "influence the learning environment that teachers create for children and for themselves" (Bussis, Chittenden, & Amarel, 1976). Relationships between teacher and pupil interactive behavior and teacher thinking about teaching and learning have been examined, and consistencies do exist (Morine-Dershimer, in preparation in 1977; published eventually in 1979b). Pupil and teacher conceptions of interactive *behavior* have also been studied, with interesting results. Morine and Vallance (1975) examined teacher concepts of pupils and pupil concepts of teaching behavior in their study comparing the information processing of more effective and less effective teachers. When pupils observed live and videotaped examples of classroom interaction, identified behaviors they observed, and organized these into groups of "similar" behaviors, it was determined that pupils were selective in their observations and that pupils of both grade levels (second and fifth) and all ability groups (high, middle, and low reading achievement) emphasized cognitive aspects of lessons most heavily. There was a correspondence between pupil observations and teacher observations of classroom interaction in this study. Both pupils and teachers emphasized teacher response to right/wrong answers, management/control of pupil behavior, and selection and organization of examples used by the teacher to convey a concept.

Clearly, both pupils and teachers in this study were alert to many of the features of classroom discourse that have been identified by classroom researchers. Further, this study demonstrated the importance of examining participants' interpretations of the classroom, for pupils differed from teachers in their interpretation of the social meaning of the same situation ("Peter's Problem"), and teachers differed from each other in the values they placed upon the same observed behavior (Morine-Dershimer, 1976). Most importantly, however, this study demonstrated the feasibility of involving pupils directly in the observation and analysis of classroom language and behavior.

Taken together, the research reviewed supports the objectives of the proposed study to examine pupil conceptions of classroom discourse, to compare these conceptions to teacher conceptions of the same discourse, and to inquire whether teachers' observations of pupils' communicative behavior are related to their behavior in interacting with pupils. In addition, the studies cited above identify several features and functions of classroom language that need to be studied from the perspective of the pupil participant.

Relevant Studies of Children's Language Development

Studies of the development of linguistic competence and linguistic performance in children have focused on the biological forces (e.g., Lenneberg, 1969), the interpersonal forces (e.g., Brown & Bellugi, 1964; Cazden, 1972; Ervin, 1965; Slobin, 1967), the acquisition of phonology (e.g., Menyuk, 1971), the learning of morphology (e.g., Berko, 1958), the acquisition of syntax (e.g., Chomsky, 1969; McNeill, 1970; Menyuk, 1969), the development of semantic meaning (e.g., Brown & Berko, 1960; Clark, 1971, 1972; Donaldson & Wales, 1970), the development of body language (e.g., Bugenthal, Love, & Gianetto, 1971; Kagan, 1964; Michael & Willis, 1968), the development of prosodic meaning (e.g., Dimitrovsky, 1964; Fenster & Goldstein, 1971), and the development of proxemic patterns (e.g., Jones & Aiello, 1973).

Psycholinguistic studies have relevance for the proposed study because they demonstrate that children continue to develop competence in language over an extended period of years (Chomsky's 1969 study of acquisition of syntax between 5 and 10 years of age is a good example of this) and because they are based on the assumption that children learn language through an active process of concept acquisition. A variety of methods have been employed to uncover children's linguistic intuitions and to identify the rules that prompt them to use language as they do. Slobin (1971) has outlined five methods, which include checking for regularities in method, testing for the extension of regularities to new instances (e.g., Berko, 1958), looking for the child's self-corrections, asking indirect questions (e.g., Chomsky, 1969), and asking direct questions (e.g., Brown & Bellugi, 1964). Nelson (1973) discusses the effects of children's early conceptions or intuitions on their language learning and presents a detailed model of the interaction between children's and parents' conceptions of the environment, carefully demonstrating the importance of "concept-matching" in children's early attempts to speak. Her analysis supports the suggestion that lack of correspondence between teacher and pupil views of the classroom setting may affect pupil learning of the rules of classroom discourse.

Studies of the development of communicative competence and performance in children have not been as extensive. Several studies have examined social-class differences in the effectiveness of communication in structured tasks such as two-person communication games. Lower-class children have consistently been found to be less explicit in their encoding (child as speaker) and less accurate in their decoding (child as listener) than middle-class children, and to use a style of encoding termed Whole Inferential in contrast to the middle-class child's Part Descriptive (Heider, 1971). These studies have considered the child as speaker (Hawkins, 1969; Heider, Cazden, & Brown, 1968), and as both speaker and listener (Brandis & Henderson, 1970; Glucksberg, Krauss, & Weisberg, 1966; Heider, 1971; Krauss & Glucksberg, 1969). Bernstein (1972) found some crossover of effectiveness. Middle-class children were more explicit in telling stories about a series of pictures, but lower-class children were more willing to role play the pictured situation and to hypothesize about what the person in the picture might be saying. Questions have been raised about the effects of the "test" situation on the accuracy of this picture of children's communicative ability (Stubbs, 1976), but Joan Tough (Cazden, 1972), taping children in play sessions, replicated Hawkins's results.

Some studies have examined children's communication without emphasizing social-class differences. Mueller (1971) videotaped play sessions of young children and found that failure of communication was best predicted by fragmentary or unclear utterances (child as speaker), whereas success was best predicted by the attention or involvement of the listener. Strandberg and Griffith (1968) found that personal involvement of the speaker in photographs being described resulted in greater structural complexity of the description. Labov et al. (1968) obtained similar results in comparing children's narration of television programs and personal experiences.

Several studies have examined children's communication in varied social situations. In addition to the studies mentioned in the earlier section on sociolinguistic methods, Carlson and Anisfeld (1969) and Weeks (1970) found that very young children varied their intonation and pitch to serve different functions in different social situations. Horner (1968) examined the types of language (mands and tacts) young children heard and used when interacting with their mothers and with other children. Verbal behavior appeared to be more patterned or standardized between child and adult than between child and child. Houston (1970) found that black children in rural Florida used a "School Register" in school and with all people in authority over them. The content expressed in this register was limited and did not reveal children's attitudes, feelings, or ideas. A different "Non-School Register" was used in other situations.

These developmental studies support the sociolinguistic thesis that the social situation is the principal determinant of verbal behavior. They also reemphasize the fact that children from different backgrounds may behave differently in the "same" situation.

Relating Developmental Research to Classroom Research

Developmental research has studied the child as speaker and as listener. Classroom research indicates that the child's principal communicative role in the classroom is that of listener rather than speaker (Flanders, 1970). We know that the child as speaker has strong effects on the teacher's attitudes and judgments (Hammersley, 1974; Leiter, 1974; McDermott, 1974; Mehan, 1974; Shamo, 1970; Wight, 1971, 1975). Although correlations exist between use of nonstandard dialects and cognitive features of language, such as vocabulary and language use (Cicirelli, 1969), use of nonstandard English has *not* been demonstrated to be a *causal* factor in school achievement (Cazden, 1972; Stubbs, 1976). However, teacher expectations based on negative judgments of pupils resulting from language differences may have an effect on school achievement (Beez, 1968; Brophy & Good, 1969, 1974; Rist, 1970). We know a fair amount about the kind of language the child as listener hears in the classroom (e.g., Bellack, 1966; Sinclair & Coulthard, 1974; Woods, 1975). We know very little about how the child as listener interprets the language of the classroom. What we do know has been largely inferred from a comparison of the child's behavior in school and in other settings (e.g., Boggs, 1972; Dumont, 1972; Houston, 1970; Philips, 1972). The point has been strongly made that the individual's interpretation of the social situation must be considered if we are to understand the behavior we observe (Hymes, 1972; Psathas, 1968; Stubbs, 1976). It has also been demonstrated that it is possible to tap individual interpretations of classroom behavior using what Slobin (1971) would term "indirect" methods, for example, having pupils identify the items of teacher behavior they observe while participating in a lesson, then group or categorize these items according to their similarities, to reveal the concepts that pupils use in organizing their observations of the classroom (Morine & Vallance, 1975), and having teachers follow the same process with regard to their observations of pupil behavior (Morine & Vallance, 1975; Morine-Dershimer, in preparation in 1977, published in 1979a).

The basic investigative procedures to be used in this study derive from the work of Inhelder and Piaget (1964), Bruner, Goodnow, and Austin (1956), and Ausubel (1963) in studying the processes of concept acquisition. The procedures used by these investigators have been adapted for use as teaching strategies by Taba (1967), Joyce and Weil (1972), and Morine and Morine (1973), among others. They have also been used to investigate the thinking of young children as it affects classroom learning (e.g., Almy & Chittenden, 1966; Formanek & Morine, 1968). The Piagetian procedures have been adapted to investigate pupil and teacher conceptions of classroom interaction (Morine & Vallance, 1975; Morine-Dershimer, in preparation in 1977, published in 1979a). The Piagetian, Bruner, and Ausubel procedures have all been utilized to assist children in analyzing their language, using concepts developed by structural linguists and transformational grammarians (e.g., Morine-Dershimer, Weil, & Vallance, 1976; Postman, Morine, & Morine, 1963; Roberts, 1966). The procedures are well developed and readily applicable to the purpose of this study, that is, to examine pupil and teacher conceptions of classroom discourse and teacher observations of pupils' communicative behavior.

Conclusion

In sum, the research cited above demonstrates that we need to know more about how pupils with different characteristics interpret and develop competence in classroom discourse, about how closely pupil interpretations of the rules of classroom discourse correspond with teacher interpretations, and about how pupils' language in the classroom affects teacher expectations for pupil performance. This proposed research is necessary because the consequences of miscommunication can be bad for children both socially and intellectually, and because a clearer understanding of the separate perspectives of the participants in classroom discourse can eventually help those participants to understand each other more fully. The guidelines for effective research have been clearly stated (Stubbs, 1976). The essentials are naturalistic observation, an analysis of classroom language as a linguistic system, an analysis of the social meanings the participants attach to classroom language, and a comparison of classroom discourse to sociolinguistic behavior in other settings. Methods have been developed that will enable us to identify the concepts pupils and teachers use to interpret classroom language and the differences that teachers observe in pupils' communicative behavior. The need, the guidelines, and the methods all exist. The time is ripe to investigate participant perspectives of classroom discourse.

Investigators	Subjects	Settings	Focus
Cole, Griffin, & Newman	One third-grade class, San Diego, California	Integrated school; classroom setting	Instruction in various types of groups (teacher-directed vs. student-directed; small vs. large; formal vs. informal)
Cook-Gumperz, Gumperz, & Simons	One first-grade and one fourth-grade class, Berkeley, California	Integrated school; classroom, home, and community settings	Discourse in lessons (reading groups, sharing time), among peers (field trips), and between parent and child
Cooper, Ayers-Lopez, & Marquis	One kindergarten and one second-grade class, Austin, Texas	Public school in working-class community; Parochial school; classroom setting	Dyadic interaction with peers during independent work and in experimental learning tasks
Erickson, Cazden, Carrasco, & Guzman	Two first-grade bilingual classes, Chicago, Illinois	Low SES school; classroom setting	Participation structures in formal vs. informal, teacher-led vs. pupil-led, and small vs. large groups; repertoires of individual children
Hymes	Two classes each of fourth, fifth, and sixth grades, Philadelphia, Pennsylvania	Three different schools	Eight substudies: three explored expectations of parents and community, three explored participation/communicative competence of pupils in school/community settings, and two explored writing instruction and written literacy
Merritt & Humphrey	Two classes each of preschool, kindergarten, first, second, and third grades	Private school; classroom setting	Secondary analysis of data collected for an earlier project; communication in servicelike events
Morine-Dershimer & Tenenberg	One second-grade, three third-grade, and two fourth-grade classes, San Jose, California	Integrated school in low SES community; classroom, home, and play settings	Comparison of pupil, teacher, and sociolinguistic specialist's perceptions of units, features, functions, and rules of classroom discourse (in language arts lessons)

FIGURE 1.3 Structural outlines of seven NIE-funded sociolinguistic studies.

SOCIOLINGUISTIC STUDIES LAUNCHED SIMULTANEOUSLY

This proposed study and six other sociolinguistic studies were funded by NIE as part of the 1978 grants program for Teaching and Instruction. These studies, and three others funded in 1979 as Reading and Language Arts studies under the unsolicited grants program, have been comprehensively reviewed by Green for several different audiences (Green, 1983a, 1983b; Green & Smith, 1983). The structural outlines of the seven studies that commenced in 1978 are described briefly in Figure 1.3 (see p. 19) to provide a more complete picture of the research context in which this particular study was embedded when data collection began in 1978. A detailed description of the design and procedures for this particular study is presented in Chapter 2.

2

The Investigation of
Participant Perceptions

FRAMING THE PROBLEM

The General Problem

The study reported here was one of seven sociolinguistic studies funded by the National Institute of Education in 1978 to examine the general question of possible causes and effects of inadequate understanding of the rules and processes of classroom discourse (verbal interaction). Much prior research (see Chapter 1) had suggested that one possible reason for lower achievement of minority group children was a discontinuity between the patterns of language use they had learned at home and those they were expected to follow and understand in the classroom. The seven studies attempted in a variety of ways to describe the classroom language events that might lead to misunderstanding by pupils of different cultural backgrounds (Green, 1983a, 1983b; Green & Smith, 1983).

The Sociolinguistic Perspective

The designation of these studies as sociolinguistic studies placed them within a particular methodological tradition. Sociolinguists study language in the context of the social setting in which it is used. They argue that the social context is the most powerful determinant of verbal behavior (Labov, 1970). An example of this would be the difference in the way you would typically interact with a stranger standing next to you at a football game, compared with the same stranger standing next to you at a cocktail party. In the latter context there would predictably be more direct interaction, and much of it would be centered on an exchange of "identification." In the former context there would be little direct interaction, and most of it would be centered on reactions to the events in the game.

Within the boundaries set by the social context in which language occurs, sociolinguists examine the relationships among social status, participation in discourse (conversation), and interpretation of the meaning of that discourse. For example, imagine a conversation in a kitchen during the preparation of the evening meal (social setting). A mother and a teenaged daughter are conversing (status: parent and child). One of them says, "No, you can't go out tonight" (participation in discourse, or contribution to the conversation). The interpretation of the meaning of that statement will be very different depending on who makes the statement. If the mother says it to the daughter, it will probably be interpreted as a directive, and it may even be seen as a legitimate directive, though this will not be true for all teenagers. If the daughter says it to the mother, it is apt to be interpreted as a sign of disrespect, a challenge to authority. Thus, how we interpret what we hear and, indeed, what we consider appropriate to say, will depend in large part on who is speaking to whom.

One of the unique characteristics of the sociolinguistic approach is the emphasis placed on the interpretation of the meaning of language by those who are participating in a conversation. Many researchers in other traditions have examined relationships between status and participation in verbal interaction. Flanders, for example, coined the "⅔ rule" (1970), noting that ⅔ of the time someone was talking in the classroom, ⅔ of the time that "someone" was the teacher, and ⅔ of the time the teacher was talking, he or she was using "direct" language. In this type of research on classroom language the teacher's dominant status in the classroom and the degree to which verbal utterances by the teacher exceeded those of pupils were directly observable. The designation of the teacher's language as "direct" or "indirect," however, was the outside observer's interpretation of the meaning of that language.

Sociolinguists have placed special emphasis on the need to study participants' interpretations of language occurring in social situations (Hymes, 1972; Stubbs, 1976). This is not an easy task. These interpretations must either be inferred from the subsequent verbal and nonverbal behavior of the participants, or they must be obtained directly by interviewing the participants subsequent to the interaction. Both of these procedures present difficulties, for neither the inference nor the self-report can ever be assumed to recreate exactly the mental processes they attempt to trace. These difficulties notwithstanding, the attempt to gather information about the participants' perceptions can add an important dimension to the analysis of verbal interaction.

A brief example may help to illustrate this added dimension. Take a common occurrence in classroom interaction, such as a child calling out an answer to a teacher's question without waiting to be recognized. In many cases, the teacher will ignore the response and call on someone else to answer the question. He or she may also restate the rule, "Raise your hand." From observation of such a transaction, it is difficult to know whether the child who called out has failed to learn the rule, or knows it but thinks it is unimportant, or is too eagerly involved in the discussion to hold back and wait to be called on. These clearly different attitudes could have very different consequences in terms of the pupil's daily performance and long-term achievement. Knowing which attitude applied could help the observer make more accurate judgments about the teacher's classroom management skills and more accurate predictions about the pupil's achievement. In one such situation in this study a child called out "A horse," in response to the teacher's question, "What animal gallops?" The teacher said, "I need to see your hand," and called on another pupil. Upon viewing this interaction during the videotape playback of the lesson, the student reported, "I started to say 'horse,' but I remembered I had to raise my hand, so I didn't say it." This reconstruction of the event demonstrated that the child not only knew the rule, but was so concerned about violating it that she transformed the incident in her report, even after being confronted by the recorded evidence. Clearly, this kind of information can add new depth to the study of verbal interaction.

When the sociolinguistic approach is applied to the study of classroom language, the social setting of primary interest is, of course, the classroom, and more specifically, the lesson in which verbal interaction occurs. The participants of interest are the teacher and the pupils. Obviously, the teacher holds a different status than the pupils, but it is also the case that individual pupils differ in status within the classroom. In examining participation in verbal interaction during lessons, then, the sociolinguist notes who says what, when, to whom, and this "who" or "whom" includes *which pupils* as well as teacher versus "pupil" in the generic sense. Of central interest is the additional question, Who interprets what how? Is an incorrect response by a high-achieving pupil interpreted differently by the teacher than an incorrect response by a low-achieving pupil? When a teacher says, "Have you finished your work?" is this interpreted as a directive (Get busy!) by a middle-class student, but misunderstood to be a real question by a child from a lower socioeconomic background? These are the kinds of questions a sociolinguist keeps in mind in the investigation of classroom language.

The Research Paradigm

The particular sociolinguistic study of classroom language reported here placed participants' perceptions in a central position in the paradigm that guided the investigation (see Figure 2.1). In this model, pupil and teacher perceptions (interpretations) of classroom language and pupil participation in class discussions were seen as mediating variables between pupil

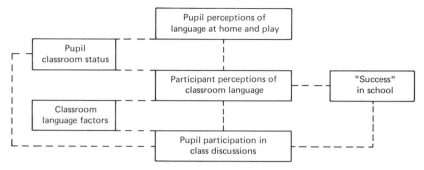

FIGURE 2.1   Paradigm guiding the study.

classroom status, or classroom language factors, and eventual success in school. That is, data were gathered on participant interpretations of the meaning of classroom language and on patterns of pupil participation in language events during lessons. This information was collected in order to provide possible explanations for prior research findings that some individual pupils achieve more than others and that some patterns of classroom language use are associated with greater "teacher effectiveness" in obtaining group gains in achievement. Information on pupil perceptions of language in home and play settings was gathered in order to provide a more complete description of pupil perceptions of classroom language, by contrasting them to pupil interpretations of similar language events in different social settings. The examination of relationships among pupil classroom status, participant perceptions of classroom language, and pupil participation in class discussions reflected the sociolinguists' emphasis on status, participation, and interpretation as critical variables in understanding language within any social setting.

Most of the boxes in Figure 2.1 represent sets of variables rather than individual variables. Figure 2.2 specifies these variables in more detail to clarify specific types of data that were collected. Additional information on specific variables studied is presented in the following section, as well as in Chapters 3 through 6.

METHOD OF INVESTIGATION

The School Setting

The study was conducted from September through June of the 1978–1979 school year in a single elementary school located in an urban area at the southern end of the San Francisco Bay. The community surrounding the school consisted primarily of stable, two-parent families of lower socio-economic status, living in small, well-kept, single-family dwellings. It was a

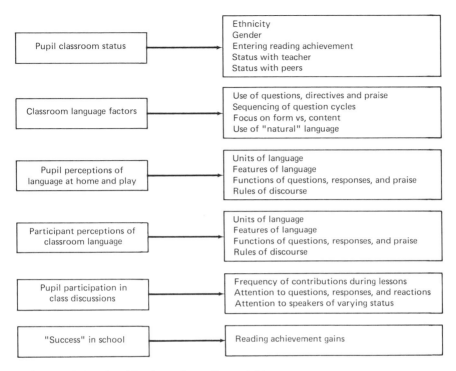

FIGURE 2.2   Identification of specific variables.

multiethnic community. About 45% of the pupils in the school were Mexican-American, 35% Anglo, 11% black, and 9% other minority groups, mainly children of Asian and Portuguese parentage.

The school served kindergarten through fifth-grade children, and there were three classes at each grade level. Teachers all had several years of experience and most had been teaching at the same school for a minimum of three to five years.

Subjects

The subjects were six teachers and 165 pupils in one second grade ($n = 27$), three third grades ($n = 25$, $n = 29$, $n = 29$), and two fourth grades ($n = 27$, $n = 28$). The teachers were all female and one was black. The teachers volunteered to participate and parental permission was obtained for the participation of the pupils. Only one student chose not to participate, so for all practical purposes the study was conducted with intact classes.

It should be noted here that all second-, third-, and fourth-grade teachers in the school were invited to participate in the study in the spring of the year before data collection began. There were three classrooms at each grade level, and two teachers at each grade level agreed to participate. During the summer there was a shift in numbers of pupils enrolling in the second and third grades, and during the first week of school one of the second-grade teachers who had agreed to participate was assigned to teach a newly formed third grade. This unexpected shift in the numbers of pupil subjects at each grade level made it more difficult to examine developmental changes in pupil perceptions of classroom language, as will be seen in later chapters, but did not otherwise affect the design of the study.

Determining Classroom Status

The five classroom status variables considered in this study were gender, ethnicity, entering reading achievement, pupil status with teacher, and pupil status with peers. Gender was readily observable. For most pupils, ethnicity was also easily determined by observation, and subjects were identified as Mexican-American, Anglo, black, or other minority group. In a few instances, school records were checked or teachers were asked about the family background of a pupil, to be certain that accurate designations of ethnicity were recorded.

Entering reading-achievement scores were obtained from results of the Metropolitan Achievement Test (1970), which was routinely administered by all teachers in the school in early October. Within each classroom, pupils were categorized as high, middle, or low in entering reading achievement, based on the mean percentile score and standard deviation for that classroom.

Pupil status with teacher was based on each teacher's grouping of pupils within her classroom, according to several characteristics that had been found to be of importance to teachers in an earlier study in the same school (Morine-Dershimer, 1979a). These characteristics included participation in discussions, attentiveness in class, tendency to follow the "no talking" rules of the classroom, use of "standard English," and probable success in reading. Teacher rankings of pupils on all these characteristics were combined to form a composite score, and each pupil was categorized as high, middle, or low in status with his or her teacher, based on this score in comparison with the scores of other pupils in that classroom.

Pupil status with peers was based on a sociometric device, in which pupils viewed a random array of photographs of their classmates and selected the three pupils most likely and least likely to fit each of several scenarios. The scenarios included the following: those you would choose as participants in a class team for a sports contest; those you would choose as participants in a class team for a television quiz show; those you think would be able to take charge and know what to do in a classroom emergency, if the teacher were out of the room; and those someone would see "hanging around with you" if they watched you on the playground. A composite score was derived for each pupil, according to the number of positive and negative selections he or she received from all other pupils in the class, for all four scenarios. Each pupil was categorized as high, middle, or low in status with peers, based on this score in comparison with the scores of other pupils in that classroom.

Thus, classroom status scores reflected the position of each pupil within the social setting of his or her own classroom and could be used to examine within-class patterns of relationships among status variables, perceptions of classroom language, and participation in class discussions. At the same time, the classroom status *categories* of high, middle, and low for the three acquired status variables (entering reading achievement, status with teacher, and status with peers) could be used to examine patterns of such relationships occurring across all six classrooms.

Language Samples

Samples of language from three familiar social settings were obtained in order to gather information on pupil perceptions of language. The three settings included classroom lessons, family conversations, and play-group interaction. Within the limitations associated with videotaping (e.g., presence of camera and microphone), these language samples were obtained in "naturally occurring situations."

Classroom Language. Six teacher-planned language arts lessons were videotaped in each classroom over the first half of the school year (early September, late September, October, November, December, and January). Teachers were asked to plan a lesson that was directed to the whole class and that involved verbal interaction (i.e., not seatwork, not oral spelling tests). Specific content and instructional procedures were determined by the teacher. The 36 lessons that were videotaped covered a variety of topics (e.g., capitalization, nouns, poetry analysis, creative writing) and a variety of activities (e.g., pantomime, a sensory awareness exercise, textbook exercises).

Each lesson was approximately 30 minutes in actual length. About 12 minutes of each lesson were videotaped, including the introduction (1–2 minutes), a segment of the "middle" (8–10 minutes), and the conclusion (usually very brief). The camera followed the flow of discussion, centering on each speaker and also providing a view of others located in the general area of the speaker. When teacher or pupil use of the chalkboard was a prominent feature of the lesson activities, the videotape included periodic shots of information recorded on the chalkboard.

The videotaped lessons were played back in three 4-minute segments to pupil participants on the same day that they were taught, and pupils were interviewed individually through use of a variety of tasks. The several tasks are described in detail in Chapter 3. A brief description of the initial task should suffice here to give a flavor of the interview. After each lesson segment was played back, the pupil was asked, "What did you hear anybody saying in that part of the lesson?" The response was recorded on a 3 × 5 card, verbatim, and the pupil was asked, "What else did you hear anybody saying?" until no further responses were forthcoming. The next lesson segment was then played, and the same procedure repeated. Teachers were interviewed using the same tasks as the pupils.

Family Conversations. Videotapes of family conversations were made in February of three of the third-grade children (one Anglo, one Mexican-American, and one black). The families were selected because each mother was considered a "leader" by other mothers of the same ethnic group, someone they came to for advice on matters pertaining to family and community life. Each of the three mothers was asked to identify a situation in which family conversations most typically occurred in her home, and those were the situations videotaped.

The conversation in the Anglo family took place in the kitchen after breakfast, as the children were preparing for school, and featured interaction among the mother, a third-grade daughter, a fifth-grade daughter, and a one-year-old baby brother. Language events included the mother asking questions that functioned as directives ("Did you make your beds?"); an argument between the two sisters, with an attempt to draw the mother in ("Mom, she's not doing it right!"); and the younger sister talking baby talk to the infant brother.

The conversation in the black family took place in the kitchen, around the supper table, and featured interaction among the mother, a third-grade daughter, a fourth-grade daughter, and a one-year-old baby brother. Language events included a lengthy report by the third grader on a fight between two boys on the playground in school that day; admonitions by the mother about table manners ("Don't eat so fast"); and attempts by both girls to amuse the baby, who was fussy due to a cold.

The conversation in the Mexican-American family took place in the living room after supper, around the television set, and featured interaction among the mother, the father, a second-grade daughter, a third-grade son, and a son and daughter of high school age. Language events included discussion of the rules of a board game being played by the mother and the two younger children; comments about the evening television news report being watched by the father and the two older children; and code switching by the two older children, who spoke English when addressing the mother and Spanish when addressing the father.

These videotaped conversations were not meant to typify family conversations in each of the three ethnic groups but rather to provide a variety of types of family interaction for pupils in the study to view. A 4–5-minute segment of interaction from each setting was selected for replay to pupils. Selections were made to provide maximum clarity of sound and maximum variety of verbal interaction. In March, these segments of family conversations were played for all pupils in the study, and each was interviewed individually by use of the same tasks as those used with videotapes of classroom lessons.

Play-Group Interaction. In April, a stratified (peer status and gender) random sample of six students from each classroom was videotaped in an unstructured indoor setting, playing with a variety of construction toys. Each of the six separate play groups was videotaped for 30 minutes, after being told that they were free to use the toys in any way they chose.

Different groups initiated different types of activities. The second graders invented a game called "Cat's Eye," which involved competition to see who could be the first to construct a figure from pipe cleaners, with the shout of "Cat's Eye" being the signal that someone was done; but soon everyone was calling "Cat's Eye" regardless of the state of completion of their figure. One third-grade group organized running, jumping, crawling, and rolling races, with accompanying arguments over who cheated by starting before "go" was called. A fourth-grade group began a competition between the girls and the boys to see who could build the tallest tower out of blocks, with ensuing accusations that "you're stealing our blocks" and eventual destruction of each tower by the competing group.

In each of the six groups, play was fairly uninhibited and verbalization was extensive. Children's comments in these settings did not always elicit a response. Much of the language was intended to gain the attention of others or to influence the actions of others, and a wide variety of language forms were used to serve these functions.

Each of these six videotapes was edited down to 12 minutes of interaction, selected for maximum clarity of sound (not a simple task) and variety of play activities. Each videotape was then played for the classmates of the group participating in the play session, and each pupil was again interviewed individually by use of tasks similar to those used with the tapes of classroom lessons and family conversations.

Pupils and Teachers as Observers

In this manner, each pupil was interviewed after viewing three different classroom lessons (early September, October, and December or late September, November, and January), as well as after viewing the videotape of three family conversations (March) and the videotape of classmates at play (April). Each teacher was interviewed after viewing each of the six lessons she taught.

Tasks used in these interviews were designed to gather information on teacher and pupil perceptions of classroom language and on pupil perceptions of language at home and at play. The units of language reported as heard, the features of language identified, the function or purpose of language occurring in question cycles (teacher question, pupil response, teacher reaction), and the "rules" governing language use (who talks when to whom) were the aspects of pupil and teacher perceptions of language that were explored using these videotaped language samples. Procedures associated with exploration of these variables are described in more detail in Chapter 3.

Outside Observers

Although the perceptions or interpretations of pupils and teachers as participants in classroom language were given special emphasis in this investigation, the perceptions of outside observers were also important. In this case the outside observers of classroom language were specialists in sociolinguistic analysis, and the information they provided comprised the data in the box called "classroom language factors" in Figure 2.1. In addition, outside observers who were specialists in child development and early childhood education viewed the videotapes of play settings and provided information on language and interaction occurring in these settings.

Three Analyses of Classroom Language. Three different approaches were used for sociolinguistic analysis of language in the 36 lessons. Each analysis differed in the aspects of language emphasized and in the type of data reported. Each was conducted by a different team of researchers.

The first team, headed by Roger Shuy of Georgetown University, used the most broadly descriptive approach. They viewed each videotaped lesson in turn and identified the linguistic features that were most marked in each lesson, then summarized the features of the six lessons for each teacher, and finally compared the features exhibited by one teacher to those exhibited by others. Thus, the "dimensions of language" that emerged grew out of the behavior exhibited rather than a preconceived category system.

The second team, headed by Arnulfo Ramirez of the State University of New York at Albany, used the most highly delineated category system and the most heavily statistical approach. They worked entirely from written transcripts of the lessons and applied a completely predetermined set of categories in their analysis of the "speech acts" that occurred in these lessons.

The third team, headed by Morton Tenenberg at California State University at Hayward, one of the chief investigators of the overall study, used the approach that emphasized sequences of discourse most strongly. Both the written transcripts and the videotapes were used by this team. A category system developed by Johnson (1979) was adapted to focus on three types of question cycles (a "cycle" includes question, response, reaction), yielding a graphic display of the structure of the lessons according to the sequencing of these cycles.

These three different approaches provided different types of information about the language in these six classrooms, so together they gave a much broader and richer description than any single approach could have given. In addition, the findings from the separate systems tended to corroborate each other, so they combined to strengthen the validity of the "final" description of classroom language factors. The systems and the findings are presented in greater detail in Chapter 4.

Observations of Language in Play Groups. Pupil perceptions of language in play settings were collected to provide a comparison to their perceptions of classroom language in order to understand more fully their interpretations of language in lessons. But similarities or differences in *interpretation* of language in the two settings could not be clearly understood unless it was demonstrated that there were similarities or differences in language *use* in the two settings. Project funds did not allow for detailed sociolinguistic analysis of the play tapes. For this reason, the videotapes of play groups were viewed by 10 outside observers who were specialists in child development and early childhood education (four professors of human development, three experienced classroom teachers of primary-grade children, and three doctoral students in early childhood education).

These outside observers were given no information about the children other than name and grade level. After viewing each videotape, they were asked to record their "predictions" as to the identity of the boys and girls within the play group who were low and high in peer status in their classroom. They were asked also to rank seven types of language events in terms of the frequency with which these language events had occurred within that play setting. The categories included word play, attention getting, information seeking, information giving, directing/influencing, teasing/taunting, and approving/congratulating. Finally, the observers were asked to rate the play group on a five-point scale on the following dimensions: cooperative versus competitive play, imaginative versus nonimaginative or routine use of materials, and variation versus repetitiveness of activities (recall that these videotapes had been edited to provide the maximum amount of variation in activities possible). All ratings were done independently and without any group discussion of perceptions.

The observers showed significant agreement on all three sets of observations (Kendall coefficient of concordance), providing some evidence of the reliability of these observations. The perceptions of the group of observers as a whole were used to provide a description of language use in play settings, and comparisons were made between classroom language events and language events in play settings. In addition, comparisons were made of the perceptions of outside observers, participants in the play groups, and classmates of those participants. These findings are discussed in Chapter 7.

The Technique of Triangulation

By this time, the perceptive reader will have detected an emerging pattern of systematic comparison of alternative perceptions of the same (or similar) interactive events. The technical name for this analytic procedure is *triangulation*. It is a method that has been applied to increase the validity of findings in descriptive studies of classrooms that use participant perceptions as data (e.g., Adelman & Walker, 1975). In this particular study the triangulation method was carried to extremes.

Figure 2.3 depicts graphically the various sets of triangulation that were used as a series of checks, all aimed at constructing as complete and accurate an understanding of the complex reality of the classroom as possible. The construction began (triangle 1) with comparison of three alternative perceptions of classroom discourse (teachers, pupils, and a sociolinguist as outside observer). It proceeded (triangle 2) with a comparison of pupil perceptions of discourse in three alternative settings (classroom, home, and play groups). Next was added the comparison of three different sociolinguists' views of the classroom discourse (triangle 3). Finally, a comparison was made of three alternative perceptions of discourse in play settings (triangle 4).

From this array of data, piece by piece, a coherent picture of discourse in these six classrooms was constructed for use in examining the major relationships under investigation (see Figure 2.1). Of course, the analysis

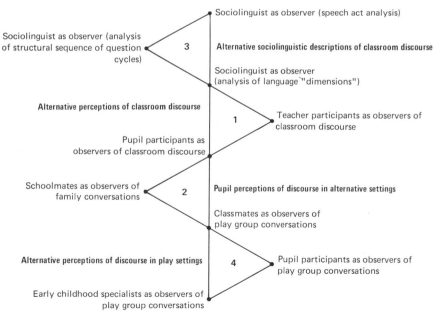

FIGURE 2.3   Triangulation.

did not really proceed in such an orderly fashion. Because participant perceptions of classroom language were considered to be central to the understanding of classroom discourse, triangle 1 (alternative perceptions of classroom discourse) was "revisited" after investigation of each of the other three triangles. Each time such a return visit was made, the data on participant perceptions were viewed from a more inclusive perspective.

The technique of triangulation, thus expanded, was perhaps the most critical and unique feature of the method of investigation employed in this study. It served to control and systematize the analysis of the masses of varied and complex descriptive data that were collected. However, triangulation was not the only important method of analysis used in this study.

Statistical Analyses

Although this was a descriptive study, statistical analyses were employed in a number of ways. Simple descriptive statistics (e.g., means, percentages) served to show general patterns of responses to each of the various data collection tasks. Nonparametric statistics (e.g., chi-square, Friedman's analysis of variance by ranks) were used to examine relationships between categorical variables (e.g., ethnicity and perceptions of the function of teacher questions) or relationships between categorical and quantitative variables (e.g., ethnicity and attention to the comments of peers). Analysis of variance was used to examine the complexity of relationships among pupil-status variables (e.g., entering reading achievement, status with peers) and variables associated with pupil perceptions of classroom language (e.g., units of language reported, features of language identified). Regression analysis (General Linear Model of the Statistical Analysis System computer program) was used to identify factors that contributed to variance in participation in class discussions and "success" in school (final reading achievement, with entering reading achievement controlled for, as recommended by Cronbach & Furby, 1970). The measure of final reading achievement was pupil scores obtained from results of the Metropolitan Achievement Test administered by teachers in October 1979, the year following basic data collection.

ORGANIZATION OF INFORMATION

Part I of this book has presented the framework within which this study was carried out. Chapter 1 explicated the framework provided by prior research on classroom language. Chapter 2 has further delineated the framework provided by the field of sociolinguistics, and has described the design of the study as it took shape within that framework.

Part II of this book presents additional information on procedures used for data collection and analysis in each separate piece of the study, as

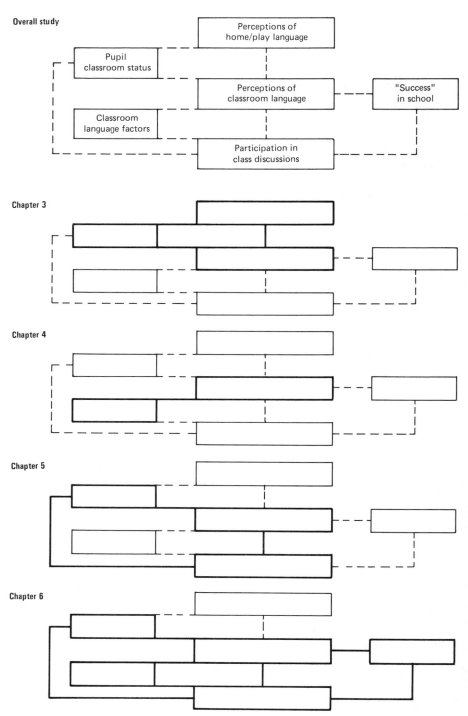

FIGURE 2.4 Development of relationships as reported in Part II.

well as presenting the findings. Each chapter explores a different set of the relationships depicted in Figure 2.1. This progression is illustrated graphically in Figure 2.4.

Chapter 3, The Meaning of Language at Home, at Play, and at School, compares pupil perceptions of language units, language features, language functions, and rules of discourse in the three social settings of classroom lessons, family conversations, and interaction in play groups. These perceptions are examined in relation to pupil status variables. Similarities and differences in the perceptions of different pupils and in the perceptions of different settings are explored. Emphasis is on the meaning of classroom language as revealed by these comparisons.

Chapter 4, Classroom Differences in Language Use and Language Meaning, compares the outside observers' descriptions of classroom language use to the perceptions of teachers and pupils regarding language units, features, functions, and rules of discourse. In addition, classroom differences in both language use and language meaning (participant perceptions) are examined in some detail.

Chapter 5, The Interpretation of Pupil Attention and Participation in Discussions, examines relationships among the three "favorite" variables of the sociolinguist: status (pupil classroom status), participation in discourse (participation in class discussions), and interpretation of discourse (perceptions of classroom language). In particular, pupil patterns of attention and of verbal participation in class discussions are explored, and a system of pupil beliefs about how to learn from class discussions is proposed as one possible explanation for these patterns.

Chapter 6, Talking, Listening, and Learning, traces the relationships of pupil status variables and classroom language factors to success in school, through the mediating variables of pupil perceptions of classroom language and pupil participation in class discussions, and examines these relationships directly. This chapter demonstrates that the mediating variables do provide new and potentially useful interpretations of some processes by which pupil-status variables and classroom language factors may affect school achievement.

Chapter 7, Talking, Listening, and "Succeeding" in Play Settings, explores an area that was not envisioned in the original design of the study, and is not included among the diagrams in Figure 2.4. A comparison is made between patterns of pupil language use in play settings and in classroom lessons. In addition, patterns of relationships among status, perceptions, and participation in discourse in the two settings are examined, and differences are revealed. Observable differences in styles of interaction in the various play groups that correspond to observable differences in patterns of interaction in the six classrooms are also discussed.

Part III of the book addresses what Lee Shulman (1974) has so aptly called the "so what?" question. Chapter 8, Potential Value for Research, considers possible meanings of results for researchers, both from the point of view of providing new insights into prior research findings and with regard to recommendations for questions to be pursued in further studies. Chapter 9, Potential Value for Teachers, considers possible meanings of results for classroom teachers, including recommendations for classroom practice that teachers might wish to test further within their own classrooms.

Part II

The Construction
of Meaning

All meaning is constructed, either consciously or unconsciously. This study involved the careful, step-by-step construction of meaning, in an attempt to understand how pupils and teachers interpreted classroom language and how these interpretations might be related to pupil learning. Part II reconstructs that step-by-step process in the belief that the conclusions of this study cannot be fully understood in isolation from the procedures used in their development.

3

The Meaning of Language at Home, at Play, and at School

UNCOVERING MEANING

The general task of uncovering the meanings that language events have for the participants in conversation in any social setting is not a simple one. Because meaning is never directly observable, investigators may either infer meanings from the behavior of participants or interview participants directly about the meanings they ascribe to the events. In this study, both of these procedures were used to some degree, but in addition, a middle-ground approach was used rather extensively. This third approach might best be described as an *indirect* interview technique. The attempt was to gather information on participants' perceptions through indirect means as well as through direct observation and direct questioning.

The Initial Questions

The general problem addressed by this study was the identification of possible causes of pupil misunderstanding of the rules and processes of classroom discourse, and the identification of possible effects of such misunderstanding on school achievement. As a descriptive study, this investigation could not specify cause-and-effect relationships, but significant correlations could be interpreted as indicators of *possibilities* of such relationships to be investigated further in follow-up studies.

The need to examine pupil *mis*understandings of the rules and processes of classroom discourse suggested an important prior question, What do pupils perceive to *be* the rules and processes of classroom discourse? Until this question was answered, the question of what pupil misunderstandings existed could not be addressed. Until such misunderstandings were identified, the problem of possible causes or effects could not be considered. Thus, the initial task to be tackled was the identification of pupil perceptions of the rules and processes of classroom discourse.

But what "pupil perceptions" ought to be tapped? Clearly this phrase needed further definition. To some extent, that definition came from issues that had for years plagued researchers studying verbal interaction in classrooms.

The first such issue was what constitutes a "unit" of language or verbal interaction. The units measured had varied drastically from one study to another. Flanders (1970) and many others had used time intervals of 3–5 seconds to mark units of interaction to be recorded. Joyce (1975) had used "thought units" as the basic units of interaction. Ramirez (1979) had used clauses as the basic units to be measured. This variation in what researchers perceived to be the units of verbal interaction in classrooms suggested the first type of pupil perception to be tapped. The first question to be raised, therefore, was, What do pupils identify as the units of language in classroom interaction?

The second annoying issue for researchers was what "features" of classroom language ought to be considered most important (studied most closely). Stubbs (1976) had criticized much classroom research because the features identified for investigation appeared to be based upon the "whim of the researcher." For example, Dumont (1972) studied silence, Torode (1974) studied topics discussed, Boggs (1972) studied children's responses to and uses of questions, and Atkinson (1975) examined "metacommunication," or talk about talk. This variation in what researchers perceived to be the important features of classroom language pointed to the second type of pupil perception to be probed. The second question asked was, What do pupils identify as the important features of classroom language?

The third issue of concern to researchers had to do with the difference between form and function in language. It was clear to sociolinguists that the same form could serve several different functions (e.g., a question form could be used to inquire, to direct, or to complain, as in "Why did you decide to go to college?" "Why don't you sit over here?" or "Why does everything happen to me?"). It was also clear that the same function could be served by several different forms (e.g., an intent to direct someone else's behavior could be framed as a command, a request, or a question, as in "Sit down," "Will you please take a seat," or "Is there some reason why you're not in your seat?"). Despite these clear distinctions, some category systems tended to classify classroom language by form rather than function. For example, Flanders (1970) and Bellack et al. (1966) made no distinction between "real" questions and questions to which the teacher already knew the answer, questions that served to test children's knowledge rather than provide the teacher with new information about the child. Other category systems focused on the function served by an utterance without noting differences in form. For example, Ramirez (1979) did not differentiate between questions and requests in identifying speech acts that functioned "indirectly" to manage the behavior of others. This variation in attentiveness of researchers to form-function distinctions indicated a third type of pupil perception that might be productively pursued. The third question asked, then, was, Do pupils perceive distinctions between form and function in interpreting or using language in the classroom?

The fourth question to be asked was more obvious than the first three. Since the basic question was, What do pupils perceive to be the rules and processes of classroom discourse? it seemed sensible to inquire directly, What would pupils identify as *specific rules* that they follow as to "who can say what when to whom" during classroom lessons?

The investigation of pupil interpretations of the meaning of classroom language was therefore defined as the examination of pupil perceptions of the *units*, *features*, *functions*, and *rules* of classroom discourse. But these perceptions could best be understood if they could be compared to perceptions of the units, features, functions, and rules of discourse in other settings, such as family conversations and play-group interaction. Thus, the relationship between pupil perceptions of classroom language (units, features, functions, and rules of discourse) and pupil perceptions of language at home and at play (units, features, functions, and rules of discourse) became the initial topic of investigation addressed in the study.

Tasks for Collecting Information

Five different tasks were used in interviewing pupils in order to gather information to investigate this initial topic. Each task was repeated in relation to each of the three settings (classroom lessons, family conversations, and play-group interaction). Three of the tasks were used in conjunction with the videotapes of actual interaction, and two were independent of the videotapes.

Identifying Units of Language. To determine what pupils would perceive to be the units of classroom language, a very open question was asked (i.e., an *indirect* interview technique was used). As noted in Chapter 2, videotapes of classroom lessons were played back to pupil participants on the same day the lessons were taught. At the end of each 4-minute segment, each pupil was individually asked, "What did you hear anybody saying in that part of the lesson?" The pupil response was rapidly recorded verbatim on a 3 × 5 card, and the pupil was then asked, "What else did you hear anybody saying?" The questioning and recording of responses was continued until no further responses were forthcoming. The next segment of the videotape was then played and the entire procedure repeated. The same process was used with the videotapes of classroom lessons, of family conversations, and of play-group interaction.

Each single pupil response to the question, "What did you hear anybody saying?" was denoted as a "unit" of language identified by that pupil. A special category system was devised to describe the various types of responses given. This system will be presented in a later section.

Identifying Features of Language.

Another indirect technique was used to gather information on pupil perceptions of the features of classroom language. When the entire videotape of a lesson had been played, and all pupil reports of "what anybody said" were recorded, the 3×5 cards thus accumulated were spread out in front of the pupil in a random array, and read back to him or her. The interviewer then said: "These are all things that you heard being said in the lesson, and some of these things are like each other, because people were saying the same kinds of things. Which of these cards do you think belong together because people were saying the same kind of thing?"

The pupil would typically point to or pick up two to four cards that "belonged together," and the interviewer would ask: "What's your idea about these? Why do you think these go together?"

Explanations given by the pupil were recorded verbatim, and a note was made on each 3×5 card to indicate the group in which it had been included. The cards were then replaced in the random array, and the pupil was encouraged to form additional groups: "What other cards do you see that you think belong together because people were saying the same kind of thing?"

Each pupil had an opportunity to form three or more different groups. This task was repeated in the same form with the videotapes of family conversations and play-group interaction.

The groups formed and the reasons given for their formation provided data on the "features" of language perceived by pupils. A category system was developed to describe pupil responses to this task. This system will be explained when results are reported in a later section of this chapter.

Identifying Functions Associated with Certain Forms of Language.

Prior research had indicated strongly that the most basic pattern of classroom language was the "question cycle" of teacher question, pupil response, teacher reaction. Therefore, investigation of pupil perceptions of the functions of classroom language focused on these particular language forms. After the two tasks described above had been completed, the pupil was presented with a set of several (four to six) 3×5 cards, each containing a question asked by the teacher during the lesson. The interviewer said: "Here are some things I heard being said in the lesson. [Cards were read aloud.] Who do you think said these things? ... Who do you think they were talking to? . . . Why do you think they said these things? What reason do you think they had?"

Pupil responses to these questions were recorded. The same procedure was then followed with a set of cards on which were recorded pupil responses to teacher questions, responses that had been given in the videotape just viewed. The same procedure was also followed with a set of cards containing teacher reactions, that is, "praise" statements that had been made during the lesson in reaction to pupil answers.

The original plan of the study was for this task to be used with videotapes of family conversations and play-group interaction as well as with classroom lessons. However, few questions were used in play settings, and these rarely elicited "responses" in the traditional sense, because they were mainly attention-getting devices. Very little praise occurred in either family conversations or play settings. In the absence of this type of interaction in the videotaped settings, it was difficult to check pupil perceptions of it. Accordingly, this task provided information on the functions of questions and responses in both lessons and family conversations, but not in play groups. Information was provided on the functions of praise in lessons only.

Categories were developed to describe the different types of functions identified by pupils. These are presented in the section reporting results of this task.

Identifying Forms Associated with Certain Language Functions.   Another type of task was used to examine pupil perceptions of appropriate forms for particular functions. In this instance, the functions examined were selected because of the high incidence of language associated with these functions exhibited in the play-group settings. In the play-group videotapes, much of the children's language was directed toward getting the attention of playmates and toward influencing playmates to engage in a particular activity (or, in some instances, cease engaging in a particular activity). Therefore, these language functions were examined in more depth.

In an interview that did not occur in conjunction with the showing of a videotape, pupils were presented with a set of sentences that might function as directives, selected because they had appeared in one or more of the videotapes shown earlier and/or had been reported frequently by pupils as language that they heard used in one or more of the three settings. The list contained several different forms (e.g., Let's watch T.V.; Get me the scissors; Did you finish your work?). The sentences were each written on a 3 × 5 card, and cards were presented to pupils in a random array. The interviewer asked, "Which of these things might someone say to you if they wanted to get you to do something?" Cards were selected by the pupil, noted by the interviewer, and returned to the array. This procedure was repeated for each of the following questions:

"Which of these things might your mother or father say to you, if [she or he] wanted to get you to do something?"

"Which of these things might your teacher say to you, if she wanted to get you to do something?"

"Which of these things might your friend say to you, if [he or she] wanted to get you to do something?"

The pupil was then asked to generate additional instances for each setting:

"Can you think of some other things your friend [mother/father, teacher] might say to you, if [he or she] wanted to get you to do something?"

"What would you say to your friend [mother/father, teacher] if you wanted to get [him or her] to do something?"

Responses to each of these questions were recorded.

The same procedures were followed with a set of sentences that might function as attention getters (e.g., Jimmy; Come here a minute; You know what?). Pupils generated additional instances of sentences to serve this function as well. Standard categories of language forms (e.g., command, request, question, suggestion) were used to analyze these responses.

Identifying Rules of Discourse. The task used to investigate pupil perceptions of the rules of discourse was developed in two stages. First, pupils were asked a series of rather open-ended questions: "Suppose a new [boy or girl] came into your classroom, and you wanted to help them understand how people talk in your class. What would you tell them? . . . When do kids talk, and what kinds of things do they say? . . . When does the teacher talk, and what kinds of things does she say? . . . What else would you want to tell a new child about how people talk in your class?"

Pupil responses to these questions were recorded and analyzed. Based on the information that seemed to be pertinent to pupils (types of events commented on most frequently), a set of uncompleted sentences was developed to gather more structured data on pupil perceptions of who talked when, and for what reasons. In a later interview, the sentence stems were read aloud to each pupil, and he or she was asked to "finish each sentence so it will tell something about how you and other people talk in your classroom." The same basic sentence stems were later used to gather information on each of the other two settings (e.g., When my teacher wants me to be quiet, she_____; When my mother wants me to be quiet, she_____; When my friend wants me to be quiet, he or she_____). The sentence stems covered a variety of types of language events (e.g., I don't talk when_____; I ask a question when_____; When I need help, I_____).

Responses to this task were used to identify pupil perceptions regarding who could talk when, how, to whom, and for what reason. Some of the sentence stems provided additional information about pupil perceptions of the functions of questions and praise.

Clarification. These five tasks have been described in some detail because, as any good teacher or researcher knows, the task presented will structure to a great degree the type of response possible. Unless the data collection tasks are clearly understood, the pupil responses (findings of the study) may be misinterpreted. The Appendix presents interview protocols for two third-grade pupils, to provide further detail for interested readers.

It should be noted here as well that, although each task was designed to provide a very specific type of information, the variety of information provided by the various tasks made it possible to examine relationships among responses to different tasks, so that in many instances interpretations of findings from one task were reinforced by findings from another task.

LAYERS OF MEANING

In one sense, uncovering the meaning of classroom language was like excavating an archaeological dig. Responses to each task had to be carefully "dusted off," catalogued, and analyzed before the next task could be "dug." Each progressive task revealed a new layer of information to be studied. As each new layer was uncovered and examined, a greater depth of understanding was acquired.

Each layer of meaning was interesting in its own right, as well as contributing useful knowledge about the total site being investigated. Therefore, the findings will be reported here layer by layer.

Units of Language

The units of language that pupils reported in response to the question, "What did you hear anybody saying?" were coded using a five-category system developed specifically to reflect the types of responses pupils gave. The major categories and examples of actual pupil reports are noted below, together with the conventions developed for recording different types of responses on the 3 × 5 cards.

> **Event:** A report of a nonverbal event, or a verbal event in which none of the actual language used was reported (marked by brackets).
>
> 1. [*One girl raised up her hand.*]
> 2. [*They were mostly talking Spanish.*]

Fragment: A report of a single word or brief phrase that was actually stated as part of a longer utterance (marked by dots).
1. ... games ...
2. ... a little boy ...

Simple Unit: A report of a verbal event given in a form that closely approximated the actual utterance, but provided no information beyond the utterance.
1. How many would like me to put another word up?
2. Before you come up, think of a word.
3. Cowboy.

Compound Unit: A report of a verbal event given in a form that closely approximated the actual utterance, and provided *one* additional piece of information, such as who said it, who it was said to, what was said in response, or what nonverbal event preceded or followed it (who said it noted in parentheses).
1. James, when did you figure out what I was looking for?
2. [Miss DeLuca rang the bell.] Now to do your assignment, you have to write the sentences. There is 14 lines.
3. I'm making Superman. (Raymond said)

Complex Unit: A report of a verbal event given in a form that closely approximated the actual utterance, and provided *two or more* additional pieces of information, such as who said it to whom or who said what in reply.
1. Cheryl, what would you say tomorrow if we asked you what a compound word was?
   Two little words put together to make a new one.
2. Sit down. (Mother said to the baby)
3. I'm gonna tell your mom, Amy. (Raymond said)
   You don't even know my mom's name. (Amy)
   Your mom's name's Karen. (Raymond)
   Huh uh. 'Cause that's my sister's name, and if her name was the same as my mom's, then Karen would be named after my mom. (Amy)

General Patterns of Response. For the most part, pupils reported what they heard people saying in simple units of language. The second most frequently reported type of unit was compound. Table 3.1 shows patterns of pupil reporting for the three classroom lessons each pupil viewed. Table 3.2 shows patterns of reporting over the three settings of classroom, home, and play. The pattern of predominance of simple followed by compound units was repeated for all three lessons and all three settings.

TABLE 3.1. Types of Language Units Reported by All Pupils over Three Lessons (Mean Number of Units per Pupil) ($N = 123$)

	Event	Fragment	Simple	Compound	Complex
Lesson I September	.57	1.13	9.01	2.95	.92
Lesson II mid-fall	.49	.92	8.20	4.80	1.55
Lesson III mid-winter	.33	1.38	7.87	5.68	1.79
Lesson average	.46	1.14	8.36	4.47	1.42

Differences over Time. There was an apparent shift over time toward reporting more compound and complex units of language, and fewer events, as the year went on (see Table 3.1). In other words, pupils seemed to be reporting more actual language and more linguistic information, and using more complicated units in reporting classroom language, as the school year progressed.

In order to examine this apparent shift further, a measure of "information load" was determined by the adding up of all the items of linguistic information contained in the responses of a given pupil (e.g., a simple unit contained one item of information, a compound unit contained two items, a complex unit contained three or more items). A measure of "degree of complexity" was also derived, by division of *information load* by the number of responses (number of units, or 3 × 5 cards) generated by the pupil that stated actual language. The number of "events" reported (no actual language repeated) was also considered, separate from these measures.

Table 3.3 presents a summary of these three measures over time in classroom lessons, together with the results of an analysis of variance. There was a significant increase in both information load and degree of complexity in the units of language reported, as the classroom became more familiar. There was no significant decrease in the number of language events reported.

The additional information that was included, as units of language

TABLE 3.2. Types of Language Units Reported by All Pupils over Three Settings (Mean Number of Units per Pupil) ($N = 123$)

	Event	Fragment	Simple	Compound	Complex
Lesson average	.46	1.14	8.36	4.47	1.42
Play settings	1.60	.80	7.12	5.27	1.22
Family conversations	2.76	1.48	5.80	4.22	1.37
Weighted average over three settings	1.61	1.14	7.09	4.65	1.25

TABLE 3.3. Summary of Means and ANOVA Values: Units of Discourse Measures over Lessons (*N* = 123)

	Time of lesson			ANOVA	Prob. F
	I (*Sept. 78*)	*II* (*Nov. 78*)	*III* (*Jan. 79*)	*F value*	*exceeds*
Number events mentioned	.569	.488	.325	.70	.481
Discourse information load	19.16	24.06	27.22	36.50	.001
Degree of complexity	1.45	1.69	1.82	14.33	.001

reported changed from simple to compound to complex, was information about the *social context* of language use (i.e., who said what to whom, in response to what comment). Therefore, the fact that information load and complexity of units reported increased as the classroom became a more familiar social setting for pupils suggested that pupil awareness of the social context of language increased as familiarity with the social setting increased. (Note 1)

Differences across Setting.   To pursue this matter further, a comparison across settings was made. The classroom settings were considered to be more "familiar" to the pupils than either the play-group settings or the family conversations, because all pupils interviewed had participated in the lessons they viewed. Only six pupils from each classroom actually participated in the play-group interaction, and only three pupils actually participated in the family conversations. Thus, although play-group interaction and family conversation in general would be quite familiar social settings to pupils, the specific instances on which they were asked to report were not so familiar, in the sense that most pupils had not been actual participants in the social interaction.

Table 3.4 presents a comparison of pupil response patterns in lesson and nonlesson (home and play) settings. Information load was significantly higher in the more familiar lesson settings. Degree of complexity was also higher, but not significantly so. Thus, this comparison lent only partial support to the supposition that pupil awareness of the social context

TABLE 3.4. Summary of Means and ANOVA Values: Units of Discourse Measures for Lesson vs. Nonlesson Settings (*N* = 123)

	Lesson	*Nonlesson*	ANOVA *F value*	Prob. F *exceeds*
Events	.46	2.18	73.03	.001
Information load	23.48	21.06	13.44	.001
Degree of complexity	1.71	1.64	2.81	.09

of language might increase along with familiarity with the social setting.

Table 3.4 also shows a significant increase in the reporting of events when nonlessons were viewed by pupils. This difference might best be explained by the degree of formality of the setting. In classroom lessons, turns at talk were carefully controlled by the teacher, and only on rare occasions was more than one person talking at a time. In play-group interaction and in family conversations, it was frequently the case that more than one person was talking at once. Thus, specific utterances were not as easy to detect. The difficulty of identifying specific utterances might help to explain pupil tendencies to report more language events without denoting the specific language used when reporting what was heard in these informal settings.

Individual Differences. When pupil patterns of reporting units of language were examined according to classroom status differences (ethnicity, entering reading achievement, status with teacher, and status with peers), only one significant difference was found. Pupils of low peer status reported units of language that carried a significantly smaller "information load" than pupils of middle or high status with peers (see Table 3.5). Since there was no significant difference in degree of complexity of the units reported, this difference in information load did not mean that pupils of high peer status were reporting more of the social context of the language used. It was the case, however, that high-peer-status pupils reported significantly more actual units of language than low-peer-status pupils.

To understand this finding more clearly, a further analysis was performed. For each pupil, the proportion of pupil comments reported (number of pupil comments "heard" divided by number of pupil comments made in lessons) was computed. These proportions were ranked, and a Kruskall-Wallis analysis of variance was performed (Siegel, 1956). In similar fashion, the proportion of teacher questions reported was analyzed. As Table 3.6 shows, there were significant differences between high- and low-peer-status pupils in their reporting of pupil comments, but not in their reporting of teacher questions. Thus, the tendency of high-peer-status pupils to give more total language information and to report more language units than low-peer-status pupils appeared to derive from their

TABLE 3.5. Summary of Means and ANOVA Values: Units of Discourse Measures by Peer Status Categories ($N = 123$)

	Peer status categories			*ANOVA* *F value*	*Prob. F* *exceeds*
	Low	*Middle*	*High*		
Information load	19.51	23.83	25.97	4.11	.019
Degree of complexity	1.45	1.69	1.72	1.302	.276
Number of units	13.46	14.10	15.10	3.353	.038

TABLE 3.6. Summary of Kruskall-Wallis Analysis: Attention to Teacher Questions and Pupil Comments by Peer Status Levels ($N = 123$)

	Average rank for peer status levels				
	Low (n = 25)	Middle (n = 72)	High (n = 26)	Value of H	Prob. H exceeds
Attention to teacher questions	50.06	63.38	67.02	3.26	.20
Attention to pupil comments	57.84	60.58	71.83	7.21	.05

tendency to report the comments of other pupils more frequently. To put this finding another way, pupils who were highly regarded by their peers tended to be more aware of the units of language contributed by their peers in classroom lessons than were pupils who were not highly regarded by their peers.

The First Layer of Meaning Laid Bare. As a result of digging into the first layer of pupil perceptions of classroom language, then, several interesting facts were uncovered. Pupils reported mainly simple and compound units of language. The information load carried by these units and the degree of complexity of these units increased significantly over time in pupil reporting on classroom lessons. The information load was significantly lower for pupil reporting of family and play-group interaction, compared with classroom lessons. Language units reported by pupils of high peer status carried a higher information load than units reported by pupils of low peer status. High-peer-status pupils also reported more total units of language and proportionately more pupil contributions to the language of these lessons.

These facts were interpreted to suggest that pupil awareness of the social context of language (who says what to whom) increased as the social setting became more familiar, and that pupils who had higher status with peers tended to be more aware of the language contributed by those peers during classroom lessons than did pupils of lower status with peers.

Language events were reported without reference to specific language utterances significantly more often after viewing of informal (home and play) settings than after viewing of classroom lessons. This fact was interpreted to suggest that pupils were less aware of specific language uttered in informal settings where several people were talking at once, and specific comments were not as readily identifiable.

Features of Language

Features of language were investigated by asking pupils, "Which of these things [units of language recorded on 3 × 5 cards] belong together because people were saying the same kinds of things?" The categories that pupils formed in response were coded using a five-category system developed to differentiate among the types of reasons they gave for their formation of groups. The major categories, together with actual examples of the units of reported language that pupils grouped together, and the reasons they gave for these groupings, are presented below.

Elemental: The reason given for forming a group focused on identical letters, words, or phrases.

1. Instances selected:
   a. I think this is how you spell *wart*.
   b. They all shouted, "Wart."

Reason for grouping: Because they both have *wart*.

Structural: The reason given for forming a group focused on features emphasized by the linguistic structure of English, such as relationship of topic (subject) or action (verb), or capacity for sentence expansion.

1. Instances selected:
   a. [When they were building that block thing] Amy, I'm gonna knock down your building. (Raymond said)
   b. [Bobby wrecked mine and Raymond's building.] I'm gonna murder you. (I said)

Reason for grouping: Because they wrecked down things in both of these.

Functional: The reason given for forming a group focused on the form/function of the comments made such as question/asking, statement/telling, or command/directing.

1. Instances selected:
   a. What if I was a person from another planet and I didn't know what a witch looked like. Could you describe it for me?
   b. Let's draw a witch. How can you describe a witch? [She called on Ricky.]
      Scary.
      I don't know how to draw scary, so I'll just write it on the board.

Reason for grouping: She was asking them how to describe a witch.

2. Instances selected:
   a. Sit down.
   b. Don't bring any friends in and don't fight.
   c. Did you clean your rooms?

Reason for grouping: The mother was telling them to do something.

Social: The reason given for forming a group focused on the person involved, such as who said things or who they were said to, or else it referred to an interchange between two people.

1. Instances selected:
   a. Do you know what a mental picture is?
      [She asked Ysa.]
      A mental picture is something that you think in your head. (Ysa said)
   b. There was a Jawa chasing after me. (Ysa)

Reason for grouping: Ysa's talking. It's about the stuff that she seen in her head.

2. Instances selected:
   a. It doesn't look very tall. (Amy said)
   b. So what? We ran out of blocks. (Raymond)

Reason for grouping: Raymond was answering Amy—telling her about the "Empire State Building."

Contextual: The reason given for forming a group included reference to a segment of activity that occurred on the videotape or to the central concept taught in the lesson.

1. Instances selected:
   a. Bill. Let's see what Bill can make.
   b. Gavino, come up and see what he can make.
   c. Robert made *mousetrap*, and that's a fun game, too.

Reason for grouping: Those people went up to make some words (on the felt board).

2. Instances selected:
   a. Doorbell.
   b. Airplane.
   c. Sidewalk.
   d. Bedroom.
   e. Fishhook.
   f. Cowboy.
   g. Milkman.
   h. Fireman.

Reason for grouping: They all have two words. (Lesson concept was compound words)

General Patterns of Response. In grouping the language units that they identified and describing the common features of those units that they thought "belonged together," pupils identified contextual features most frequently. Structural features placed second in frequency of mention. Functional features were the least frequently mentioned. This pattern held across all three lessons, and it was also true for the three settings considered as a group (weighted average—i.e., the three lessons counted only one-third).

TABLE 3.7. Types of Language Features Identified by All Pupils over Three Settings (Mean Number of Features per pupil) (N = 123)

	Elemental	Structural	Functional	Social	Contextual
Lesson average	.76	.82	.17	.28	1.31
Play settings	.58	.76	.24	.89	.72
Family conversations	.55	1.11	.12	.53	.93
Weighted average over three settings	.63	.90	.18	.57	.99

Table 3.7 also presents the figures for the three settings considered separately. Here it can be noted that social features predominated over both contextual and structural features in play settings, whereas structural features predominated over contextual features in family conversations.

To examine these patterns more carefully, three proportional measures were computed: the proportion of *elemental features* identified (average number of elemental groups formed, divided by total groups formed, for each pupil each replay session), the proportion of *linguistic features* identified (average number of structural plus functional groups formed, divided by total groups formed), and the proportion of *social-contextual features* identified (average number of social plus contextual groups formed, divided by total groups formed). The linguistic features were those "forced" on one's attention by the structure and function of the language itself. The social-contextual features were those brought to the foreground of one's attention by the social setting in which the language occurred.

Differences over Time.   If pupil awareness of the social context of language did indeed increase as the social setting became more familiar, then one could conjecture that the social-contextual features of classroom language might also be focused upon more frequently by pupils as the school year progressed. That, in fact, was precisely what happened. Table 3.8 presents these findings, based on Friedman's analysis of variance by ranks. There were significant changes over time in proportionate identification of social-contextual features of language units. There were no significant changes in focus on elemental or linguistic features.

TABLE 3.8. Summary: Analysis of Variance by Ranks for Language Features over Classroom Lessons (N = 123)

	Lesson I September	Lesson II mid-Fall	Lesson III mid-Winter	X_r^2	Prob. X_r^2 exceeds
Elemental features	2.09	1.97	1.94	3.59	.20
Social-contextual features	1.90	2.04	2.07	6.08	.05
Linguistic features	1.93	1.96	2.11	2.06	.50

TABLE 3.9. Summary of Results: Language Features, Lesson vs. Nonlesson
($N = 123$)

	Lesson > nonlesson	Nonlesson > lesson	No difference	Z value	Prob. Z exceeds
Elemental features	54	33	36	2.14	.032
Social-contextual features	61	47	15	1.25	.211
Linguistic features	40	62	21	2.07	.038

Differences across Settings.   Awareness of social context in relation to familiarity with social setting was examined further with regard to differences across settings. The SIGN test was used for this comparison. As Table 3.9 illustrates, social-contextual features were not emphasized significantly more in classroom lessons than in home and play settings, though there was a trend in that direction. Thus, for both units of language and features of language, the classroom data over time supported the possible relationship between awareness of the social context of language and familiarity with the social setting more strongly than did the data comparing classroom and home/play settings.

Table 3.9 also indicates that the linguistic features of language were emphasized significantly more in nonlesson settings, whereas elemental features were emphasized significantly more in lessons. The former finding is not readily explainable, but the latter one is. Focus on elemental features occurred when pupils grouped language units because they contained exactly the same words, or words beginning with the same letters. That is, they focused on the written elements of the language units reported rather than on their social or linguistic meaning. Pupils might reasonably be more aware of these features in classroom settings, because it was in these settings that they were taught to focus on the written elements of language (i.e., they were taught to read).

Individual Differences.   To pursue this possibility further, pupil classroom status differences in identification of language features were examined. There were no significant differences in features identified based on ethnicity, status with teacher, or status with peers, but there were significant differences according to entering reading achievement. Pupils lower in reading achievement were more apt to identify elemental features of language than pupils higher in reading achievement ($r_s = -.293$, $p < .002$). Thus, pupils whose classroom reading instruction was probably more heavily focused on elemental features (e.g., grapheme/phoneme correspondence) emphasized these types of features in their analysis of classroom language (when their reports of oral language were recorded in written form).

Exposing the Second Layer of Meaning. In the uncovering of the second layer of pupil perceptions of classroom language (i.e., the features of language identified), these pertinent facts were revealed: that contextual features were most frequently mentioned, that social-contextual features of classroom language were focused on more frequently as the school year progressed, that elemental features were focused on more frequently in lessons than in home/play settings, and that pupils lower in reading achievement focused more often on elemental features than pupils higher in reading achievement.

These facts lent some additional support to the interpretation of the data on units of language, further emphasizing the possibility that pupil awareness of the social context of language increased in relation to familiarity with the social setting. In addition, it appeared that pupils less adept at reading focused more on the written form of the language units they reported hearing than did more adept pupils. Finally, it was clear by this point in the analysis that pupil perceptions of classroom language were not random or haphazard. This finding suggested that there were indeed certain identifiable patterns of pupil understanding of classroom discourse that could provide a framework for the investigation of pupil *mis*understanding.

Rules of Discourse

Pupil perceptions of the general "rules" governing discourse in classroom lessons supported this contention further. In responding to the sentence-completion task, pupils were reporting their understanding of how people *ought* to behave during lessons. In most areas there was strong agreement on what was the expected form of behavior. The following sentences are illustrative of these patterns of agreement.

Being Quiet and Not Talking
1. When the teacher wants me to be quiet, she ... rings the bell.
2. When the teacher talks, I ... be quiet.
3. I don't talk when ... the teacher's talking.
4. The teacher doesn't talk when ... we're talking.
5. At recess, I talk to ... my friend.
6. When I finish my work, I talk to ... my friend/neighbor.

Getting Information/Assistance/Praise
1. When I want to ask something, I ... raise my hand.
2. When I need help, I ... raise my hand.
3. The teacher says "good" when ... someone gives a good answer.

Asking and Answering
1. If I know the answer to a question, I ... raise my hand.

There were also some areas in which there was not strong pupil agreement about the expected form of behavior. In these instances, there were generally two or three types of responses that were almost equally favored. The following sentences are illustrative.

Being Quiet and Not Talking
1. When I'm doing my work, I talk to . . . the teacher aide/no one.

Asking and Answering
1. I ask a question when . . . the teacher's not talking/I need help.
2. The teacher asks a question when . . . she wants to tell us something/ we're doing math.
3. If I don't know the answer to a question, I . . . don't raise my hand/listen/keep quiet.

The fact that lack of agreement centered on the rules for asking and answering questions suggested that this area might be a prime candidate for pupil misunderstanding of the rules of discourse in lessons. Since prior research (see Chapter 1) had indicated that pupil misunderstandings might stem from differences between expectations at home and at school, pupil reports of discourse rules in home and play settings were examined next.

Discontinuities in Rules across Settings.   It may seem inappropriate to talk about "rules" of discourse in informal settings such as family conversations and play-group interactions, but it is the case that there are certain expectations of appropriate verbal behavior in any ongoing social group. In general, children in this study perceived definite differences in the rules of discourse at school and in more informal settings. For example:

1. When a teacher wanted quiet, she was expected to use a signal (turn out lights, ring the bell), but mothers and playmates were expected to give commands, and they were seen as giving sharp commands (Shut up!) proportionately more often than teachers.
2. Children said that when teachers and mothers talked, they kept quiet, but when playmates talked, they listened.
3. It was expected that children would ask questions at school, home, or play when they needed help, but at school there was the added expectation that they would do this at the "allowed" time.
4. Teachers were expected to ask questions in order to teach (tell), whereas mothers asked when they wanted to know something, and playmates asked when they wanted help.
5. The expectation was that children would directly acknowledge not knowing the answer to a question (say, "I don't know") at home or play, whereas at school the acknowledgment was quite indirect (don't raise my hand/listen/keep quiet).

There were also certain similarities in expectations across settings. For example:

1. Both at home and at school, children expected to talk to friends/siblings when they were playing, or when their work was done.
2. Signaling to get attention before asking for information was essential at school (raise my hand), but getting attention first was also a clear expectation in home and play settings ("Hey, Mom, come here" or "Hey, you guys").
3. Asking questions was seen as a situational activity for mothers as often as for teachers (the teacher asks a question when we're doing math, my mother asks a question when she's cooking supper).

This clear awareness on the part of pupils of the similarities and differences in expectations across settings was reassuring, for children could not function in the school setting if they were not aware of the similarities and differences. A more important question was whether different children perceived these congruencies and discrepancies differently. For pupils in this study, there were no significant differences by either ethnic background or entering reading achievement in pupil perceptions of home-school congruence in the rules of discourse.

The issue of home-school discontinuities was not dropped here, however. Three different types of rules were identified in relation to home-school congruency of expectations. There were rules with fairly high congruency across settings (i.e., *individual* pupils reported the same type of expectation in both instances), such as:

1. When I'm playing, I talk to ... my friend.
2. When my teacher/mother talks, I ... be quiet.
3. My teacher/mother doesn't talk when ... someone else is talking.

There were also several rules with highly agreed-on discrepancies (i.e., individual pupils perceived similar differences in rules in the two settings). For example:

1. If I know the answer to a question, I ... raise my hand (school)/say it (home).
2. When I need help, I ... raise my hand (school)/ask my mom (home).
3. My teacher/mother says "good" when ... *someone* gives a good answer (school)/*I* do something right (home).

There was no confusion about the difference between the two settings in the above instances. However, there were rules for which expectations were muddled, that is, expectations were not similar across settings and in addition, there was no strong agreement among pupils on the specific discrepancies across settings. The expectations that were most muddled for these pupils had to do with questioning. They included the following sentence stems:

1. If I don't know the answer to a question, I....
2. I ask a question when....
3. My teacher/mother asks a question when....

It appeared, therefore, that the area of asking and answering questions might be the most likely candidate in a search for pupil misunderstanding of classroom discourse processes. That is, possible detrimental effects of home-school discontinuities in the rules of discourse might be most readily observed in relation to classroom questioning. Fortunately, the fourth layer of meaning to be uncovered dealt specifically with the functions of questions, responses, and reactions in class discussions.

Functions of Classroom Questioning

Two different tasks were used to examine pupil perceptions of form-function relationships in classroom language. The first task presented pupils with examples of teacher questions, pupil responses, and teacher reactions from the videotaped lesson, and asked, "Who said these things? ... Who were they talking to? ... Why did they say these things—what reason did they have?" Categories were developed to describe the types of language functions pupils identified in response to this last question. The categories and sample pupil definitions coded within each category are presented below.

QUESTIONS

Informative: Questions were asked because the teacher wanted to know something.
1. She wants to know how you would feel.
2. She wants to know what a witch is like.
3. She knows we say things different, and she wants to know what we'll say.

Instruction: Questions were asked because the teacher wanted to tell/teach something, wanted to know if the pupils knew something, or wanted pupils to think.
1. To make us understand.
2. To find out if we knew what to do.
3. To see if we could think harder.

Routine Interactive: Questions were asked to get answers or because "that's what we were doing."
1. She wanted us to answer them.
2. It was in our lesson.

RESPONSES

Informative: Answers were given because pupils wanted the teacher or other pupils to know something.
1. They wanted her to know about the Haunted House.
2. To tell the class what happened.
3. So the kids would know.

Instructional: Answers were given because pupils wanted to learn, or wanted the teacher to know they knew something.
1. To think harder.
2. They're seeing if they're right.
3. To show her they know about a witch.

Routine Interactive: Answers were given because the teacher asked a question.
1. Mrs. Case asked the question.
2. To answer her.

PRAISE

Informative: Teacher praise was given because it was deserved, that is, pupils provided good information or had good ideas.
1. 'Cause the answers were good.
2. Because people were saying good things.

Instructional: Praise was given to help pupils learn or to provide positive motivation.
1. So we can know how to say mental pictures.
2. She wanted them to feel happy.
3. Trying to show us we can do it.

Routine Interactive: Praise was given because pupils participated in the discussion or in order to get pupils' attention.
1. They said an idea.
2. So they'd listen.

Functions of Questions, Responses, and Praise in Lessons. Most pupils readily noted that questions and praise were given by teachers, whereas responses were made by pupils. Table 3.10 shows the percentage of pupils who reported each type of function. Two points stood out clearly.

First, pupils apparently did not view the question cycle (question, response, reaction) in any functionally coordinated way. A coordinated view might say that questions, responses, and praise *all* served an informative function. But the general perception of these pupils was that teachers asked questions in order to *tell* pupils something (instructional), that pupils gave answers because teachers asked questions (routine interactive), and that teachers gave praise because pupils gave good answers, that is, answers that provided correct or useful information (informative). Was this further evidence of a lack of understanding of classroom questioning?

TABLE 3.10. Pupil Perceptions of the Functions of Questions, Responses, and Praise in Classroom Lessons

	Questions (N = 155)	Responses (N = 155)	Praise (N = 139)
Informative	14%	22%	59%
Instructional	43%	8%	23%
Routine interactive	27%	33%	3%
No codable function	26%	38%	15%

The second important point revealed in Table 3.10 was that many pupils could not explain the functions served by questions, responses, and praise in lessons. Most surprising was the fact that more than one-third could not provide a function for pupil responses, since giving answers was the major pupil role in these discussion lessons. This certainly substantiated the idea that classroom questioning could be a source of misunderstanding.

Functions of Questions and Responses in Family Conversations. To pursue this issue further, pupil perceptions of the functions of questions and responses in family conversations were examined. (Praise occurred so infrequently in these videotapes that data on perceptions of praise in home settings were not available from this task.) Table 3.11 presents the patterns of reporting functions in this setting. The lack of functional coordination between question and response was repeated in pupil perceptions of family conversations. Mothers asked questions because they wanted to know something (informative), and children gave answers because questions were asked (routine interactive). Furthermore, many children could not explain the functions of questions and responses in this setting any better than they could in classroom lessons.

The puzzles posed by pupil response patterns were not peculiar to lessons and could not be interpreted as merely a lack of understanding of classroom discourse, though they might suggest a lack of understanding of the functions of question cycles in general. However, the fact that pupils readily identified the very real differences in the functions of questions in lessons and in family conversations, noting that teachers asked questions to

TABLE 3.11. Pupil Perceptions of the Functions of Questions and Responses in Family Conversations

	Questions (N = 158)	Responses (N = 158)
Informative	56%	21%
Influencing	1%	11%
Routine interactive	14%	40%
No codable function	29%	28%

teach something whereas mothers asked questions to learn something (an understanding that was clearly articulated in both the sentence completion task and the "functions" task), suggested that an important degree of understanding of these functions did in fact exist. Further analysis was called for.

Individual Differences in Reporting Functions of Questions, Responses, and Praise. To pursue the matter further, patterns of pupil responses were examined in relation to pupils' classroom status (ethnicity, entering reading achievement, status with teacher, and status with peers). There were no significant differences in pupil perceptions of the functions of questions or responses at school or home for any one of these status variables.

There were significant differences in pupil perceptions of the functions of praise, according to entering reading achievement ($x^2 = 14.39, p < .01$, contingency coefficient or $C = .31$), status with teacher ($x^2 = 11.11$, $p < .05, C = .29$), and status with peers ($x^2 = 16.33, p < .005, C = .33$), but not according to ethnicity. Pupils of high status on each of these variables were more apt to define praise as serving an informative function (i.e., denoting good answers), whereas pupils of low status were more apt to report instructional or interactive functions (i.e., to motivate or reward participation) or to give no codable function.

These clear patterns did not suggest a general lack of understanding of the functions of praise, but suggested rather that teacher praise might be seen as serving different functions for pupils of different classroom status. Prior research, for example, had indicated that high achievers did receive praise for correct answers, whereas lower achievers might receive praise for mere participation (Brophy, 1981). This finding on perceptions of praise prompted further analysis of patterns of reporting the functions of questions and responses in lessons.

Although there were no pupil status differences, there were significant *classroom* differences in pupil reporting of the functions of questions ($x^2 = 30.68, p < .001, C = .41$). In three classrooms questions were reported to serve a primarily instructional function, in one they were perceived as serving an informative function, and in two classrooms one-third of the pupils could give no codable function. There were also classroom differences in teacher *use* of questions as noted by sociolinguistic observers. (These differences are explored in detail in Chapter 4.) Thus, pupil differences in reporting functions of classroom questions might reflect real differences in classroom use of questions.

There were also significant grade-level differences in perceptions of the functions of pupil responses in classroom lessons ($x^2 = 9.8, p < .05$, $C = .25$). Second and third graders were much more apt to give no codable function than were fourth graders, suggesting that there was a developmental factor in pupil ability to explain the function of pupil responses.

Support for Pupil Understanding of the Functions of Question Cycles.
Taken all together, a number of facts suggested that pupils did have some
basic understanding of the functions of questions, responses, and praise in
classroom lessons. They readily distinguished between the instructional
purpose of teachers' questions and the informative purpose of questions in
family conversations. There were significant classroom differences in
functions of questions reported by pupils, and there were also classroom
differences in teacher use of questions, as reported by sociolinguistic
observers. Pupil differences in perceptions of teacher praise were related
to classroom status differences in ways that corresponded to prior research
findings on teacher use of praise. Apparent inability to explain the
functions of pupil responses was related to grade level, but not to
classroom status.

None of these findings showed systematic pupil status differences in
understanding of classroom questioning that might provide useful clues as
to sources of misunderstanding. More importantly, none of the findings
indicated that pupil perceptions of the functions of questions, responses,
and praise were *inaccurate*, in either school or home settings. But the fact
remained that their perceptions of the functions of questions, responses,
and praise in lessons were functionally uncoordinated, because questions
were seen as instructional, responses were seen as routine interactive, and
praise was perceived as informative. Was it possible that this apparently
uncoordinated perception had some inner logic that was not immediately
discernible? This was a question worth considering, but it could not be
answered until more information was available.

Form-Function Relationships

The final task used to reveal pupil perceptions of classroom language
required pupils to generate forms of address that might be used to "get
someone's attention" or "get someone to do something" in school, home,
or play settings. These two language functions were clearly important to
pupils in all three settings.

Pupils generated a wide variety of sentence forms, including commands, requests, suggestions, and questions, as appropriate for serving
both the attention-getting and influencing functions. Within each of the
three settings of school, home, and play, the forms of address identified as
appropriate varied according to the relative status of the speaker and
listener in that social setting. For example, command forms were generated as instances of what mothers and teachers would say to children (Do
your chores now; Go get me some paper), but questions and request forms
were generated as instances of what pupils would say to these adults (Did
you fix my bike yet? Please help me with my work).

In effect this difference in use of forms of address was a way of
acknowledging the differential status positions of the adult and child. In

general, pupils generated forms of address designed to influence others that accorded more differential status to the teacher, relative to the child, than to the mother. But this was not true for all pupils. Pupils low in reading achievement, and blacks and other minority group children (not Mexican-Americans), did not accord as much differential status to the teacher versus the mother in the forms of address used to influence. That is, they did not display as much awareness of a home-school discontinuity here, which suggested that they might not understand the status rules associated with forms of address in formal settings as well as other pupils.

In addition, in the forms of address used to influence others, Anglo pupils and pupils high in reading achievement accorded more differential status to their teacher (relative to themselves) than did Mexican-American pupils or pupils low in entering reading achievement. Of particular interest was the fact that low-peer-status pupils accorded more differential status to their playmates, relative to themselves, than did pupils of middle and high peer status.

These findings indicated that pupils in general were very aware of the relationship between social status and appropriate forms of address in each of the settings most familiar to them, and of the very real differences between appropriate forms of address in school settings compared to home settings. Pupils who did not perceive the appropriate forms of address used to influence others as being very different in the formal versus informal setting tended to be those from minority groups and those who had encountered achievement problems.

Thus, the data on form-function relationships further strengthened the evidence that these pupils in general had a fairly clear understanding of the rules and processes of classroom discourse as well as an understanding of the differences between classroom discourse and discourse in home and play settings. These data also revealed systematic differences in the understanding of forms of address used to acknowledge differential status, and these differences were tied to differences in classroom status.

COORDINATING THE MEANING OF CLASSROOM LANGUAGE

This chapter has examined the data on pupil perceptions of classroom language in order to address the question, What do pupils perceive to be the rules and processes of classroom discourse? In addition, it has examined possible relationships among these perceptions, pupil perceptions of language in home and play settings, and pupil classroom status, in order to identify possible sources of pupil misunderstandings of classroom discourse. Figure 3.1 indicates the place of these major variables within the context of the study as a whole.

The confirmed sociolinguist would undoubtedly be delighted with the

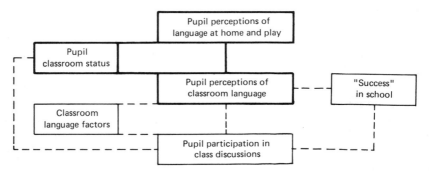

FIGURE 3.1   Initial questions in context of the overall study.

results of this initial phase of the investigation. The sociolinguist argues that social context is the most powerful determinant of verbal behavior, and pupils in this study demonstrated both that they had clear ideas about appropriate behavior in each of the three settings and that their expectations for appropriate behavior did indeed vary from the formal setting of the classroom to the informal settings of home and play. The sociolinguist looks for relationships among social status, participation in social discourse, and interpretation of the meaning of that discourse. The reports of these pupils showed evidence of these types of relationships. Pupils higher in peer status were more aware of language contributed by their peers in classroom lessons (i.e., interpreted it as having special meaning). Pupils high in entering reading, status with teacher, and status with peers interpreted the function (meaning) of teacher praise differently than those lower in status on these variables. Lower achievers and minority group children accorded less differential status to the teacher than other children did in the forms of address they generated to "get her to do something" (participation in discourse). In general, the forms of address used to get attention or influence others clearly acknowledged differential social status in all three settings. Perhaps the most interesting finding to the sociolinguist would be the fact that participant awareness of the social context of language (who said what to whom) appeared to increase as the social setting (the classroom) became more familiar, for this type of awareness would be essential in order for participants to interpret the meaning of discourse in terms of the social status of those who were interacting.

The beleaguered educator might not be so sanguine about these initial results. True, classroom questioning was revealed as a potential area within which pupil misunderstandings of classroom discourse might develop. Many pupils could not explain the functions of questions or responses in either school or home settings. Pupils did not view the elements of the question cycle in any functionally coordinated way. Pupil perceptions of congruencies and discontinuities in rules of discourse at home and school were most muddled with regard to the asking and answering of questions. But there were no clear relationships between these possible misunderstandings and pupil status variables that might be considered to provide clues about sources of these misunderstandings. There were, for example, no significant differences in pupil perceptions of rules or functions of questioning at school, or in perceptions of home-school congruence in rules and functions of questioning, according to either pupil ethnicity or entering reading achievement. If pupil misunderstanding of classroom questioning did exist, it could not be easily tied to variables associated with classroom status differences in pupils.

There were, however, indications that differences in pupil perceptions of the functions of classroom questioning might be explained on other grounds. Pupil inability to give explanations for pupil responses to teacher questions was related to grade level and might be explained in terms of developmental factors in interpretation of discourse. There were classroom differences in pupil perceptions of the functions of teacher questions, and there were also classroom differences in teacher use of questions, as noted by sociolinguistic observers. Perhaps an important source of differences in pupil understanding of classroom discourse was the actual use of language in the classroom by the teacher. This possibility guided the investigation in the second phase of the analysis of data, the analysis of classroom differences in language use and language meaning.

4

Classroom Differences in Language Use and Language Meaning

SOURCES OF DATA

The identification of classroom differences in language use and language meaning involved the analysis and coordination of data from two of the "triangles" that comprised this study. Three alternative approaches to sociolinguistic analysis of classroom discourse were used, and descriptions derived from these three systems were first tested against each other, then synthesized, to produce a comprehensive comparison of language use in the six classrooms under investigation. Teacher and pupil perceptions of classroom language were compared and synthesized to develop an understanding of the meanings ascribed to classroom discourse by the participants in these six classrooms. These two sets of data were then coordinated to identify possible relationships between language use and language meaning.

Systems for Analyzing Classroom Language

The three alternative approaches to sociolinguistic analysis were selected with an eye to maximizing differences in both the analytic procedures and the form of reporting descriptive findings. The analyses were carried out by three different teams of investigators, but in each case the principal investigators of the study provided input to insure that the final descriptions provided data relevant to the major questions under investigation. In particular, each description provided detailed information on classroom questioning patterns, although each approached questioning from a different perspective.

The Language Dimensions Approach. Roger Shuy, of Georgetown University, assisted by Steven Cahir, used the most broadly descriptive approach to analysis. This team viewed each videotaped lesson in turn and identified the linguistic features that were most marked in each lesson, then summarized the features of the six lessons for each teacher, and finally compared the features exhibited by one teacher to those exhibited by others. Thus, the "dimensions" of language that emerged grew out of the behavior exhibited rather than a preconceived category system.

Shuy had strong views about how language *ought* to be used most effectively in classrooms, however, so his descriptions of these six classrooms were presented in comparison to an "ideal type" that was clearly explicated. Shuy argued that talk about content should be emphasized over talk about management; that questioning should follow a probing sequence from more open to more narrow questions, in order for teachers to diagnose pupil understanding before presenting new information; and that effective classroom language in the primary grades should include some elements of "home language," in order to reduce the mismatch between school and home talk styles. This analysis addressed not only language function (questions, management), but also language content (topic) and language style (use of self-referencing, intonation, and naturalness).

The Speech Act Analysis Approach. Arnulfo Ramirez, of the State University of New York at Albany, assisted by three graduate students, used the most highly delineated category system and the most heavily statistical approach. This team worked entirely from written transcripts of the lessons and applied a completely predetermined set of categories in their analysis of the "speech acts" that comprised these lessons.

Speech act analysis (Sinclair & Coulthard, 1974) divides classroom language into exchanges, moves, and acts. An "exchange" can be initiated by either the pupil or teacher and typically consists of three different types of "moves": an opening move (e.g., a teacher question), an answering move (e.g., a pupil response), and a follow-up move (e.g., a teacher praise statement). Each move can consist of one or several "acts." For example, in an opening move, a teacher might give a direction, then provide some information, then ask a question. Each of these would be considered a separate speech act. Speech act analysis focuses primarily on language function as inferred by the outside observer.

In this study, some important but not necessarily common distinctions were made in categories of speech acts. These are noted below.

1. *"Real" versus "known-information" questions*
    A real question was one that might be used in normal conversation, where the person asking the question did not know the answer and was really seeking information from the responder.
    A known-information question was the type more typically used in

classroom questioning, where the teacher asking the question did know the answer and was asking in order to learn whether pupils also knew the answer.

2. *"Personal" versus "nonpersonal" informatives*

A personal informative provided information that reported personal experiences or opinions of the person speaking.

A nonpersonal informative provided impersonal or abstract information (e.g., "a noun is a person, place, or thing").

3. *"Metastatements"*

A metastatement informed pupils about the plan or organization of the lesson and indicated "where we are" in relation to that plan at a given point in time.

Based on these types of distinctions, exchanges, moves, and speech acts were coded for all 36 lessons. Ratios were formed and Friedman's two-way analysis of variance by ranks was used to examine classroom differences and differences over time in patterns of language use. Ratios included pupil-initiated exchanges to teacher-initiated exchanges, real questions to known-information questions, personal informatives to non-personal informatives, indirect management to direct management, praise to accept, and correct/paraphrase to accept.

The Question Cycle Sequences Approach. Morton Tenenberg, of the California State University of Hayward, assisted by Gary Galluzzo, a doctoral student at Syracuse University, used the analytic approach that emphasized sequences of discourse most strongly. Both the written transcripts and videotapes were used by this team. A complex category system (Johnson, 1979) was adapted to form a simpler three-category system, which yielded a graphic display of the lessons, according to the sequencing of question cycles. This system defined three types of cycles in terms of structural relationships.

The "independent," or "topical," relationship was one in which two adjacent question cycles were structurally separate though frequently related by topic. The first cycle was closed out with a reacting move, and a new cycle was begun with a question addressed to a new pupil. The following is an example of this type of relationship.

Question—MRS. ESTES:	On page 106 is a poem that we're going to read and discuss this morning. What is the title of the poem? Elli?
Respond—ELLI:	Antonio.
React—MRS. ESTES:	Antonio.
Question—MRS. ESTES:	And the person who wrote this poem is who? Horace?

| Respond—HORACE: | By Laura E. Richards. |
| React—MRS. ESTES: | By Laura E. Richards. OK. |

The "conjunctive" relationship was one in which two or more question cycles were tied together because the same question was asked of more than one pupil. This could occur when a question was unanswered or was answered incompletely or incorrectly. In these lessons, this relationship was found also to occur when divergent questions were asked and a variety of correct responses were given. An example of this type of relationship, which did involve "incomplete" answers, is given below.

Question—MISS DeLUCA:	What is a sentence? Janie?
Respond—JANIE:	It's a little story.
React—MISS DeLUCA:	It's a little story. OK.
(Same Q)—	(*Nods at Jim*)
Respond—JIM:	It tells you something.
React—MISS DeLUCA:	Jim says it tells us something.
(Same Q)—	Carol.
Respond—CAROL:	It's a little story that starts with a capital letter and ends with a period.
React—MISS DeLUCA:	Starts with a capital and ends with a period.
Question—MISS DeLUCA:	What are the three things we need to make a good sentence, then? Mike?

The "embedded" relationship was one in which one question cycle was contained within another, because the react move involved a new solicitation, as in the case of a probing question, or a question of clarification. The following is an example of this type of relationship.

Question—MRS. FLOOD:	Has anyone here ever accidentally swallowed anything? John?
Respond—JOHN:	Dirt.
React (Question)—MRS. FLOOD:	How did you do that?
(Respond)—JOHN:	Climbing up a hill on my motorcycle and I hit a rock and uh ... the front wheel popped up and I turned around so the bike wouldn't fall, but it fell on me and my head hit the dirt, and I ate some dirt.
(React)—MRS. FLOOD:	Your face told me how you liked the taste of that. (laughter)

In diagramming lessons, each of the three cycle types was displayed in a different manner. A series of topical or independent question cycles was displayed in a vertical sequence, as below:

1
2
3

A series of conjunctive cycles was displayed in a horizontal sequence as follows:

1 2 3 4

An embedded cycle was shown as a subscript. Thus, a single probing question occurring in reaction to one response in a conjunctive series would be diagrammed this way:

1 2 3_1 4

A series of three probing questions occurring in reaction to a response in a nonconjunctive cycle (*each* probe would begin a new embedded cycle) would be displayed in the following manner:

1
2_3
3

The following brief interactive sequence further illustrates the procedure. The passage includes all three types of question cycles; below it is the diagramming for the sequence.

Interactive sample:

Question—Miss DeLuca:	Can you give me some nouns that are people? Mickey.
Respond—Mickey:	Presidents.
React—Miss DeLuca:	Presidents are persons.
(same Q) Respond—Ron:	Butchers.
React—Miss DeLuca:	A butcher is a person.
(same Q) Respond—Matt:	Directors.
React—Miss DeLuca:	A director is a person.
(Question)—	What do they do?
(Respond)—Matt:	They direct movies.
(React)—Miss DeLuca:	OK, movie directors.
(same Q) Respond—Manuel:	Parents.
React—Miss DeLuca:	Parents are persons.
(same Q) Respond—Carl:	Ancestors.
React—Miss DeLuca:	Ancestors are persons.
(Question)—	Would most of them be living or dead?
(Respond)—Carl:	Dead.

(React)—Miss DeLuca:	They would be dead, huh?
(Same Q)—	Jill.
Respond—Jill:	Sisters.
React—Miss DeLuca:	Sisters are persons. Very good.
Question—Miss DeLuca:	Now, can you remember what a noun is? Let's do it again.
Respond—Pupils:	A noun is a person, place, or thing.
React—Miss DeLuca:	Very good. That was a very good review.

Diagram:

1 2 3_1 4 5_1 6
2

In this sequence, then, a series of six conjunctive (horizontal) question cycles occurred, and two of these contained embedded (subscript) cycles within them. This conjunctive series was followed by a new, structurally independent, but "topically" related cycle (vertical). The diagram that displays these relationships is quite simple in design, so that the "bare bones" of the lesson structure stand out. The sequence of the question cycles, for purposes of reading the diagram, moves from left to right and from top to bottom.

The 36 lesson diagrams that resulted from this analysis were compared in terms of graphic structure. Data contained in these diagrams were also quantified to examine particular aspects of lesson structure. Two different measures were developed for this purpose. The measure of *conjunctive development* of the lesson (Note 2) was designed to give some quantification of the degree to which questions were developed "horizontally" (giving several pupils an opportunity to respond to the same question). The measure of *embedded development* of the lesson (Note 3) was designed to quantify the degree to which pupil responses were developed, expanded, or refined through use of probing or clarification questions.

Friedman's two-way analysis of variance by ranks was used to compare conjunctive and embedded development of lessons across classrooms and over time. In addition, this description examined language function (inferred teacher intention) in relation to form (type of question cycle used), and considered the possible pupil misunderstandings that could arise from form-function complexities.

Information on Teacher Perceptions

Data on teacher perceptions of the meaning of classroom language were obtained in the same way as data on pupil perceptions. Teachers were interviewed individually after each of the six lessons that they taught, and they responded to the tasks on units, features, and functions of classroom language described in Chapter 3. In addition, each teacher responded to the sentence-completion task on rules of discourse, completing each sentence in the way she thought a pupil would who "really understood the procedures" in her classroom.

General patterns of teacher perceptions were compared to general patterns of pupil perceptions, and individual teacher perceptions were compared to the perceptions of pupils within the individual classrooms.

This chapter presents information on general patterns as well as individual classroom patterns of language use and meaning. Fictitious names are used, and teachers are designated as Mrs. Addams, Mrs. Brown, Mrs. Case, Miss DeLuca, Mrs. Estes, and Mrs. Flood.

GENERAL PATTERNS

Language Use

Many prior studies (see Chapter 1) had identified the question cycle (question, response, reaction) as the basic pattern of classroom interaction. Furthermore, the analysis of pupil perceptions of classroom language (see Chapter 3) had indicated that classroom questioning was an area with strong potential for the occurrence of pupil misunderstanding or misinterpretation of discourse. For these reasons, particular attention was given to patterns of questioning in each of the three sociolinguistic analyses of classroom language use.

Questioning consumed a great deal of classroom time in these 36 lessons. About one-third of teacher utterances were questions. Teacher-initiated question cycles predominated strongly over pupil-initiated cycles, with lesson means of 38.67 to 6.5. When teachers initiated questions, the question cycle typically went full circle (e.g., with a lesson mean of 38.67 teacher-initiated exchanges, there were lesson means of 41 pupil answering acts and 34.8 teacher follow-up acts). When pupils initiated questions, the cycles were truncated (e.g., with a lesson mean of 6.5 pupil-initiated exchanges, there were lesson means of 8.8 teacher answering acts and .38 pupil follow-up acts). To put this another way, teachers almost always reacted to pupil responses to their questions, but pupils almost never reacted to teacher answers to their questions.

Questions were used mainly in the parts of lessons where new information was introduced and rehearsed and where teachers were encouraging pupils to consider how they knew what they knew (metacognition). They occurred much less frequently in the initial or final parts of lessons (transitioning in and transitioning out).

Questions in these lessons did *not* follow Shuy's proposed model of an effective probing strategy. Shuy proposed moving from an open-ended

TEXTBOOK EXERCISES ON WORD ORDER AND SENTENCE MEANING		POETRY INTERPRETATION		REVIEW AND PRACTICE OF BASIC CONCEPTS	
Mrs. Estes, early September	Mrs. Flood, early September	Mrs. Estes, December	Mrs. Flood, October	Miss DeLuca, January (nouns)	Mrs. Flood, January (compound words)
1	1	1 2_3	1_1	1	1
2_2	2_2	2	2	2	2
3	3	3	3	3 2 3 4 5 6 7 8 9 10 11	3
4	4	4	4_2 2_1 3_1 4_1	4	4
5	5_1 2_2	5 2 3 4 5	5	5_1	5
6_2	6	6 2 2 3 4 5 7 8 9 10_1	6_1 2 3	6	6_1 2 3_2 4
7	7	7	7	7	7
8_2	8	8_2 3_1 4 5 6 7	8 2	8_1	8
9	9	9_1 2 3_1 4 5 6 7		9	9
10_3	10	10		10	10_3
11	11_3	11 2 3_1 4 5 6 7 8 9 10_2 11 12 13		11_1	11
12_1	12	12 2_1 3 4_1 5_1 6 7		12_1	12_1
13_1	13			13	13
14_1	14_4			14	14
15	15			15 2_1 3 4 5 6_1 7_1 8 9_1 10_1 11 12_1 13	15
16_2	16_2			16 2 3 4 5 6 7 8 9_4	16
17	17			17 2 3 4 5 6 7_1 8 9 10_1 11 12 13 14	17
18	18				18 2 3 4 5 6 7 8 9
19_1	19_1				19_1 2 3 4_1 5
20_2	20				20
$21_{1,2}$	21				21_1 2 3_1 4_1 5 6 7 8 9_1
22	22				
23_1	23_1				
24	24				

FIGURE 4.1 Comparing lesson structures.

question such as "Tell me about the industry of Bolivia," to progressively more narrow questions such as "What is the leading export of Bolivia?" (a "what is" question), "Is tin the leading export of Bolivia?" (a "yes-no" question), and "Tin is the leading export of Bolivia, isn't it?" (a rhetorical question). Instead, the flow of questions in these lessons was more "level." That is, a series of "what is" questions were asked before proceeding to a "yes-no" question. "What is" and "yes-no" questions both predominated strongly over open-ended questions.

Teachers' known-information questions predominated over "real" questions, but not as strongly as one might expect (only 1.25 to 1). Pupils' responses provided primarily nonpersonal rather than personal information, and this was a strong predominance (2.5 to 1). Teacher reactions tended to be simple acceptance of a response (e.g., "Okay"). Acceptance predominated over repeating of a response (3 to 1), over praise (6 to 1), and over corrective feedback (9 to 1).

The structural sequencing of question cycles varied across lessons for each of the six teachers and tended to reflect the instructional process being used. Figure 4.1 presents six lesson diagrams to illustrate this point. The two lessons based on textbook exercises were primarily vertical in development, with each textbook question representing a new topical cycle. The two lessons on poetry interpretation showed more conjunctive development, because several pupils were asked to provide their interpretations or experiences relative to the content of the poem. The two "review and practice" lessons showed initial vertical development because a series of "independent" or topical cycles reviewed definitions and examples pertinent to the concept, but the final portions of these lessons showed extensive conjunctive development, because pupils practiced applying the concepts by providing examples of their own.

Complexities and Possible Confusion. Several types of form-function complexities that might be confusing to pupils were identified in the question cycle analysis. For example, a conjunctive cycle could mark an incorrect answer, but it could also be used following a correct answer. Here is a lesson sequence that included two conjunctive cycles, each initiated by the same question. The first followed an incorrect answer; the second, the correct answer.

MRS. ADDAMS:	Why is it important that we put our words in the right order? Who can tell me? Chan?
CHAN:	So it can rhyme?
MRS. ADDAMS:	Why is it important that we put our words in the right order? Why, Manuel?
MANUEL:	So it makes sense.
MRS. ADDAMS:	Let me ask that question again and see how many people know the answer. Why is it important that we

	put our words in the right order? Oh, good! Lots of people know this time. Would you tell us, Renaldo?
RENALDO:	To make sense.
MRS. ADDAMS:	So the words make sense.

Two other types of cycle events with the potential for misunderstanding were also identified. One was the use of answer-repeats by the teacher. This occurred when the teacher repeated the pupil's response as the initial part of the react move:

MRS. FLOOD:	OK. In the morning when you get up, what are all the things you do? What's one of the things that you do? Something you do, Mike?
MIKE:	Eat breakfast.
MRS. FLOOD:	You eat breakfast. OK. What do you do, Sam?
SAM:	Get dressed.
MRS. FLOOD:	You get dressed.

In these lessons, the use of repeats was quite frequent. Potential confusion for pupils who had trouble following the flow of discourse might come from the fact that repeats could and did convey as many as four distinctly different meanings: (a) simple acknowledgment that an answer had been given, (b) definite indication that an answer was correct or appropriate, (c) definite indication that an answer was *in*correct or *in*appropriate (usually but *not always* given with rising/question intonation), and (d) indication that the teacher was unsure whether she (the teacher) had correctly heard the response (always given with rising/question intonation, meaning, "Is that what you said?").

The third type of potentially confusing cycle event involved what appeared to be an incongruity between a teacher question and a teacher reaction within the same cycle. Sometimes in these lessons teachers asked questions for which there were many possible appropriate answers (such as the question in the sample above: "In the morning when you get up, what are all the things you do?") or questions soliciting a pupil's personal or "inner" experiences (e.g., "Can you think of anything that has happened to you where you felt silly or embarrassed by it?"). Usually pupil responses to such questions were met with teacher react moves conveying simple acknowledgment that an answer had been given or that the answer was appropriate *in type* to the question asked (conveying, "Yes, that's the *kind* of answer to give,"). At times, however, the teacher react move contained a substantial indication that the *particular* answer given was an especially "good" one, or was, in contrast, incorrect. In these cases, the nature of the react move would be difficult to predict from the surface meaning conveyed by the question, and the meaning of the whole cycle (or a sequence of several cycles) could be obscured. Presumably for the type of question being asked, *any* pupil answer that was appropriate *in kind* would be as "correct" or as "good" as any other pupil's answer; and, presumably, the pupil would know more about his or her own personal experiences than the teacher would. However, these assumptions were sometimes contradicted by teacher reactions such as the ones in the following sequences:

MRS. BROWN: When did you figure it out? That my rule was, "all names begin with capital letters." Do you remember when?

CAROLINE: After you wrote "Don."

MRS. BROWN: Oh, that was pretty quick. Ken, when did you figure it out?

KEN: When you wrote "Tom."

MRS. BROWN: Oh, but I asked you a question somewhere down here, didn't I, and you didn't quite get it, so I think it was a little further down, wasn't it? I think you got it when I wrote "Roger."

MRS. CASE: All right, let's pretend that you are a cup. How would you look, Juan?

JUAN: Light colors.

MRS. CASE: Light colored. OK. How would you look, Lana? (no answer) How would you look, uh—

RITA: Round.

MRS. CASE: Huh?

RITA: Round.

MRS. CASE: Round. All right. How would you feel if you were a cup? Um, Sara?

SARA: Wet.

MRS. CASE: Beg pardon?

SARA: Wet.

MRS. CASE: Oh, that's a good word.

All of the six teachers in this study exhibited instances of these types of form-function complexities, although they were more prevalent in the lessons of certain teachers.

Changes over Time. The statistical analyses provided by the speech act approach and the question cycle sequence approach showed several instances of changes over time in patterns of questioning in these six classrooms. To begin with, the "density" of speech acts in the opening move decreased over time (i.e., teachers gave fewer directions and items of information in introducing their questions), and this change was significant ($x_r^2 = 12.16$, $p < .05$). Furthermore, conjunctive development of lessons increased over time ($x_r^2 = 11.85$, $p < .05$), and embedded development of lessons also tended to increase, though not significantly ($x_r^2 = 9.39$, $p < .10$). These shifts in pattern suggested that the pace of lessons was increasing, because individual questions received less teacher structuring, and also that answers to questions were being developed in more depth, because several pupils were asked to respond to the same question or an individual pupil was questioned further to clarify an initial response.

Two other interesting shifts over time were revealed. Within the opening move, the ratio of general management (e.g., "Raise your hand and wait to be called on.") to lesson-related management (e.g., "Turn to page 46 in your textbook.") went from a high in September to a low in December, then increased again in January ($x_r^2 = 11.28$, $p < .05$). Within the answering move, a reciprocal shift occurred when the ratio of personal responses to nonpersonal responses moved from a low in September to a high in December, then decreased again in January ($x_r^2 = 16.99$, $p < .01$). These shifts in pattern suggested that teachers in the fall devoted more time to establishment of classroom routines, including a businesslike approach to questions, focusing more on obtaining abstract information from pupils. By December, classroom routines were well established, requiring less general management, and questions were somewhat more informal, drawing more on pupils' personal experiences. In January, after the winter holidays, teachers created an atmosphere of "back to business," including more comments designed to reestablish class routines and asking questions that focused once again on more abstract or nonpersonal information.

Form over Content. This periodic increase in emphasis on general classroom management was reflective of a basic issue disclosed by Shuy's analysis of language dimensions. He noted that all classrooms have multiple purposes, because school is supposed to develop learning of content but it is also designed for learning acceptable social behavior. These two concerns, he argued, are sometimes at odds with each other. Shuy reported that teachers in this study tended, on the whole, to focus on socialization aspects of lessons rather than on content aspects. That is to say, much of the classroom talk in these lessons dealt with social aspects of being in school, such as management, directions for taking out books, and being quiet. Although topics of language arts content were introduced in these lessons, Shuy contended that only two of the teachers regularly developed these topics to any point of resolution.

Similarities Summarized. In general, then, these six classrooms exhibited certain basic similarities in language use, many of which would tend to indicate that they were fairly typical of classrooms observed in prior studies. Question cycles formed the basic pattern of interaction. Teachers initiated questions much more often than pupils. Questions were primarily known-information questions, although "real" questions were asked fairly often. Pupils answered most questions by providing nonpersonal information. Pacing of lessons, and extended development of question cycles through repeated or probing questions, increased as the school year progressed. Language use reflected more businesslike procedures in September and January and more informal procedures in December.

The potential for pupil misunderstanding of form-function relationships in questioning cycles was present in all six classrooms, although some classrooms exhibited this potential less than others. The tendency to focus on talk dealing with socialization aspects of lessons rather than content aspects was present in all six classrooms to some extent, although some classrooms exhibited this tendency less than others.

Language Meaning

Teachers in this study exhibited many perceptions of classroom language that were similar to those exhibited by pupils (reported in Chapter 3). In reporting units of language they heard "anybody saying" in lessons, teachers reported primarily complex units rather than simple ones, but they showed increases over time in information load (57.25 in September to 78.50 in mid-winter) and degree of complexity (3.92 in September to 4.21 in mid-winter), just as pupils did. In identifying salient features of classroom language, teachers emphasized contextual features, just like pupils, but functional features were a close second for teachers, whereas these were the least often mentioned by pupils. Proportions of social-contextual features of language identified by teachers increased over time (2.17 in September to 2.50 in mid-winter), similarly to those identified by pupils (1.90 to 2.07). Since only six teachers were involved, these patterns were not tested for statistical significance. However, since they were so comparable to pupil changes and showed even stronger shifts than pupils in all instances, they were interpreted as providing support for the suggestion that participants (both pupils and teachers) showed increasing awareness of the social context of classroom language as the classroom increased in familiarity over time.

There were interesting subtle differences between teachers' and pupils' reports of both units and features of language. Pupils' simple units typically reported a pupil response to a teacher question, without noting the question. Their compound units typically reported a pupil response, plus the source of the response, still without noting the teacher question that initiated the response. Their complex units typically reported a teacher question with a pupil response, and the source of that response. Since complex units were less frequently reported than simple or compound units, pupils tended to report hearing pupil responses *in isolation from* the teacher question that initiated them.

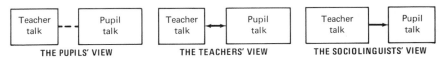

FIGURE 4.2   Perceived units of classroom language.

In contrast, teachers' simple units typically reported teacher directions or structuring of the lesson. Their compound units typically reported a teacher question and a pupil response to that question. Their complex units were generally extended interchanges, initiated by a teacher question and containing multiple pupil responses. Since complex and compound units were reported most frequently by teachers, they rarely reported pupil responses in isolation from teacher questions or teacher talk in isolation from pupil talk.

In identifying features of classroom language, pupils tended to organize their contextual groupings by lesson segment (e.g., these things were said at the beginning of the lesson) or by lesson activity (e.g., these were all said when we were writing words on the board). For teachers, contextual groupings tended to be organized by lesson concept (e.g., these were the ordinary examples of compound words that the kids gave; these were the unusual and interesting examples of compound words that they gave). For pupils, functional groupings tended to be simple, standard categories (e.g., questions, answers). For teachers, functional groupings tended to include references to instructional purpose (e.g., questions I asked to get out facts; questions I asked to get expressions of their opinion).

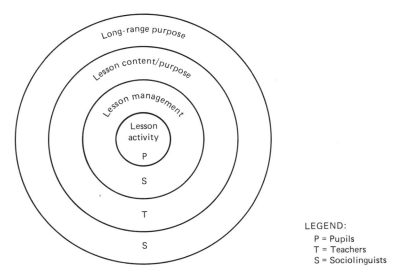

FIGURE 4.3   Features that organize perceptions of classroom language.

These differing perceptions of pupils and teachers are compared to the perceptions of the sociolinguistic observers in Figures 4.2 and 4.3. Figure 4.2 shows that with regard to "units" of language attended to, for the pupil, pupil talk predominated, and there was no clear relationship between teacher question and pupil response. For the teacher, both teacher and pupil talk were attended to, with pupil comments being reported somewhat more frequently than teacher comments, and teacher questions were usually reported in conjunction with pupil responses. For the sociolinguists, teacher talk predominated and functioned primarily to direct the flow of pupil talk (e.g., teacher questions were seen as initiating most teacher-pupil interchanges).

Figure 4.3 shows differences in perception related to the "features" of language identified. The figure can be interpreted as follows: Ideally, any lesson is designed to serve some long-range goal or purpose; at the same time, the lesson has a content and purpose of its own; this content or purpose determines the management procedures appropriate to the lesson; the management, in turn, is designed to facilitate the activities that occur within the lesson. The findings of this study suggest that pupil perceptions of classroom language were organized by the "inner circle," the lesson activities. Teacher perceptions were organized from a broader perspective, by the content and purpose of the lesson. The sociolinguists perceived classroom language from two perspectives, one more narrow (management of the flow of talk), and one more broad (the long-range goals of classroom communication, such as learning of content or socialization to procedures of classroom discourse). In a sense, then, the sociolinguists' views were at once more encompassing and more penetrating than the teachers' perspective, and, indeed, this should be expected from an outside observer, just as it should be expected that the teachers' views would be more encompassing than the pupils'.

Functions of Question Cycles.   In reporting on the functions of questions, responses, and praise in lessons, teachers differed only a little from pupils (as reported in Table 3.10). In no instances did teachers fail to report codable functions. For the 12 lessons with which this task was used, teachers reported that questions served an informative function in two lessons, an instructional function in six lessons, and a routine interactive function in four lessons. They reported that pupil responses served an informative function in six lessons, an instructional function in three lessons, and a routine interactive function in three lessons. With one exception, they reported that praise served an instructional function in these lessons. Thus, teacher perceptions of the functions of question cycles tended to be as uncoordinated as pupils' perceptions. They tended to concur with pupils that teacher questions served primarily instructional functions, but differed in their thinking that pupil responses served primarily informative functions. Teacher reports that praise served an instructional function were categorically different from pupil reports that praise was given because it was deserved, that is, because pupils gave good answers (informative function). However, teachers said that praise was used for purposes of feedback (instructional function), that is, to let pupils know they had the right idea. Thus, teacher praise was apparently functioning as teachers intended, for pupils did perceive that praise occurred because their ideas were good.

These teachers differed from each other in their perceptions of the functions of question cycles. These differences in teacher perceptions reflected the classroom differences in pupil perceptions of the functions of questions, noted in Chapter 3. They were also related to differences in teacher use of classroom questions, as described by the three sociolinguistic analysis systems. The next section of this chapter reports on these classroom differences, in the form of six brief case studies.

VARIATIONS ON A COMMON THEME

Mrs. Addams

Mrs. Addams had a second-grade classroom with 27 pupils. One of the outstanding features of Mrs. Addams's classroom was the ritualized use of language. The day was opened with a series of rituals: saluting the flag, singing "America," taking lunch count, and reciting an opening poem complete with "finger play." During transitions to language arts lessons, much time and attention were devoted to getting pupils seated in an exact circle, sitting up straight, hands to themselves, and eyes front. Mrs. Addams's lessons, therefore, appeared to focus more on "doing school" than on doing language arts. That is, much teacher talk dealt with socialization aspects of learning rather than with subject matter content. Pupil talk in this classroom also tended to be less content oriented. (The ratio of pupil informatives to noninformatives was 2.67, the lowest of all six classrooms.)

Mrs. Addams spoke very slowly and in a monotone. For language arts lessons, she typically sat in a low chair while pupils sat around her on the floor. She gestured frequently as she spoke, and used her hands to manage the class, "much as an orchestra leader might conduct an orchestra," according to Shuy.

Shuy also noted that Mrs. Addams's questions had "little continuity or direction." She initiated fewer exchanges than any of the other teachers (30.67 lesson mean, while other teachers ranged from 38.33 to 43). Pupils in this classroom initiated many exchanges, however (11.33 lesson mean). The ratio of pupil-initiated exchanges to teacher-initiated exchanges was significantly higher in this class than in other classes.

This combination of characteristics might suggest that pupils had some freedom to direct the flow of talk in this classroom, but Shuy found this not to be the case. In fact, he noted that pupils were so insecure about what a "safe topic" was, that in one "sharing time" lesson they continually recycled to old, safe topics. The following topic cycling occurred: lunch money, BB guns, snow, BB guns, snow, lunch money, Thanksgiving, snow.

Mrs. Addams may have contributed to this lack of pupil assurance by failing to indicate clearly when pupil responses were appropriate or inappropriate. She was significantly lower than other teachers in the use of teacher reactions to pupil responses, and she was also lowest in use of correct/paraphrase versus acceptance. Instances of positive feedback were very infrequent (62 instances in six lessons, while other teachers ranged from 146 to 167).

Mrs. Addams was the only teacher to ask many more "yes-no" than "what is" questions. To put this another way, her questions permitted a narrower range of answers. Most pupils in this classroom reported that questions served an instructional function, but almost one-third gave no codable function for these questions, and over one-third gave no codable function for pupil responses. Praise reportedly served an informational function or denoted "good ideas."

Mrs. Addams, herself, reported a coordinated instructional function for her question cycles. Teacher questions were asked to "get pupils to think about/understand what we're doing." Pupil responses were given "to let me/everyone know they know the answer." Praise was given to motivate or "encourage children to talk." Thus, Mrs. Addams would appear to be focusing fully on content, rather than management, in her perceptions of the functions of classroom questioning. It should be noted, however, that in the two lessons where she reported on the functions of her questions, "what we're doing" referred to practicing a Thanksgiving play and writing stories for their mothers about cats; thus, instruction was focused on procedural issues rather than subject matter content.

This tendency to focus on procedural (socialization) aspects of lessons was also obvious in Mrs. Addams's reporting of the language that she heard in lessons. For example, in the "sharing time" lesson discussed above, she reported hearing 16 units of language (all complex). Seven of these focused on personal information children were contributing ("I forgot my lunch pail this morning. So my mother's going to come back at lunch time and bring my lunch pail," Julie said. "That's nice. We're glad your mother's going to come."). Five units focused on pupils' classroom behavior ([Brian was making a noise with his feet.] "Brian, can you be quiet so we can hear what Danny's saying?" "Yes." [Then he was quiet]). Four focused on comments about appropriate behavior *outside* the classroom ("Should you shoot a gun in the city?" "No," everybody said. "Should you shoot a gun where there are animals?" "No," everybody said. "There are some places where they have targets 'specially set up so you can shoot with a gun.''). Thus, over half of the language units Mrs. Addams identified in this lesson focused on language associated with socialization.

The language features that Mrs. Addams identified were mainly functional (11 out of 30 groups) and contextual (8 groups). One interesting fact was that, unlike other teachers, Mrs. Addams formed five groups of language units based on elemental features (I said, "Let's get started" in both of these). Second graders identified elemental (written) or repetitive features significantly more often than third or fourth graders, and this was interpreted as related to the heavier emphasis on developing initial reading skills in second grade. The fact that this second-grade teacher was also more aware of the written or repetitive features of language lends additional support to this interpretation.

The three sets of perceptions of Mrs. Addams's classroom, then, were in fairly close agreement. The sociolinguistic observers saw Mrs. Addams as a teacher who focused on the socialization aspects of lessons rather than the content, and Mrs. Addams seemed to concur. She was highly attentive to classroom language dealing with appropriate behavior. Although she defined her question cycles as serving an instructional function, the instruction involved was procedure oriented rather than content oriented. Pupils who could explain the functions of questions and responses said that these served an instructional and routine interactive function, but many could not explain the function that these important language forms played in their lessons. This might have reflected the fact that Mrs. Addams's questions had "little continuity or direction," an observation reported by Shuy.

The ritualization of language and the emphasis on socialization over content in this classroom is referred to again later, in relation to pupil patterns of attention and achievement (Chapter 6) and pupil activities in play sessions (Chapter 7).

Mrs. Brown

Mrs. Brown taught a third-grade classroom with 25 pupils. An outstanding feature of this classroom was the variation in instructional strategies used. Teachers in this school had participated in a Teacher Corps project involving in-service training in "models of teaching," a series of varied strategies explicated by Joyce and Weil (1972) and designed to achieve varied instructional goals, particularly development of varied types of thinking skills. Five of the six videotaped language arts lessons in Mrs. Brown's classroom were "model" lessons. Not surprisingly, then, Mrs. Brown's lessons appeared to focus on "doing content." Pupil and teacher talk in this classroom were heavily content oriented. (The ratio of pupil informatives to noninformatives was 6.0, the second highest of all six classrooms. The ratio of teacher management to teacher information was significantly lower than in other classrooms.)

Mrs. Brown was described by Shuy as "talking teacherese." That is, she used intonation and self-referencing ("I have a good one. *Mrs. Brown* is thinking about a teacher in this school. And I want you to ask me some questions . . .") both to separate her role as teacher from her role as friend or helper, and to set off certain parts of her lesson (e.g., intonational range increased in the instructional segments compared with the opening exercises).

Shuy also noted that Mrs. Brown was a skillful manager of classroom talk. Topics were controlled by the teacher, although she was "amenable to suggestions from pupils." This observation was corroborated by the fact that the ratio of pupil-initiated exchanges to teacher-initiated exchanges was significantly lower in this classroom than in other classrooms. Pupils in this classroom were not left in doubt about the appropriateness of their responses. Mrs. Brown was significantly higher than other teachers on both the use of teacher reactions to pupil responses and the ratio of praise to acceptance.

Shuy noted that Mrs. Brown was also a skillful questioner. She varied her question types, tending to ask more "what is" than "yes-no" questions and moving from "what is" to "yes-no" questions in a flow rather akin to his recommended probing sequences. She displayed an ability to work on both form and content of pupil language, as in the following sequence where pupils were learning to ask effective (yes-no) questions in order to discover an idea the teacher had in mind.

AMANI: What shape is it?
MRS. BROWN: Can you say that another way?
AMANI: How big is it?
MRS. BROWN: No, why don't you ask me what shape you *think* it is? Ask me that.
AMANI: Is it square?
MRS. BROWN: No. But that's a good question.

Most pupils in this classroom reported that teacher questions served an instructional function, but one-third gave no codable function and over half gave no codable function for pupil responses. Two-thirds reported that praise served an informational function (i.e., was "deserved"). Thus, pupils in this classroom were somewhat muddled about the purpose of the classroom question cycle.

Mrs. Brown reported that her questions served an instructional function ("to make sure that they understood what a group was"; "to evoke descriptive words"). She saw pupil responses as serving a routine interactive function ("they were answering my questions"). She defined praise as serving an instructional function ("it was reinforcement"; "to let them know that their replies were correct"). Thus, Mrs. Brown's view of the function of the classroom question cycle was consistent across lessons, but somewhat uncoordinated. She saw *her* role as instructional (questions and praise), but the pupil role was described as simply to respond (routine interactive) rather than to learn or to demonstrate knowledge.

In her reporting of the units of language she heard in lessons, however, Mrs. Brown clearly focused on pupil responses in relation to the cognitive task. For example, in a lesson on grouping or categorizing she reported hearing 12 units of language (mostly complex). Seven of these units reported pupil responses to the various categorizing tasks they were given ([I gave Tammy and Manuel colored counting blocks.] "Here are some blocks. Sort them or put them in groups any way you would like to." [They sorted according to colors. Tammy had four groups and Manuel had two groups.]). Four units reported teacher comments structuring or explaining the task ("We're going to put items in groups. I will pass out items that you can sort or put in groups any way you want"). Only one unit was not fully content or task oriented ("Now we're going to do something on the board. We're going to do some grouping." [Then I bawled them out.]).

This strong focus on the cognitive content of the lesson was repeated in Mrs. Brown's identification of the features of classroom language. She formed 49 groups, 25 of which were contextual, dealing mainly with the concepts or skills being taught (e.g., These were all instances where a child *guessed* with their question, and I asked them to rephrase it, or asked them if they had enough information to ask that question).

At least two sets of perceptions were in close agreement in this classroom. The sociolinguistic observers saw Mrs. Brown as a content-oriented teacher, and Mrs. Brown clearly concurred. She defined her questions and praise as serving instructional functions, and she focused heavily on units and features of language that were related to lesson content.

Pupils in this classroom were less clear about the function of question cycles. This might be seen as related to the high variation in instructional strategy. As Shuy noted, Mrs. Brown varied in the types of questions she asked. Two lessons required pupils to use inductive thinking, two involved thinking in analogies, and two involved deductive thinking. This variation could well have been confusing to pupils, contributing to their rather muddled perceptions of the functions of classroom questioning.

Another related explanation comes from the analysis of question cycle sequences. Tenenberg noted that incongruities between the question and react moves of the same cycle occurred most often in lessons that had several levels of learning objectives. He cited two of Mrs. Brown's lessons as examples. One was the lesson noted earlier, which had a surface objective of having students figure out what the teacher had in mind but also had an underlying objective of having them learn how to ask good questions, questions that would zero in on the solution.

All of Mrs. Brown's "model" lessons involved achieving simultaneous objectives dealing with both content knowledge and thinking skills. Thus, her question cycle sequences were more apt to contain form-function complexities. This characteristic *derived from* her use of varied instructional models and could also have contributed to pupils' muddled perceptions of the functions of question cycles. As can be seen later (Chapter 6), Mrs. Brown's pattern of instructional variation did have interesting relationships to pupil patterns of attention and achievement in lessons.

Mrs. Case

Mrs. Case taught a third-grade classroom with 29 pupils. Perhaps the most outstanding feature of this classroom was the teacher's reliance on the textbook as a guide for instruction. Four of Mrs. Case's lessons were straight from the textbook, with children reading directions or explanations aloud and the teacher reading questions directly from the teacher's guide. Despite this fact, Shuy described this as a classroom where the teacher focused on "doing school" rather than on teaching content. The data from the speech act analysis do not fully support this description. Mrs. Case was neither high nor low on the ratio of management to information. Pupils in this classroom had the third highest ratio of pupil informatives to noninformatives (5.9). These figures would suggest that lessons in this classroom fell in the middle of this group of six classes, with regard to content orientation.

Shuy further asserted that Mrs. Case displayed "an as yet undeveloped ability to do 'teacher talk' effectively." For example, she failed to set the ground rules of her lessons with clarity, so students were not always clear what they were to do. Mrs. Case attempted to overcome this confusion by seeking the help of one of her better students, a boy on whom she could depend for participation and cooperation. Shuy suggested that Mrs. Case had "appointed an assistant manager." Some support for this lack of clarity was provided by the speech act analysis. Mrs. Case was significantly lower than other teachers on the ratio of metastatements to lesson-related management, indicating that she rarely informed pupils about "where they were" in the lesson.

Despite this lack of clarity, Mrs. Case was generally in control of the flow of talk in her classroom. This classroom was significantly lower on the ratio of pupil-initiated exchanges to teacher-initiated exchanges, and also on the ratio of teacher indirect management to direct management.

Mrs. Case asked more "what is" than "yes-no" questions overall, but in the instructional parts of her lessons, where new information was introduced and practiced, she followed the same pattern as Mrs. Addams, asking two "yes-no" questions for every "what if" question. Thus, during actual instruction her questions (the textbook questions?) permitted a very narrow range of responses.

Less than one-third of the pupils in this classroom reported that teacher questions served an instructional function. Instead, they reported that Mrs. Case's questions were asked to "get an answer" (routine interactive). Over one-third of them gave no codable function for questions, and *more than half* gave no codable function for pupil responses. Less than half of the pupils in this classroom reported that praise served an informational function (was given because pupils gave good answers). Of the six classrooms, this was the one where the most pupils exhibited the least clarity with regard to the functions of the question cycle.

Two characteristics of Mrs. Case's classroom language provided insight into this pattern of pupil perceptions. The first was her habit of reading questions directly from the teacher's guide of the textbook. In effect, there *were* no *teacher* questions in many of these lessons. Pupils were aware of this. In fact, one high-achieving boy commented during one interview, when he was presented with the set of teacher questions, that *he* never said these kinds of things in lessons. When asked why, he replied, "Because I don't have the *list*" (i.e., the list of questions contained in the teacher's guide).

The second characteristic involved Mrs. Case's use of praise. Mrs. Case was lowest of all six teachers in her proportional use of praise. Only 10% of her "positive feedback" was praise. The rest was simple repetition (69%) or acceptance (21%) of a pupil response. Furthermore, Mrs. Case's acceptance was typically an "Okay," a term that was used as often to signal a shift in topic or activity as to indicate an acceptable pupil response.

Thus, both Mrs. Case's questions and her praise lacked a certain clarity, as did her attempts to set up the ground rules in introducing her lessons. In fact, Mrs. Case's reports of the functions of questions, responses, and praise in her lessons acknowledged the possible confusion inherent in her use of corrective feedback.

Mrs. Case defined her questions as serving an instructional function ("to get them to think critically"; "to review all the things we learned about this, to clarify"). She reported that pupil responses served an informative function in the first lesson ("They're telling me how they'd feel if they were this object"), but in the second lesson she identified the pupil responses as *comments of her own*, a reflection of her tendency to repeat most pupil responses verbatim. Praise was defined as instructional in the first lesson ("giving positive reinforcement, because they had the answer I was looking for"). In describing the function of her feedback statements in the second lesson, she said, "I say 'Okay' or 'All right' either to let them know 'I agree,' or to say, 'Let's move on.' " Thus, she demonstrated her awareness of the dual functions served by these language forms, though she seemed unaware of the confusion this might cause for pupils.

In identifying what she heard being said in lessons, Mrs. Case demonstrated her reliance on the textbook. For example, in one textbook lesson on use of signs and symbols, she reported hearing 19 units of language (six simple, seven compound, six complex). Fifteen of these involved language directly from the textbook or pupil reference to something in the textbook ("Which one would we go to if we wanted help?" "The one at the bottom of the page, because he's a crossing guard."). The other four units involved pupil ideas that were only one step removed from the textbook, as they discussed how you could tell a man's occupation by his uniform ("A fireman wears a big heavy jacket," Donald said). Not one of these units contained any language that was *original* with the *teacher*. This fact tends to support Shuy's contention that she had not yet learned how to "do teacher talk," and might even be construed as support for his assertion that she is "doing school" rather than teaching content. This focus on textbook language is reminiscent of children's attempts to play school.

In identifying features of classroom language, Mrs. Case focused most strongly on contextual features (20 groups), then on functional features (14 groups). Many of the contextual features referred to information in the textbook somehow, and in two instances Mrs. Case explicitly differentiated between textbook language and participant language (Here I'm asking a question, read from the book—they will have to answer; Here I'm asking questions where they have to draw from their own experience). Thus, she indicated some awareness that the textbook did not have to be the sole source of information in a lesson.

On close inspection, there was agreement between the perceptions of the sociolinguist and the teacher with regard to the language in this classroom. The sociolinguist noted a lack of clarity and an inability to talk like a teacher. Mrs. Case acknowledged the dual purposes served by her use of positive feedback, was confused herself about the source of pupil responses, and focused most of her attention on the language of the textbook rather than that of the participants in the lesson. Pupils in this classroom had good reason to be confused about the functions of questions, responses, and praise, and they exhibited this confusion to a marked degree. The restricted nature of language in this classroom is noted further in the discussion of children's language in play sessions (Chapter 7).

Miss DeLuca

Miss DeLuca taught a third-grade classroom with 29 pupils. An outstanding feature of this classroom, according to Shuy, was the fact that Miss DeLuca encouraged "highly specific and descriptive language use in her students, possibly as much by her own dramatic verbal behavior as by her official requests for it."

Many of Miss DeLuca's lessons did make "official requests" for descriptive language. For example, in her December lesson, pupils were asked to close their eyes and think of something "red and running," then to report what they imagined. Responses included the following:

1. This red ball ... was chasing somebody.

2. I seen this three-headed red snake.
3. I saw a red horse running around 'cause a cowboy was chasing him.
4. I seen this guy carrying a red rectangle and there was blood coming off of it.

Shuy suggested that this lesson incorporated a conversational technique, known as "one-upping," which is a rather useful language function, particularly at adult cocktail parties. He noted, however, that it was unclear whether Miss DeLuca was intentionally working on development of this particular communication skill in this lesson.

Lessons in this classroom did engage pupils in use of much descriptive language, and the ratio of pupil informatives to noninformatives reflected this. (It was 6.56, the second highest of all six classrooms.) However, Shuy commented that *teacher* language tended to focus on lesson form rather than lesson content. Miss DeLuca consistently informed her pupils about where they were in the lesson plan. Speech act analysis corroborated this description, for Miss DeLuca was significantly higher than other teachers in use of metastatements.

Shuy reported that topics in this classroom were controlled by the teacher, but that pupils had some input as well. This description was also corroborated by speech act analysis, for Miss DeLuca was significantly higher than other teachers on the ratio of indirect to direct management and on the ratio of pupil-initiated to teacher-initiated exchanges. In fact, in several lessons there were short segments in which pupils played the teacher role, calling on and asking questions of other pupils. In each case, however, the topic area on which these pupil questions focused was defined in advance by Miss DeLuca.

Miss DeLuca used "what is" and "yes-no" questions with almost equal frequency overall, but in the instructional parts of her lessons, "what is" questions dominated four to one. She tended to ask the same question type (e.g., "what is") several times before moving on to another type (e.g., "yes-no").

Questions in this classroom showed rather more conjunctive development than in the other five classrooms. However, Miss DeLuca exhibited few instances of form-function complexity or incongruity in her use of these cycles. Thus, her language provided clarity for pupils here as well as in her delineation of the progress of the lesson through its various parts.

Most pupils in this classroom reported that teacher questions served an instructional function, and more than four-fifths were able to explain their views on the functions that these questions served. Furthermore, pupils in this classroom tended to report that both pupil responses and teacher praise served informative functions. Thus, they had a more coordinated perception of the functions of question cycles than did pupils in most other classrooms in this study.

Interestingly enough, Miss DeLuca's view of the function of question cycles was less coordinated than that of her pupils, although it was consistent across both lessons. She reported that her questions served a routine interactive function ("to get a response from the kids"), whereas pupil responses served an informative function ("they were describing the witch"; "telling us how things looked to them"), and praise served an instructional function ("to show I thought all the answers were good"; "to let kids know they're on the right track"). One interpretation of this pattern was that Miss DeLuca's view of the question cycle was centered on pupil responses, with teacher questions serving to elicit these responses and praise serving to acknowledge their accuracy or value.

This impression was substantiated by Miss DeLuca's reporting of the units of language she heard in her lessons, where she focused very strongly on pupil responses. For example, in her December lesson on "one-upmanship," she reported hearing 33 units of language (9 simple, 6 compound, 18 complex). Nineteen of these focused almost exclusively on pupil responses, and three others included pupil responses, although they began by reporting teacher directions. All of these units highlighted pupils' descriptive language (i.e., focused on the communication skill being practiced). The other 11 units did not deal with question cycles at all but focused instead on teacher structuring of the lesson, including specific directions about the task (lesson management) as well as information about the sequence of procedures to be followed (metastatements). This latter pattern was reflective of her attention to informing pupils about "where they were in the lesson," which was noted by Shuy and confirmed by the speech act analysis.

Miss DeLuca exhibited one other interesting characteristic in her reporting of language units. She was the only one of the six teachers to show a strong concern for reporting the language heard *in the order in which it occurred* in the lesson, and she also tried valiantly to report *everything* that had been said. Given Shuy's reference to her "dramatic verbal behavior," and her penchant for metastatements, this might well be interpreted to suggest that Miss DeLuca "scripted" her lesson in advance, periodically located her position within that script during interaction, and recapitulated the interaction later by attempting to reproduce both her own initial script and the pupils' "improvisations" in careful detail.

This interpretation was supported by Miss DeLuca's reporting of the features of language in her classroom. She identified 49 features, about equally divided between contextual (23) and functional (21). Eleven of these (almost one-fourth) located language units within the lesson "script," (e.g., "summing up after my first segment") or acknowledged the function of metastatements in "scripting" the lesson for the students (e.g., "telling what we're going to do, what the lesson's going to be"; "letting them know they're going to get a chance to play the role of teacher"). One grouping (the first group formed for the January lesson on nouns, which was graphically depicted earlier in Figure 4.1) even organized *all* the language units into subgroups to describe the exact sequence of lesson segments. The subgroups within this organization were as follows:

1. "Telling what I'm going to be doing."
2. "I had them read from the board."
3. "I asked someone what a noun was."
4. "We were dealing with the first chart."
5. "We were dealing with the second chart."
6. "They were naming places."
7. "They were naming people."
8. "The culmination."

The shift in pronouns as this sequence of subgroups progresses is an interesting one, given the earlier suggestion that Miss DeLuca centered her attention within the question cycle on pupil responses. This lesson was diagrammed (Figure 4.1) as having heavy conjunctive development in the final segments, with well over half the question cycles in the lesson occurring in these segments. In Miss DeLuca's subgroups, the "actors" shifted from "I" to "we" to "they," so that pupils were the clearly designated major actors in the final segments of the lesson, where most question cycles occurred, whereas the teacher was the major actor in the initial segments, where the "script" was being introduced.

With regard to the management functions of language within this classroom, the sociolinguistic observers and the teacher were in rather close agreement. Miss DeLuca was described as using metastatements consistently to inform her pupils about "where they were" in the lesson plan (or script), and Miss DeLuca herself both reported the language units she heard in scriptlike form (i.e., in the sequence in which they occurred) and organized them into groups that emphasized both the location of language within the lesson sequence and the use of language to denote the lesson sequence.

With regard to the instructional functions of language within this classroom, the teacher and pupils showed interesting patterns of agreement. One sociolinguistic observer (Tenenberg) noted that form-function incongruities were noticeably absent in Miss DeLuca's use of question cycles. Pupils in this class were clearer and more coordinated in their perceptions of the functions of question cycles than were pupils in most of the other classrooms. Although Miss DeLuca and her pupils disagreed about the function of teacher questions (she saw them as routine interactive, whereas they saw them as instructional), they agreed that pupil responses served an informative function and that teacher praise served to designate good answers. Thus, in this classroom, where the form-function relationships of question cycles were more consistent, there was also more teacher-pupil agreement about the overall function of the question cycle. Also, within this classroom, which featured highly descriptive language use by pupils, there was teacher-pupil agreement that pupil responses carried important *information* in the lesson. Patterns of attention and achievement within this classroom were interesting in this regard, as is noted further in Chapter 6.

Mrs. Estes

Mrs. Estes taught a fourth-grade class with 27 pupils. An outstanding feature of this classroom was teacher management by "withholding information." Shuy reported one particular sequence of interaction to illustrate this pattern.

> HERMAN: What page of the book?
>
> MRS. ESTES: I haven't told you yet. (Pause) Would you please open your books to page 18.

Shuy described Mrs. Estes as "always in control, inching forward slowly, never fully revealing the right answers, and often giving only hints of them." She exhibited well-controlled turn-taking procedures, with pupils bidding (raising hands) to be called on and receiving short turns to talk. There was a wide range of class participation but very little obvious progress toward a content goal, because Mrs. Estes provided few reactions to indicate whether any answers were right or wrong. As a result, lessons in this classroom appeared to focus more on management than on content.

Speech act analysis confirmed these descriptions, for Mrs. Estes was significantly higher than other teachers on the ratio of management to information. She was significantly lower in the ratio of praise to accept. Furthermore, the ratio of pupil informatives to noninformatives was very low (3.4). Thus, neither teacher talk nor pupil talk was very content oriented, and the teacher did little to signify the accuracy of whatever content was contained in pupil responses.

Mrs. Estes asked four times more "what is" questions than "yes-no" questions, both overall and in the instructional portions of her lessons. She tended to move from "what is" to "yes-no" questions, so her questioning strategy looked more like Shuy's recommended probing strategy than did the strategies of most other teachers. Coupled with her failure to designate correct pupil responses (i.e., to inform other pupils which responses conveyed good ideas), these observational data might be interpreted to suggest that Mrs. Estes used questions mainly to test students' knowledge (diagnose, evaluate).

Pupils in this classroom reported overwhelmingly (three to one) that teacher questions served an instructional function, but they were divided in their perceptions of responses. One-third of them reported that pupil responses served an instructional function, whereas another one-third reported the more common (general) interpretation that responses were routine interactive. Praise was seen as serving an informative function, despite the fact that it occurred infrequently.

Mrs. Estes differed from both her pupils and the sociolinguists in her perceptions of her questions. She reported that her questions served a routine interactive function ("so that I won't always be the one giving the information, or doing the talking"). She concurred with her pupils in displaying "divided" perceptions of the functions of pupil responses. In one lesson she reported that they served an informative function ("to share with me an experience they had"), although in another lesson she reported dual functions ("I think when kids respond it's for two reasons: (1) because they're expected to answer, and (2) because they get some satisfaction from being able to answer"). The first of these dual functions was routine interactive, the second was instructional. Mrs. Estes defined teacher praise as serving an instructional function ("It's giving reinforcement to children—I never want to put anyone down"; "to let them know they're on the right track").

What was most interesting in these perceptions was that in this classroom, where there was wide pupil participation in contributing responses to the lesson but little teacher feedback to denote which pupil responses were "good ideas," both pupils and teacher appeared to be unclear about the purpose that pupil responses served, even though the teacher suggested that those responses were central to the lesson, because her questions were reportedly asked primarily to engender responses.

Mrs. Estes's reporting of the units of language she heard in lessons placed these several sets of conflicting perceptions in a new light. She did focus on pupil responses (e.g., 17 out of 21 units in the October lesson), supporting the idea that these were central to the lesson. Furthermore, she focused on *inaccuracies* in pupil responses (10 of the 17 units noted above), always reporting inaccurate responses *first*, supporting the idea that she used question cycles to diagnose or evaluate pupils. Most revealing of all, however, the inaccuracies that she keyed in on were not inaccuracies of content, but rather of grammatical form and pronunciation (e.g., [Herman wanted to say *investigate*, but he didn't pronounce it correctly]; Enrique said, "*Sch*eck it"; Bridgett said, "My sister, *she* went in and she was scared"). These inaccuracies were rarely corrected by Mrs. Estes, for, as she said, "I never want to put anybody down." Thus, Mrs. Estes displayed no clear sense herself that either teacher questions or pupil responses contributed toward any content goals of her lessons. Her patterns of reporting language units suggested that the real function of pupil responses, as well as of teacher questions, was "so that I won't always be the one doing the talking."

The features of classroom language identified by Mrs. Estes corroborated this interpretation to some degree. Although 29 of the 44 features identified were contextual, they tended to focus on the various topics on which pupils gave opinions rather than on any particular concepts or skills that were seen as goals of the lesson. For example, in the November lesson on poetry interpretation, 10 features were identified. Six of these grouped pupil comments according to the topic on which they were expressing an opinion (e.g., all have to do with the animal being in the tree; have to do with whether or not the animal can swim; have to do with the animal being confused when he escapes). One group focused on the observation that pupil opinions tended to be stated as fact (these were all said with no "maybe" or "I think"—as if there was no doubt about it), but in the lesson Mrs. Estes never pointed out the difference between fact and opinion in the process of interpreting a poem.

Mrs. Estes's features of classroom language also underscored her tendency to focus on pupil errors in language use. Ten of the 44 groups formed were based on this type of feature (e.g., all words from the poem that the children pronounced incorrectly; incorrect use of a word; they know what the word is, but they still say it incorrectly). Perhaps this pattern of teacher perceptions revealed (and reinforced?) an inherent belief that pupils in this classroom lacked the basic language skills essential to any real development of language arts content, so pupil participation became the only viable goal to be pursued.

In this instance, as in others, the views of the sociolinguists and the teacher showed congruency. The sociolinguists reported that the language of management took precedence over the language of content in Mrs. Estes's lessons. Neither teacher talk nor pupil talk was content oriented. Mrs. Estes's reports of the units, features, and functions of language in her classroom all de-emphasized the importance of content in lessons. Both teacher questions and pupil responses appeared to function in a routine interactive way, so the ultimate goal of lessons became pupil participation. Teacher attention was focused on pupil inaccuracies in grammar and pronunciation, perhaps reinforcing a sense of the futility of any attempts to teach content.

Pupils in this classroom saw teacher questions as serving an instructional function, but they were divided in their views of the functions of pupil responses. This was not surprising, since Mrs. Estes provided little feedback to indicate that pupil responses were leading toward any content resolution, although she indicated that pupil responses were important somehow, by widely distributing opportunities to talk and by encouraging pupils to offer their own opinions. Pupil patterns of participation and attention in class discussions shed further light on the meaning of language in this classroom. These are discussed in Chapter 6, along with information on pupil achievement.

Mrs. Flood

Mrs. Flood taught a fourth-grade class with 28 pupils. An outstanding feature of this classroom was the teacher's natural use of language. Rather than using the more animated and widely ranging intonation typically associated with teacher/lesson talk, Mrs. Flood was more conversational in tone.

She was also very adept at "topic branching," according to Shuy. She seemed to be very attentive to a need for topics to flow smoothly from one to another. She responded to pupil comments in a way that built on what the pupil contributed, while at the same time she designed where the topic would go next. For example, in each of the three comments that follow, Mrs. Flood was referring to a comment made by a pupil as she moved the lesson on to the next topic she wished to discuss.

1. I'd like to turn something around a minute, then. Did the elk see *you*?
2. Now I'm going to come back to you, because you sort of triggered something in my thinking there.
3. Well, something that Rachel said sort of ties in with a short little poem that I'd like to read to you today.

In addition to building on pupil comments in this way, Mrs. Flood regularly invited pupils to link their own experiences to the concept being taught in the lesson. For example, a lesson on commands (emphasizing the importance of word order in identifying sentence form) began with pupils reporting on the order in which they did things when they got up in the morning. A lesson on poetry interpretation involved the following open-ended instructions: "What I'm going to ask you to do is think of an experience you've had that's similar to the poem, that you might like to share with us . . . ." Mrs. Flood joined the students in this type of reporting. Her lessons frequently began or ended with her own personal anecdote, and this contributed to the similarity between her lessons and normal conversations.

Despite this conversational tone and discussion of personal experiences, Mrs. Flood's lessons focused on "doing content," according to Shuy. Speech act analysis confirmed this impression. (The ratio of pupil informatives to noninformatives was 6.76, the highest of all six classrooms.) The speech act analysis also supported the description of language in this classroom as more "natural," for Mrs. Flood was *moderate* in *all* of the speech act ratios that showed significant classroom differences. She was the only one of the six teachers who was not significantly higher or lower than other teachers on any of the speech act measures.

Tenenberg noted that Mrs. Flood tended to avoid extremes in use of question cycle sequences also. For example, she showed moderate use of conjunctive development in all of her lessons. (This was illustrated by the fact that the overall mean for all six teachers on the measure of conjunctive development was 1.3, with a standard deviation of 1.2. Mrs. Flood had a mean of 1.0, with a standard deviation of .4.) In addition, Mrs. Flood showed more consistency between cycle form and cycle meaning than most of the other teachers. Thus, pupils were confronted with fewer language events containing the potential for pupil misunderstanding.

This was the *only* classroom in which the majority of pupils reported that teacher questions served an informative function, that is, were asked because the teacher wanted to know what they thought. Of those who reported functions of pupil responses, about half followed the general view and saw these as serving a routine interactive function, but the other half saw them as serving an informative function (i.e., pupils answered because they wanted to tell the teacher or other pupils something). Praise was also seen as serving an informative function, that is, it was given because the pupils had such good ideas. Pupils in this classroom had the most highly coordinated view of classroom question cycles of all six classrooms, and in addition, about one-third of the pupils in this classroom reported that questions at home and at school served congruent functions (other classes ranged from .03 to .16 on this measure). Pupil perceptions, therefore, tended to support the sociolinguists' reports of the clarity of question cycles and the "natural" use of language.

Mrs. Flood concurred with her pupils in reporting that teacher questions served an informative function (I'm asking for their opinion; I'm asking them to tell me their feelings) and that pupil responses also served an informative function (they wanted to share information from their knowledge; they wanted to tell about something that had happened to them). She reported that praise served an instructional function (positive reinforcement; talking to a youngster that needs encouragement badly).

In reporting on the units of language she heard "anybody saying" in lessons, Mrs. Flood always began by reporting pupil responses, but unlike Mrs. Estes, she focused on "good" responses. The December lesson on imagining what it might feel like to be an animal was a good illustration of Mrs. Flood's focus on pupil responses. She reported 18 units (10 complex and 8 compound). Every one of these contained one or more pupil responses. In all, 28 pupil comments were reported, and the pupil who made the comment was *named* in all but one instance. No teacher comments were reported in isolation from pupil comments, and no managerial comments of the teacher were reported, only questions and reactions to pupil responses. This suggested that Mrs. Flood was highly content oriented in her attention to lesson language, and also that she was tracking individual pupils carefully throughout the lesson.

Mrs. Flood's identification of the features of classroom language also reflected attention to pupil responses, with an emphasis on the types of thinking pupils displayed in generating these responses (e.g., recalling from poem/picture; not just recalling, but opinions; sharing experiences— what happened to them; sharing feelings—what embarrassed them; compound words generated by putting pictures together; compound words *original* from the kids). This pattern of organization emphasized Mrs. Flood's perception of pupil responses as informative, for here she stressed the type of information that pupils were contributing to the lesson as they responded.

The views of the sociolinguistic observers, the teacher, and the pupils were all quite similar with regard to the use and meaning of language in this classroom. The sociolinguists reported on the content orientation, the natural use of language, and the lack of form-function incongruities in use of the question cycle. Teachers and pupils agreed that teacher questions served an informative function, much like questions at home. The teacher and many pupils also saw pupil responses as serving an informative function. Mrs. Flood's reporting of the units and features of classroom language showed strong attention to the information contained in pupil comments. This pattern of attention would seem to be an essential element in Mrs. Flood's technique of "fluid topic branching," that is, building on pupil responses to move the lesson along from topic to topic. Pupil patterns of attention in this classroom also emphasized the information contained in pupil responses. These are reported in Chapter 6 and examined in more detail in Chapter 9.

RECAPITULATION

This chapter has examined classroom differences in language use and language meaning to determine whether differences in pupil perceptions of the functions of classroom questioning might be explained by classroom differences in teacher use of questions. Figure 4.4 indicates the place of these major variables within the context of the study as a whole.

This was the second phase of the investigation. It focused on classroom questioning because the initial analysis of pupil perceptions of the functions and rules of classroom discourse indicated that this was an area of potential pupil misunderstanding. It focused on classroom differences because the initial analysis showed that there were significant classroom differences in pupil perceptions of the functions of classroom questions.

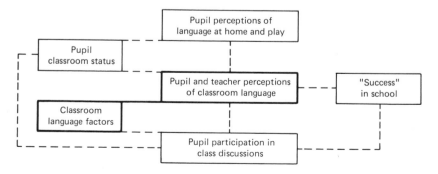

FIGURE 4.4   Phase-two questions in context of the overall study.

There were definite differences among these six classrooms in the way language was used by teachers and pupils. Teacher perceptions of language were closely akin to sociolinguistic descriptions of discourse in their classrooms. In four classrooms pupils demonstrated some confusion over the functions of the question cycle, reinforcing the suggestion (see Chapter 3) that classroom questioning provided the potential for pupil misunderstanding. In each of these four classrooms the descriptions of language use proferred possible explanations for the pupil confusion about language meaning.

In two classrooms pupils were clearer in their understanding of the classroom question cycle. These were the two classrooms (Miss DeLuca and Mrs. Flood) singled out in the sociolinguistic analysis of question cycle sequences as having fewer form-function incongruities in use of question cycles. In both Miss DeLuca's and Mrs. Flood's classrooms there was teacher and pupil agreement that pupil responses served an informative function.

The majority of pupils and four of the six teachers (Mrs. Brown, Miss DeLuca, Mrs. Estes, and Mrs. Flood) focused their attention on pupil responses in reporting on the units of language they heard in classroom lessons. This fact, and the fact that pupils as a whole showed uncertainty about the function of responses (over one-third reported no codable function), suggested that phase three of the investigation should examine patterns of pupil participation and attention in lessons.

5

The Interpretation of Pupil Attention and Participation in Discussions

CLUES TO COMMUNICATIVE COMPETENCE

Teachers have long understood the importance of speaking and listening skills in classroom lessons. In effect, pupil participation and attention in class discussions can provide clues about pupil competence in the use of these two important communication skills.

Attention and Participation as Communication Skills

The special form of communication that characterizes discussion lessons in classrooms revolves around the use of question cycles. Within the question cycle, pupils have an opportunity to exhibit speaking skills by providing responses to questions. Skill in speaking in this situation involves knowing what to say when. Many educators would argue that it also involves knowing how to say it in "standard English" (Stubbs, 1976). Sociolinguists would point out that effective speaking skills in classrooms also require a knowledge of how to get a turn to talk, for unless a pupil can get called on in most classrooms, he or she will not have a legitimate role in the discussion.

Educators typically discuss listening skills in terms of pupil attention to teacher talk, because most research on classroom interaction has indicated that teacher talk dominates verbal interaction in lessons (see Chapter 1). Sociolinguists would define listening skills more broadly and suggest that the skillful listener not only knows who and what to listen to in a discussion, but also understands that this "who" and "what" may vary as the social situation shifts or as the instructional procedures of the lesson shift.

Since attention and participation involve the use of skills in classroom communication, information about patterns of attention and participation can provide clues to pupil expectations about appropriate ways to communicate in class discussions. Where there is agreement about what these expectations are, this agreement can provide evidence about pupil understanding of the "rules of discourse" in classrooms. Where there is disagreement, there may be evidence of real differences in what behavior is appropriate. Differences in patterns of attention and participation from one classroom to another, for example, could suggest that appropriate behavior does vary by classroom and that pupil expectations vary as well. Thus, classroom differences (or "disagreement") could show that pupils are competent in adapting their speaking and listening skills to the requirements of the instructional setting in which they find themselves.

Differences among pupils of different status within the same classroom could indicate that different pupils are expected to behave in different ways within the same setting. On the other hand, such within-classroom differences could provide evidence that some pupils misunderstand the rules of communication within that setting. In any case, patterns of attention and participation indicate the rules of discourse that pupils are actually following, and thus they provide useful clues in the investigation of pupil perceptions of the meaning of classroom language.

This chapter explores general patterns of participation and attention exhibited by pupils in this study, and it explores classroom differences and individual differences associated with classroom status variables, as well. Patterns of participation and attention are interpreted in the light of pupil reports of the functions and rules of classroom discourse, and a set of pupil beliefs about classroom communication, suggested by these data, is proposed.

Techniques of Tracing Participation and Attention

To identify patterns of participation and attention, transcripts were made of each of the 36 videotaped lessons, and pupils making comments in each lesson were identified by name within the transcript. A measure of relative frequency of participation was obtained for each pupil by counting the number of times the pupil made a verbal or nonverbal (e.g., writing on the chalkboard) contribution over the course of the six lessons in his or her classroom and dividing this number by the total number of contributions for the whole class. Within each classroom, pupils were categorized as low, medium, or high in participation, based on their individual scores in comparison to the mean and standard deviation for that classroom.

The units of discourse reported by pupils (i.e., their responses to the question, "What did you hear anybody saying?") were compared to the lesson transcripts. These units provided data on pupil patterns of attention (who was heard and what was heard). For pupil comments that were reported, ratios of attention were computed by determining what proportion of the comments made by a given pupil were reported as heard by each of the other pupils in the class (Note 4). These data were then analyzed according to the classroom status (each variable separately) of the speaker and listener. For example, for Maria, a high-achieving Mexican-American girl who participated little in class discussion and was high in status with both the teacher and peers, there were 17 ratios of attention computed. These measured Maria's attention to high, middle, and low achievers; Mexican-American, Anglo, and other minority pupils; girls and boys; frequent, moderate, and infrequent participants in class discussions; pupils high, medium, and low in status with the teacher; and pupils high, medium, and low in status with peers.

In addition, pupil reports of teacher questions were analyzed according to the classroom status of the pupil reporting and according to the type of teacher question asked (management, rhetorical, lower or higher convergent, and lower or higher divergent). Reports of pupil answers to teacher questions were further analyzed according to the type of teacher question that engendered the response, the type of question cycle (independent, conjunctive, or embedded) in which the response occurred, and the type of teacher reaction to the response (use or nonuse of teacher praise). In these instances, ratios of attention were computed in each category (e.g., lower convergent questions) for each pupil, by dividing the number of comments reported by the number of comments actually made.

Based on these data, it was possible to examine who participated in class discussions, who heard what, and who heard whom, and to explore some of the ways in which patterns of teacher talk might influence patterns of pupil attention.

PATTERNS OF PARTICIPATION

Within any classroom setting, patterns of pupil participation are governed by both explicit and implicit rules. In this study, the explicit rules were revealed by pupil responses to the sentence-completion task on the rules of discourse (see Chapter 3). The implicit rules were revealed by the patterns of actual participation. Both of these types of rules must be understood in order to interpret pupil perceptions of the function of participation in class discussions.

Rules Articulated

The explicit rules for participation in lessons were strongly agreed upon by pupils and teachers in these six classrooms. They were as follows: I don't talk when the teacher or someone else is talking (83% of pupils responding); when I want to ask something, I raise my hand (81% of pupils responding); if I know the answer to a question, I raise my hand (75% of pupils responding); and if I don't know the answer to a question, I don't raise my hand/I listen/I keep quiet (83% of pupils responding). In the last example, pupils showed some disagreement with regard to use of passive behavior (don't raise my hand or keep quiet) versus active behavior (listen), but they were in agreement that they would not attempt to contribute verbally to the discussion when they didn't know the answer.

Note that these rules define both when it is appropriate for a pupil to talk in the classroom and how a pupil must behave in order to get a turn to talk. Teachers explicitly taught pupils in these classrooms that they should raise their hand and wait to be called on if they wanted help or wanted to answer a question. And teachers in these six classrooms followed their own rules, for they rarely called on a student who had not volunteered.

These teachers did not explicitly tell pupils that they should keep quiet if they didn't know the answer, or that they *ought* to volunteer if they did know the answer, but pupils explicitly stated these as basic rules governing classroom communication (Note 5). Thus, these might be seen as pupil-induced rules of participation rather than teacher-stated rules. The implicit rules revealed by actual patterns of participation suggest that pupils did tend to follow these pupil-induced rules.

Who Participated

There were clear relationships between classroom status variables and pupil participation in class discussions. Boys participated more frequently than girls ($x^2 = 9.79$; $df = 2$; $p < .01$; $C = .24$), pupils high in entering reading achievement participated more frequently than pupils low in entering achievement ($x^2 = 12.96$; $df = 4$; $p < .025$; $C = .28$), and pupils high in status with teacher participated more frequently than pupils low in status with teacher ($x^2 = 12.09$; $df = 4$; $p < .025$; $C = .27$). The last two variables can be taken as indicators of academic status in the classroom, suggesting that the most frequent participants were students with higher academic status. This interpretation is underscored by the fact that neither peer status nor ethnicity was significantly related to pupil participation in discussions.

Participation in discussions in these classrooms, then, appeared to require two different types of ability or speaking skills. The first skill involved knowing how to get a turn to talk, that is, knowing the rules for raising hands and being quiet. The second skill involved knowing the answers to questions that were asked, for the rules were that only pupils who knew the answer should volunteer and that teachers would only call on those who volunteered. Therefore, knowing the answer was a critical communication skill for pupils in these classrooms, and pupils who were high in academic status were the pupils who exhibited this skill and who participated more in class discussions as a result.

PATTERNS OF ATTENTION

Rules about listening in classrooms are rarely stated explicitly, except in a very general way, such as, "Pay attention when I'm giving directions." Furthermore, the implicit rules are not readily observed in operation, for listening is a covert activity. In this study, the patterns of attention revealed by pupil reports of what they heard "anybody saying" provided evidence about the implicit rules governing that covert activity. There were clear patterns with regard to both what was heard and who was heard.

What Was Heard

For both teachers and pupils, ratios of attention were higher for pupil responses than for teacher questions in an overwhelming majority of these lessons (33 lessons for pupils, 32 lessons for teachers). Pupils reported hearing speech acts occurring in the answering move proportionately more often than acts in the opening (questioning) or follow-up (reacting) moves (Friedman's two-way analysis of variance by ranks, $x_r^2 = 12.02$; $df = 2$; $p < .001$). Although teacher reactions to pupil comments were not reported very frequently, praise drew more attention than simple acceptance or repeats of pupil responses, and strong and extended praise drew more attention than mild praise (percent of instances occurring that were reported as heard: acceptance, 8%; repeats, 9%; total praise, 21%; mild praise, 17%; strong praise, 25%; extended praise, 29%).

Although teacher talk was reported proportionately less frequently than pupil talk, there were indications that teacher talk served to focus attention on certain pupil responses. For example, there were no significant differences in pupil attention to teacher questions of varying types, but there were significant differences in attention to pupils' *responses* to questions of varying types. More pupil attention was given to responses to lower convergent questions (i.e., factual or comprehension questions with one right answer) and higher divergent questions (i.e., questions requiring more complex thought, for which many different answers could be considered correct) than to other types of questions, such as higher convergent, lower divergent, or management questions (Friedman's analysis of variance by ranks, $x_r^2 = 71.78$; $df = 5$; $p < .001$). Pupil comments that were followed by teacher praise were reported more often than those that were not (overall ratio of attention was .33 compared to .21). Furthermore, pupil responses occurring in conjunctive cycles (i.e., cycles where the same question was asked of several children) were reported as heard more often than those in independent or embedded cycles (probing questions to the same pupil), and this was a significant difference (Friedman's analysis of variance by ranks, $x_r^2 = 10.35$; $df = 2$; $p < .002$). Responses occurring in cycles where probing occurred were also reported more frequently than responses that were not probed or responses to the probing questions themselves ($x_r^2 = 12.02$; $df = 2$; $p < .001$). Thus, pupils were attending more closely to the comments of other pupils when these comments were responsive to particular kinds of teacher questions, when they were praised by the teacher, and when they were "pursued" by the teacher through use of conjunctive cycles or probing questions.

Who Was Heard

There were also clear implicit rules for listening selectively to particular participants in class discussions in these six classrooms, if pupil reporting of the comments of other pupils can be taken as behavioral evidence of this essentially unobservable activity. Children reported hearing the comments of high achievers proportionately more often than those of lower achievers ($x_r^2 = 13.15$; $df = 3$; $p < .01$), and they reportedly heard the comments of frequent participants in class discussions proportionately more often than those of less frequent participants ($x_r^2 = 12.81$; $df = 2$; $p < .01$). Note that it was the pupils of higher academic status who tended to participate more in class discussions. The use of a proportional measure controlled for this participation, however, so they were not "heard" more simply because they talked more. Rather, the similarity of findings here suggests that pupils were following similar rules for both speaking and listening in class discussions. These rules implied that pupils of high academic status had something important to contribute to the lesson. This interpretation is underscored by the fact that pupils high in peer status were not reported as heard any more than those low in peer status, which is a pattern that might be expected. Thus, pupils were not simply listening to comments of their friends.

In addition, there was significantly more attention given to comments of Anglo pupils than to those of Mexican-American or other minority pupils ($x_r^2 = 10.82$; $df = 2$; $p < .01$). This is at least partially attributable to the relationship between ethnicity and entering reading achievement. Anglos were significantly higher in reading achievement than Mexican-Americans ($x^2 = 9.75$; $df = 4$; $p < .05$; $C = .24$). Boys were not heard proportionately more than girls, although they did participate more in class discussions. Pupils high in status with the teacher were not heard significantly more often than those lower in status, except at the fourth-grade level, where such a significant pattern did emerge ($x_r^2 = 14.79$; $df = 2$; $p < .001$). This might be interpreted as evidence that, as they grew older, more pupils followed an implicit rule to listen more closely to pupils of higher academic status.

Clearly, patterns of attention to the language of lessons in these six classrooms were not random. Rather, these patterns suggested that pupil attention was guided by verbal cues of the teacher and by academic status of the pupils who participated. Thus, listening skills in these classrooms apparently required that pupils be attentive to the comments of their peers, that they be alert to teachers' verbal cues, and that they be aware of the academic status of other pupils in the classroom.

INTERPRETING PUPIL BELIEFS

Taken by themselves, pupil patterns of attention and participation are interesting, but when they are combined with the data on pupil perceptions of the rules of discourse and the functions of the question cycle, they provide strong evidence of a set of pupil beliefs about classroom communication. The pertinent findings can be reiterated as follows:

1. Teachers' questions were reportedly asked in order to give information (to tell or teach) rather than to get information (agreed to by most pupils and most teachers).
2. Pupil responses were reportedly given because the teacher asked a question (agreed to by most pupils and most teachers).
3. Pupils who knew the answer to a teacher question were expected to volunteer to respond, and pupils who did not know the answer were expected to stay quiet (agreed to by most pupils and most teachers).
4. Pupils who were high in academic status (entering reading achievement and status with the teacher) were more frequent participants in class discussions than pupils low in academic status.
5. Pupil responses were attended to (reported as heard) proportionately more often than teacher questions, and this was true for both teachers and pupils.
6. Pupil responses to lower convergent (e.g., factual) questions and higher divergent (e.g., reasoned opinion) questions were reported as heard more often than responses to other types of questions (e.g., management).
7. Responses contributed by pupils of high academic status (entering reading achievement and participation in class discussions) were reported as heard more often than responses given by pupils of lower academic status.
8. Praise was reportedly given because pupils had good ideas (pupil view) or because teachers wanted pupils to know that their ideas were good/correct (teacher view).
9. Pupil responses that were praised were heard more often than responses that were not praised.
10. Pupil responses that were "pursued" by the teacher by asking the same question of another pupil, or by asking probing questions of the same pupil, were heard more often than responses that were not.

How might these perceptions and behaviors be integrated within a common set of beliefs? Clearly, the critical feature of classroom communication in these discussion lessons was the pupil response. Although pupils *said* that the function of a pupil answer was merely a routine response to a question, and many pupils could not readily define *any* function, they *behaved* as if pupil answers were the central part of the lesson. Although they reported that teacher questions were asked in order to tell, or to instruct, the information that they attended to was the information contained in pupil responses. It is the behavior that should be most revealing of implicit beliefs, but even the apparently contradictory explicit statements should have some logical consistency with the behavior in any interpretation attempting to explain these findings.

A coherent set of pupil beliefs might be framed in the following way. Teacher questions instruct by triggering an interactive sequence and by signaling what information pupils are expected to know or learn. Pupils respond to these questions because that is the "natural" course of communicative events—a question is asked, an answer is given. The answers to questions convey the real information, so pupils must attend to the responses of other pupils in order to learn what should be known. Pupils who know the answers to questions have a responsibility to provide this information so that other pupils may learn the answer. Pupils who are not sure that they know the answer should not confuse other pupils by answering with what may be misinformation. Therefore, pupils who are high in academic status can be expected to volunteer more and participate more in lessons.

Responses to factual questions are most apt to convey the type of information that pupils are expected to learn and remember, so they should be given special attention. Responses of pupils who are high in academic status are most apt to convey accurate information, so they should be given special attention. Responses that are praised by the teacher probably convey more accurate information, so they should be given special attention. When responses are pursued in some way by the teacher, by use of probing questions or by asking other students to add to or expand on a response, the question being discussed is probably a particularly important question, so these responses should be given special attention.

The central belief that unites these ideas into a set of beliefs is the idea that pupils can learn from other pupils. It is this belief that designates the pupil response as the critical feature of classroom communication and that spawns a series of corollary beliefs to guide pupil behavior. Within this belief system, both the explicit and the implicit rules of discourse followed by pupils in these classrooms can be seen as reasonable and appropriate.

It is doubtful that any pupil or teacher in this study would explain his or her behavior and thinking in precisely these terms, yet it is the case that this explanation provides a means for integrating a large number of discrete descriptive findings and presents a fresh perspective from which the outside observer might view classroom communication. From this perspective, the primary role of the pupil as effective speaker is to provide accurate information, or "good ideas," in order to assist other pupils in the learning process. The primary role of the pupil as effective listener is to attend differentially to the comments of other pupils, focusing particularly on those comments that might be expected to convey the most accurate and most important information. The role of the effective teacher, from this perspective, is to ask questions that clearly designate what information pupils need to learn, to call on pupils who can be expected to provide answers from which other pupils may learn, and to signal clearly by their reactions to pupil responses which answers are the most accurate and which questions are the most important.

The researcher who attempts to view classroom communication from this perspective must ask whether pupils who display these types of speaking and listening skills do in fact learn more from class discussions, and whether teachers who display these types of communication skills are in fact more effective in helping students to learn. Both of these questions will be addressed in Chapter 6, but first there are two prior questions to be addressed: (1) Were there individual differences in attention and participation? and (2) Did the general patterns of participation and attention hold for all classrooms?

PUPIL STATUS AND DIFFERENTIAL ATTENTION

Although the general patterns of attention for both teachers and pupils in these classrooms involved attending more to pupil responses than teacher questions, these patterns did not hold for all pupils. To begin with, there were significant grade-level differences, which suggested that pupils learned these attention patterns over time. Attention to pupil responses varied systematically by grade level, with third graders paying more attention than second graders, and fourth graders paying more attention than third graders (Kruskall-Wallis analysis of variance, $H = 8.03$; $p < .02$). Attention to teacher questions also varied, with fourth graders paying less attention than either second or third graders ($H = 6.29$; $p < .05$) (Note 6). Furthermore, patterns of attention to the comments of pupils with high academic status were consistently and significantly high for fourth-grade pupils considered separately, but not for third-grade pupils considered separately. Fourth-grade pupils attended more to comments made by pupils of high entering reading ($x_r^2 = 15.42$; $df = 3$; $p < .01$), pupils high in status with the teacher ($x_r^2 = 14.79$; $df = 2$; $p < .001$), and pupils high in frequency of participation in discussions ($x_r^2 = 12.79$; $df = 2$; $p < .01$). Thus, fourth graders clearly followed patterns of attention consistent with a belief that they could learn from other pupils, whereas third graders did not demonstrate these patterns as clearly or consistently, suggesting that perhaps these communication patterns were learned in the course of schooling.

It was also the case that pupils who varied in academic status varied in their patterns of attention. Pupils who were high in entering reading attended to teacher questions more than pupils low in entering reading ($H = 24.36; p < .001$). Furthermore, pupils high in entering reading attended significantly more to the comments of other pupils high in entering reading than to those of pupils low in entering reading ($x_r^2 = 19.73$; $p < .001$), whereas pupils lower in entering reading showed tendencies in this direction, but not statistically significant differences. Finally, pupils high in frequency of participation attended significantly more to the comments of other pupils high in participation than to those of pupils low in participation ($x_r^2 = 10.87$; $p < .01$), but pupils lower in frequency of participation showed no such significant differences. Thus, pupils of higher academic status (i.e., pupils who had been more successful in school to this point) more closely followed patterns of attention to comments of other pupils consistent with a belief that they could learn from responses of other pupils, and also attended more closely to teacher questions, which presumably signaled the types of information that should be learned.

One other interesting status difference in pupil patterns of attention was revealed, and this pattern was noted briefly in Chapter 3. Pupils high in peer status attended to comments of other pupils significantly more than did pupils lower in peer status ($H = 7.21$; $p < .05$). However, their attention was distributed quite equally across peer status levels. In this instance, attention patterns may have been serving social functions rather than academic functions. (This is discussed further in Chapters 7 and 9.)

To summarize, then, pupils in these classrooms exhibited individual differences in patterns of attention such that pupils with more experience and more academically successful experience in school showed significantly stronger tendencies to follow patterns of attention consistent with beliefs that pupils could learn from comments of other pupils.

PARTICIPATION AND DIFFERENTIAL MEANING

There were also interesting individual differences in patterns of participation relative to interpretations of the functions of teacher praise. Pupils who participated more frequently were more apt to define teacher praise as "deserved" (i.e., given because they had "good answers"), whereas pupils who participated less frequently were more apt to say that praise served an instructional function (i.e., was given to help them learn) ($x^2 = 12.58$; $df = 4$; $p < .025$; $C = .29$). This finding supported the proposed pupil belief system, for pupils who participated less were those who were less academically able and less apt to know the answers to teacher questions. These students tended to be the "audience" in class discussions. If they were attempting to learn from the answers of other pupils, teacher praise would serve to mark the "best" answers, and would indeed serve an instructional function for them. On the other hand, pupils who saw teacher praise as deserved tended to be the recipients of that praise, that is, the pupils who participated more, who were academically more able, and who were more apt to give "good answers" to questions. Thus, these differences in interpretation of the meaning of teacher praise were consistent with differences in the roles that pupils played in class discussions.

CLASSROOM DIFFERENCES IN PATTERNS OF PARTICIPATION AND ATTENTION

In addition to these individual differences in patterns of participation and attention, there were some classroom differences. Table 5.1 presents these patterns. There was only one classroom in which pupils consistently followed patterns of participation and attention associated with beliefs that pupils could learn from the comments of other pupils. In Mrs. Flood's class, pupils high in entering reading and status with the teacher participated most and were heard most. In Mrs. Brown's class, pupils high in entering reading and status with the teacher participated most, but pupils *low* in entering reading and status with the teacher were heard most. Both of these classrooms were described earlier (Chapter 4) as emphasizing content in lessons. Both were high in overall pupil attention to the comments of other pupils.

The other four classrooms were all lower in overall ratios of attention to pupil comments. These were the four classrooms described earlier (Chapter 4) as emphasizing "form over content." In Mrs. Addams's classroom, participation and attention were both unassociated with academic status variables. In Miss DeLuca's classroom, pupils high in reading achievement participated most, but pupil patterns of attention were unassociated with academic status variables. In Mrs. Case's classroom, pupil participation was randomly distributed across status variables, but pupils high in entering reading achievement were heard most. In Mrs. Estes's classroom, pupil participation was randomly distributed, and pupils high in status with the teacher and in frequency of participation were heard most.

Thus, while the general pattern for pupils in this study was that pupils high in academic status participated significantly more and were heard significantly more in class discussions, this general pattern was enacted somewhat differently in each of the six classrooms.

TABLE 5.1. Classroom Patterns of Participation and Attention

Classroom	Focus on form vs. content	Who participated	Who was heard	Overall attention[a]
Mrs. Addams (n = 27)	Form	Random distribution	Random distribution	.19
Mrs. Brown (n = 25)	Content	Pupils high in entering reading achievement and status with teacher	Pupils *low* in entering reading achievement and status with teacher	.26
Mrs. Case (n = 29)	Form	Random distribution	Pupils high in entering reading achievement	.18
Miss DeLuca (n = 29)	Form	Pupils high in entering reading achievement	Random distribution	.16
Mrs. Estes (n = 27)	Form	Random distribution	Pupils high in status with teacher and in frequency of discussion	.17
Mrs. Flood (n = 28)	Content	Pupils high in entering reading achievement and status with teacher	Pupils high in entering reading achievement and status with teacher	.21

[a] Mean proportion of comments made by each individual pupil that were reported as heard by every other individual pupil.

COMMUNICATIVE COMPETENCE: THE PUPIL VIEW

This chapter has examined pupil patterns of participation and attention in lessons, and interpreted these in the light of pupil reports of the functions and rules of classroom discourse, in order to identify pupil beliefs or expectations regarding appropriate behavior during class discussions. The importance of pupil responses within the classroom question cycle, and the relationships among classroom status, pupil participation, and patterns of attention have been emphasized particularly. Figure 5.1 illustrates the position of these variables within the total study.

This was the third phase of the investigation. It focused on patterns of pupil attention and participation because both teachers and pupils reported pupil comments more than teacher questions in identifying units of discourse they heard in classroom lessons, and because pupils as a whole showed uncertainty about the function of pupil responses. Thus, the role of pupil responses within a lesson appeared to be the key to pupil under-standing or *mis*understanding of classroom discourse.

Pupils high in academic status (entering reading achievement and status with teacher) participated more in discussions than pupils low in academic status. Also, the comments of pupils high in academic status (entering reading achievement and frequency of participation) were heard proportionately more often than those of pupils low in academic status. Answers to lower convergent questions, answers that were praised by the teacher, and answers that were pursued by the teacher (asking another pupil to respond to the same question, or asking a probing question of the same pupil) all received special attention from pupils.

These findings were explained by a proposed set of pupil beliefs. The central belief was that pupils could learn from the comments of other pupils in class discussions. According to this set of beliefs, communicative competence involved both speaking and listening skills. The competent speaker could provide accurate information or good ideas from which other pupils could learn. The competent listener could focus attention on

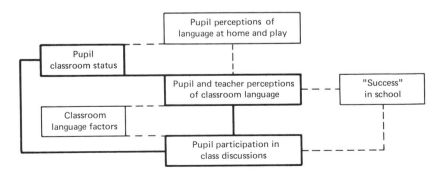

FIGURE 5.1 Phase three variables located within the study.

pupil comments that might be expected to convey the most important and/or accurate information.

Individual differences related to patterns of attention and participation provided support for the proposed explanation and suggested that these beliefs might be learned over time. Fourth graders behaved in ways consistent with these beliefs more frequently than second or third graders. Academically successful pupils (those high in entering reading achievement and frequent participants in class discussions) behaved in ways consistent with these beliefs more frequently than less successful pupils. Pupils who were less frequent participants, and therefore the "audience" for class discussions, defined teacher praise as instructional, a function consistent with the belief that they could learn by listening more carefully to pupil responses marked by teacher praise.

There were also classroom differences in patterns of pupil participation and attention. At first glance, these classroom differences would appear to contradict the proposed explanation that pupils in these classrooms believed that they could learn from the comments of other pupils in class discussions. However, another possibility is that the learning tasks differed in these classrooms, and that pupil patterns of participation and attention were consistent with the different learning tasks in which they were engaged. The classroom differences in language use and meaning described in Chapter 4 provide evidence that communication tasks did indeed differ in these classrooms. Chapter 6 explores these task differences in relation to patterns of participation and attention in more detail and also discusses their relationship to classroom achievement.

6

Talking, Listening, and Learning

THE ULTIMATE QUESTION

In the final analysis, most studies of classroom processes seek to discover the factors that contribute to student learning. This study was no exception. Pupil perceptions of classroom language and pupil participation in classroom discourse were explored in detail because they were viewed as possible contributors to pupil success in school. More specifically, they were seen as mediating variables between pupil classroom status, or classroom language factors, and eventual success in school. Prior research had shown that certain types of students achieved more and that certain patterns of classroom language were associated with greater achievement gains. This study was designed to examine possible relationships between classroom status or classroom language factors and pupil interpretations of and participation in classroom discourse, in the expectation that these relationships might help to explain differences in pupil success in school. In the six classrooms that were studied, there were individual pupil differences in perceptions of classroom language and in participation in class discussions that were associated with differences in classroom status. There were also classroom differences in language use that were associated with differences in pupil perceptions of classroom language and with differences in patterns of pupil participation in lessons. This chapter deals with the ultimate question and traces these differences in perceptions and participation to differences in eventual success in school.

The Identification of Variables Associated with Final Achievement

Since prior studies had identified both individual differences and classroom differences in achievement gains, pupil status variables and classroom assignment were tested to determine whether they were associated with variation in final achievement. In addition, since the pupil belief system about learning from class discussions highlighted certain pupil speaking and listening skills, as well as certain teacher communication skills, use of these skills was examined to determine whether this was associated with variation in final achievement. In all instances, final achievement was examined by use of regression analysis (General Linear Model of the Statistical Analysis System computer program), and entering reading achievement was controlled for by determining the proportion of variance in final achievement contributed by other variables over and above that contributed by entering reading achievement (procedure recommended by Cronbach & Furby, 1970). Final reading achievement was measured by pupil scores on the Metropolitan Achievement Test administered by teachers in the fall following the year of data collection, to eliminate possible effects of teachers' "teaching to the test."

There were three major contributors to variance in final reading achievement. These were identified by testing a regression model using fall 1978 reading achievement, frequency of participation in class discussions, "information load" (the number of items of discourse information reported by pupils after viewing each videotape), and classroom to predict fall 1979 reading achievement. The regression equation was significant [$F = 28.07$ (8, 97), $p < .001$, $R^2 = .698$], and entering reading, frequency of participation, and classroom each contributed significantly to the explained variance. Frequency of participation and classroom each accounted for 7% of the variance after entering reading achievement was controlled for. (This is equivalent to a partial correlation of .26.)

Classroom Status and Success in School. As would be expected, the classroom status variable of entering reading achievement was the best predictor of final achievement. Other pupil status variables (gender, ethnicity, peer status, and status with teacher) were also tested in regression models, but none contributed significantly to explained variance in final reading while accounting for an acceptable proportion of the variance after controlling for entering reading achievement. Even pupils of Mexican-American background, who entered with significantly lower reading achievement, did not have significantly lower final reading achievement than other pupils after entering reading was controlled for. Thus, the only pupil status variable that contributed directly to final reading achievement was entering reading achievement.

However, some pupil status variables contributed indirectly to pupil success in school through the mediating variable of pupil participation in class discussions. As noted in Chapter 5, gender, entering reading achievement, and status with teacher were all significantly correlated with frequency of participation in discussions. Because participation in discussions was a significant contributor to final reading achievement, even after entering reading achievement was controlled for, gender and status with teacher contributed indirectly to success in school by contributing directly to frequency of participation in discussion. To state this more explicitly, boys and pupils high in status with the teacher were more likely to be frequent participants in class discussions, and as frequent participants, they were more likely to show higher gains in reading.

Speaking and Listening Skills as Contributors to Success in School. The data on pupil perceptions of classroom language suggested that pupils believed they could learn from class discussions by attending to the comments of other pupils. Achievement data showed that this belief was not completely accurate. Pupil speaking skills identified as important, according to the proposed pupil belief system, were clearly associated with final achievement, for frequent participation in class discussions required that pupils both know the answers to questions being asked and know how to get a turn to talk. Pupils who had these skills and participated more frequently did achieve more. Pupil listening skills identified as important in the pupil belief system (attending more to the comments of pupils high in entering reading, high in frequency of participation, and high in status with the teacher) were not clearly associated with final reading achievement. Pupils who followed these patterns most closely did not achieve significantly more than pupils who were more haphazard in their patterns of attention to pupil comments. However, it was the case that the two classrooms with highest overall ratios of attention to pupil comments were two higher-achieving classrooms. Thus, at the classroom level, attention to comments of other pupils was associated with higher achievement.

Classroom Language Factors as Contributors to Success in School. The classroom differences in final reading achievement suggest that some of the six teachers who participated in this study were more effective than others. Table 6.1 presents entering and final reading achievement scores for the six classes. The three classrooms that were the highest achieving (entering reading controlled for), as indicated by a test of linear restriction, were Mrs. Addams's, Mrs. Flood's, and Mrs. Brown's. The lowest-achieving classroom was Mrs. Estes's, while Miss DeLuca's and Mrs. Case's classrooms showed more moderate achievement gains.

These classroom differences in final achievement might be explained in a variety of ways, but they will be analyzed here to determine whether they were associated with teacher use of effective communication skills as identified by the pupil belief system. These skills included asking questions that clearly designated what pupils needed to learn, calling on pupils who could be expected to provide answers from which other pupils could learn, and signaling clearly by their reactions to pupil responses which answers conveyed the most useful information and which questions were the most important. The remainder of this chapter is devoted to a comparison of

TABLE 6.1. Entering and Final Reading Achievement (Mean Standard Scores)

	Classes					
	Mrs. Addams (N = 19)	Mrs. Brown (N = 19)	Mrs. Case (N = 23)	Miss DeLuca (N = 24)	Mrs. Estes (N = 21)	Mrs. Flood (N = 21)[a]
Entering reading achievement (Fall 1978)	42.8	49.7	54.1	58.5	59.6	60.1
Final reading achievement (Fall 1979)	61.6	60.4	61.1	65.4	64.7	71.7
Difference (final achievement minus entering achievement)	18.8	10.7	7.0	6.9	5.1	11.6

[a] Only pupils for whom both entering and final reading achievement scores were available are included here.

higher-and lower-achieving classrooms in relation to teacher use of these types of skills.

TEACHER COMMUNICATION SKILLS
AND CLASSROOM TASKS

One useful way of thinking about teacher communication skills in relation to the classroom question cycle is to note that they serve to define the classroom communication task. The teacher's questions identify what it is that should be known; the teacher's selection of pupils to respond indicates which pupils might be expected to know; the teacher's use of praise identifies pupil responses that are particularly good, thus further specifying what it is that should be known; and the teacher's use of conjunctive or embedded cycles, or tendency to "pursue" certain questions, adds further specification about what are the most important things to know. When a teacher uses all of these skills in a coordinated fashion, the communication task should be rather clearly defined for pupils, and we might expect more learning to occur. However, although a clearly defined task may be essential for learning, it is not necessarily sufficient. Some communication tasks may contribute more than others to pupil learning. Thus, in comparing higher- and lower-achieving classrooms, it is important to consider both the teachers' skills in defining classroom communication tasks clearly and the exact nature of the communication tasks that the teachers have set. Both of these matters are addressed in the descriptions that follow.

Two Higher-Achieving Classrooms

In two higher-achieving classrooms, the teachers used skills that defined the communication task quite clearly, and they engaged pupils in communication tasks that were clearly cognitive in nature. Mrs. Flood and Mrs. Brown used somewhat different communication tasks, but pupils in these classrooms did not differ significantly from each other in final achievement. They did differ in patterns of attention to comments of other pupils, and in each case the patterns of attention were appropriate for the communication task in which they were engaged.

Mrs. Flood. In Mrs. Flood's classroom the communication task was to understand textbook concepts in relation to pupils' own experiences. Some teacher questions invariably invited pupils to report their own experiences related to the concept under discussion, whereas other teacher questions focused on defining and applying the concept. Pupils who participated most in these discussions were those who were high in entering reading achievement and status with the teacher, but pupils low in these status variables also participated actively. The dual nature of Mrs. Flood's questions permitted pupils of lower academic status to contribute useful information by reporting on their own experiences, and pupils of higher academic status could participate by defining, exemplifying, and applying the concept (Note 7).

Mrs. Flood was skillful in signaling which responses conveyed the most useful information and which questions were the most important. Her positive feedback was about equally divided among repeats, acceptance, and praise. Compared with other teachers in this study, she repeated pupil responses much less and praised them more; thus her signals about which responses were most informative were clearer than those of most of the other teachers. Furthermore, she was the only teacher to exhibit regular use of conjunctive cycles in all her lessons, and she showed more frequent use of embedded cycles than the other teachers. In pursuing selected questions in this way, she provided clear and regular signals to pupils about what information was most important to learn or to focus on within a given lesson. In addition, Mrs. Flood was one of two teachers identified as showing consistency between cycle form and cycle meaning. For example, when she used a conjunctive cycle to ask a variety of pupils to report on their experiences, she did not then identify some reports as "better" than others. This added further to the clarity of her feedback to pupils.

Through her questioning, selection of pupils to respond, and reactions to pupil responses, Mrs. Flood clearly defined the classroom communication task, and the task was a clearly cognitive one, not only involving learning concepts but also relating those concepts to pupils' own experiences. The evidence suggests that this task was clearly understood by both the teacher and the pupils. Mrs. Flood's reporting of the units and features of language in her classroom focused strongly on pupil responses and organized these according to the type of thinking pupils were exhibiting in their responses (giving opinions, sharing experiences, giving original ideas). Pupils indicated an awareness that pupil reports of experiences contributed useful information to the lesson, for many of them defined both teacher questions and pupil responses as informative, indicating that pupils were providing information not already known to the teacher. Furthermore, pupil attention was directed mainly toward responses of pupils high in entering reading and status with the teacher, but pupils low in academic status were not ignored, for their responses received more attention than pupils of middle academic status. Thus, even pupil attention patterns appeared to acknowledge the dual nature of the classroom communication task.

In this higher-achieving classroom, then, the teacher displayed communication skills that would be effective within the framework of pupil beliefs about learning from class discussion, and also engaged pupils in communication tasks that were cognitive in nature. Pupil patterns of participation and attention were well matched to the communication tasks, with pupils of high academic status participating most and being heard most, and pupils of lower academic status also being accorded opportunities to contribute useful information. An added feature of communication in this classroom was that conversation was very "natural," displaying many characteristics similar to conversations at home.

Mrs. Brown.   The communication task in Mrs. Brown's classroom was also twofold. Here pupils were engaged in learning concepts while practicing specific higher-order thinking skills, especially divergent thinking skills. Mrs. Brown taught lessons organized around "models" of teaching (Joyce & Weil, 1972), so that the specific thinking skill being practiced varied from lesson to lesson. In one lesson, teacher questions required pupils to identify various ways of categorizing manipulative materials. In another lesson, teacher questions involved pupils in identifying similarities between two very different types of things, such as a turkey and a ball. Although the types of questions varied from lesson to lesson, Mrs. Brown's questions clearly specified the kind of thinking pupils were to do. To answer these questions, Mrs. Brown called mostly on pupils high in entering reading achievement and status with the teacher. However, pupils low in academic status also had opportunities to participate, since the divergent questions encouraged many pupils to respond to the same question, and no one answer was considered "right."

Mrs. Brown was generally skillful in identifying pupil responses that conveyed useful information. Usually her praise denoted "that's the right *kind* of answer to give," not "that's the right answer." She used relatively high proportions of praise (.39 of positive feedback was praise) and relatively low proportions of verbatim repeats of pupil responses (.49). Her use of conjunctive and embedded question cycles varied from lesson to lesson, according to the lesson model she was using. Thus, in some lessons the most important questions were clearly marked for pupils, but in other lessons they were not. Mrs. Brown did not always show consistency between cycle form and cycle meaning. On occasion she would ask pupils to explain their thinking, for example, and then "correct" their answer, suggesting that she knew what they were thinking better than they did themselves. This may have reflected the dual nature of the task in which pupils were engaged, requiring them to display both knowledge of content and skill in particular forms of thought. At any rate, Mrs. Brown's reactions to pupil responses did not serve to define the communication task quite as clearly as Mrs. Flood's.

In general, Mrs. Brown defined the classroom communication task fairly well for her pupils, through her use of specific questions, by calling on pupils who might be expected to provide useful information, and by her use of praise. The task in which pupils were engaged was a clearly cognitive one, requiring that concepts be learned and that various thinking skills be practiced. This task was clear to Mrs. Brown, for her attention to classroom language was carefully focused on pupil responses, and she organized these according to the types of thinking skills pupils were practicing in the lesson. The task was not quite so clear to pupils, and this was in part perhaps a function of the variation in use of models, for the particular thinking skill to be practiced changed from day to day. Pupils defined teacher questions as instructional, but many could not explain the function of pupil responses. Pupil patterns of attention were well defined, however. Pupils low in entering reading achievement and status with the teacher were heard proportionately more than pupils high in academic status. Furthermore, attention was directed to responses to higher-order divergent questions. These patterns suggest that pupils did understand the importance of divergent thinking as a part of the communication task in this classroom. Indications from teachers skilled in use of Joyce's models of teaching are that high-achieving pupils who are used to knowing the "right" answer may be hesitant in responding to divergent questions, whereas lower-achieving pupils may be more willing to take the risks involved and may provide more interesting and divergent responses. Thus, pupils of lower academic status may well have provided the most informative responses in these lessons.

In Mrs. Brown's higher-achieving classroom, the teacher also displayed communication skills that were consonant with pupil beliefs that they could learn from class discussion, and the communication tasks were also clearly cognitive in nature. Pupil patterns of participation and attention were well suited to the communication tasks. Pupils high in academic status participated most, but pupils low in academic status and responses to divergent questions were heard most, in line with the teacher's emphasis on divergent thinking skills.

Common Features. The features that were common to these two higher-achieving classrooms included teacher use of communication skills associated with pupil beliefs about learning from class discussions, pupil engagement in clearly defined communication tasks of a cognitive nature, pupil patterns of participation and attention appropriate to the communication tasks, and teacher provision of opportunities for pupils of lower academic status to contribute important information to the discussion. The classrooms differed in the specific nature of the cognitive tasks in which pupils were engaged and in patterns of teacher use of conjunctive and embedded question cycles.

A Low-Achieving Classroom

The lowest-achieving classroom in this study was Mrs. Estes's. Pupils in this class showed significantly less growth in reading achievement over the school year than pupils in Mrs. Flood's and Mrs. Brown's classrooms. Mrs. Estes did not display effective communication skills associated with pupil beliefs about learning from class discussion, nor did she engage pupils in communication tasks of a cognitive nature. Pupil patterns of participation and attention were appropriate for the communication tasks in which they were engaged, however.

The communication task in Mrs. Estes's classroom was simply to participate. As Mrs. Estes explained during one interview, she didn't want to be the only one talking, so she tried to get pupils to talk. This emphasis on getting pupils to talk became so extreme in one lesson that she spent a great deal of time trying to get students to state correctly the procedures to be followed in a writing assignment, rather than simply give specific directions herself. Mrs. Estes's questions were generally clearly stated, but they focused on getting pupils to give opinions, and in several lessons a number of pupils were called on to respond to the same question, so that a variety of opinions were stated in response to a given question. The opinions requested were not "reasoned opinions" in the sense that pupils were asked to explain their thinking or provide evidence to support their ideas. Rather, any and all opinions were treated as equally valid. Mrs. Estes's patterns of calling on pupils to participate underscored this interpretation, for she distributed turns to talk in a random fashion, so that no particular status group received more opportunities than others to contribute to the discussions.

In reacting to pupil responses, Mrs. Estes tended to repeat the comments verbatim (.63 of instances of positive feedback were repeats), and she rarely provided real praise (only .20). Thus, few pupil responses were marked as particularly good ideas for other pupils to remember or learn from. Her use of conjunctive and embedded cycles tended to be erratic. In one lesson there would be long sequences of conjunctive cycles, and in the next lesson none at all; thus, these cycles could not serve to mark particular questions as important within a given lesson. These patterns of teacher reactions to pupil responses made it difficult for pupils who might be trying to learn from the responses of others, for there were no clear signals provided as to which responses conveyed the most useful or important information.

In Mrs. Estes's classroom, then, teacher questions, distribution of opportunities to participate, and reactions to pupil responses all worked together to convey the impression that the major communication task was to participate rather than to learn particular facts or concepts. Mrs. Estes's patterns of attention to the language of lessons also indicated a lack of focus on cognitive content, for she tended to concentrate on pupil errors in language usage or pronunciation. She was clear about the task being to participate, because she reported that her questions served a routine interactive function (to get students talking). Pupils in this class reported that teacher questions served an instructional function, but they were divided in their interpretations of the function of pupil responses, with some thinking that these were instructional and others perceiving them as routine interactive. Of course, since the communication task was to participate rather than to learn particular concepts, an "instructional" response in this classroom might be seen as showing other pupils how to participate, and thus might be roughly similar to a routine interactive function. Pupil patterns of attention were clearly appropriate to the communication task, for pupils who were heard most were those high in status with the teacher and those who participated most. In this classroom, pupils could presumably learn how to participate by attending more to those pupils who were the most frequent participants.

Critical Variables

Mrs. Estes's low-achieving classroom provided a sharp contrast to the two high-achieving classrooms in that the communication task was not a cognitive task. Teacher questions, distribution of turns to talk, and reactions to pupil responses did not assist pupils in their attempts to gather information from the comments of others. It was the case, however, that pupil patterns of participation and attention were appropriate to the communication task that characterized this classroom, which was merely to participate. It was also the case that pupils of lower academic status were provided with opportunities to participate in class discussions. This finding suggests that the critical variables associated with classroom achievement differences were teacher use of communication skills that assisted pupils in their attempts to learn from class discussion and teacher designation of communication tasks that were clearly cognitive in nature. This interpretation of the findings for these sharply contrasting classrooms can be tested against the findings for the other three classrooms.

Two Middle-Achieving Classrooms

The two middle-achieving classrooms in this study were those of Miss DeLuca and Mrs. Case. Pupils in Mrs. Flood's class scored significantly higher in final reading achievement than pupils in these two classrooms, but pupils in Mrs. Brown's class did not. Patterns of communication in these two classrooms support and extend the interpretation presented above.

Miss DeLuca. The communication task in Miss DeLuca's classroom was somewhat cognitive in nature, for it engaged pupils in using descriptive language. Teacher questions clearly specified that descriptive language was called for. Pupils who were called on to participate most were not necessarily those who might be expected to use the most descriptive language, but they were pupils high in entering reading achievement, so they had demonstrated some facility with written language. Pupil responses were typically repeated verbatim by the teacher (.66 instances of positive feedback were repeats), but praise was given in moderate amounts (.25). Thus, some pupil responses were marked by the teacher as particularly good. Miss DeLuca used embedded cycles fairly consistently throughout her lessons, but she was highly erratic in her use of conjunctive cycles, so teacher "pursuit" of particular questions did not serve well to mark these questions as having special importance in the lesson. Teacher communication skills in this classroom, then, were less sharply tuned to marking informative answers and important questions as a way of assisting pupils in their attempts to learn from class discussion.

What Miss DeLuca's language did mark most carefully for pupils was the segments of the lesson through which they were progressing. The importance of this lesson "script" to Miss DeLuca was demonstrated by her attention to lesson language, for she consistently reported what she heard in the exact sequence in which it occurred. Pupil responses were also clearly important to Miss DeLuca. She reported hearing many pupil responses, she indicated that her questions served a routine interactive rather than an instructional function, and she perceived pupil responses as informative. Pupils saw teacher questions as instructional, but they concurred with Miss DeLuca in viewing responses as serving an informative function. Pupil patterns of attention were not closely tied to the communication task in this classroom, however. No particular status group was seen as providing better responses than any other group. Thus, pupil attention to the responses of other pupils was not clearly directed by teacher signals about the quality or importance of the response, and it was not clearly directed by the status of the pupils responding. In fact, overall pupil attention to the responses of other pupils in this classroom was the lowest of all six classrooms.

In short, communication in Miss DeLuca's classroom was similar to that in the two higher-achieving classrooms in that the communication task was cognitive in nature. It was different in that teacher comunication skills did not clearly mark the pupil responses that conveyed the most useful information or the questions that were most important. Although pupil participation patterns may have been associated with the communication task of using descriptive language, pupil attention was randomly distributed. Pupils in this classroom had little apparent direction in their attempts to learn from the responses of others.

Mrs. Case. The communication task in Mrs. Case's classroom was presumably cognitive in nature, for pupils were primarily engaged in following the textbook. Mrs. Case's questions were read directly from the teacher's edition of the textbook for the most part, so they did clearly define this task. Participation in class discussions was randomly distributed, however, so that pupils who might be expected to provide better responses to these questions were not called on more often. Mrs. Case was highest of all six teachers in verbatim repetition of pupil responses and lowest in use of real praise; thus her reactions to pupil responses failed to denote those that were most informative. In addition, she did not use conjunctive or embedded cycles on a regular basis in her lessons, so pupils were not given helpful signals about which questions were the most important. The communication skills exhibited by Mrs. Case, therefore, did not provide much assistance to pupils in their attempts to learn from class discussions.

Mrs. Case's patterns of attention to the language of her lessons suggested that she was clear about the communication task she emphasized, for she tended to focus on the language of the textbook rather than on pupil or teacher language. Pupils in this classroom saw teacher questions as routine interactive, and they were confused about the function of pupil responses. Their patterns of attention, however, suggested that they had some awareness of the communication task, for they attended most to pupils high in entering reading achievement. Since the task involved reading exercises aloud from the textbook, pupils high in reading ability were probably pupils who could provide the "best" responses.

Communication patterns in Mrs. Case's classroom were similar to those in the two high-achieving classrooms in that there was a clearly designated cognitive task. In this instance, the task was centered around following the language arts textbook. Patterns in Mrs. Case's classroom were different in that the communication patterns exhibited by the teacher provided little support for pupils who were trying to learn from the comments of others. Pupil patterns of participation were not clearly appropriate for the communication task, but pupil patterns of attention were associated with the task. Thus, pupil attempts to learn in this classroom were assisted by the textbook and by attention to the comments of pupils high in reading achievement rather than by the communication skills of the teacher.

Corroboration

The findings regarding communication patterns in Miss DeLuca's and Mrs. Case's classrooms provide corroboration for the suggestion that the critical variables associated with classroom achievement differences were teacher use of communication skills that assisted pupils in their attempts to learn from class discussions and teacher designation of communication tasks that were clearly cognitive in nature. Miss DeLuca and Mrs. Case differed from Mrs. Flood in that they did not provide such clear signals about which pupil responses were most informative or which questions were most important. They differed from Mrs. Estes in that they did engage pupils in communication tasks that were cognitive in nature. Pupils in Miss DeLuca's and Mrs. Case's classrooms achieved more than those in Mrs. Estes's class and less than those in Mrs. Flood's class. Although they were lower in achievement than pupils in Mrs. Brown's class, they were not significantly lower. But note that Mrs. Brown shared with Miss DeLuca and Mrs. Case the tendency not to use conjunctive cycles on a regular basis, so there were few signals to mark the most important questions for pupils. In this respect, all three teachers differed from Mrs. Flood.

In all five of these classrooms, pupils of lower academic status had opportunities to participate in class discussions, either because of the nature of the task or because of teacher tendencies to distribute turns to talk in a random fashion. When these opportunities were associated with a communication task that was cognitive in nature (i.e., the task was one to which these pupils could contribute useful information), as in Mrs. Flood's, Mrs. Brown's, and Miss DeLuca's classrooms, then some pupil attention was clearly given to responses of these lower-status pupils. When these opportunities to participate were simply associated with the teacher's random distribution of turns (i.e., it was not clear that these pupils could contribute particularly useful information), as in Mrs. Case's and Mrs. Estes's classrooms, then little pupil attention was given to the responses of these lower-status pupils. In Mrs. Case's class, where the task was to follow the textbook, attention was given to responses of pupils high in reading achievement. In Mrs. Estes's class, where the task was to participate, attention was given to pupils high in status with the teacher (who controlled access to participation) and high in frequency of participation. Thus, pupil patterns of attention were associated with the communication task in all five classrooms.

The data from these five classrooms demonstrate the importance of teacher use of communication skills that could assist pupils in their attempts to learn from class discussions, and of pupil engagement in communication tasks that were clearly cognitive in nature. These were the two variables that best distinguished among higher- and lower-achieving classrooms. Teacher provision of opportunities for pupils of lower academic status to contribute useful information to the discussion also helped to distinguish between some of the higher- and lower-achieving classrooms.

Pupil patterns of participation and attention were appropriate to the communication task in all five classrooms. It was not the appropriateness of these patterns so much as the nature of the communication task itself, therefore, that distinguished among higher- and lower-achieving class-rooms. This finding highlights the designation of pupil perceptions and participation as mediating variables between classroom language factors and success in school. The classroom communication task specified what patterns of pupil participation and attention were appropriate, and in following these patterns, pupils were more or less successful in final achievement, according to the nature of the task in which they were engaged and the skillfulness with which the teacher defined the task.

The Anomaly of Mrs. Addams

The findings and interpretations presented above would be quite per-suasive if it were not for the anomaly of Mrs. Addams. Unfortunately, Mrs. Addams's class was the highest achieving of all six classes and scored significantly higher in final reading achievement than every class except Mrs. Flood's, so the data on her classroom can hardly be ignored.

Mrs. Addams presents a severe test of the explanations given to date, for the communication task in her classroom was definitely not cognitive in nature. Mrs. Addams engaged her pupils in learning to "do school." The questions that she asked in language arts lessons did designate this task rather clearly, for they were mainly procedural in nature. The pupils who participated were fairly randomly distributed across status groups. This pattern might have been suitable for the task, because it is not immediately clear what abilities might make pupils adept at providing procedural information. Mrs. Addams was very low in overall use of positive feedback (only 62 instances over 6 lessons, compared with other teachers who ranged from 146 to 167), but almost half of her positive feedback was real praise (.47). Thus, pupil responses that were particularly informative were identified. In addition to this positive sanctioning of pupils' verbal responses, she was frequently engaged in both positive and negative sanctioning of pupils' behavior (sitting up straight, hands to themselves, eyes front), so that pupil behavior that was appropriate or inappropriate was also identified. She used conjunctive and embedded cycles to some extent in each of her lessons, so that pupils did receive signals about which questions were the most important. In sum, Mrs. Addams used communication skills that defined the communication task quite clearly, but the task was not a cognitive one.

The evidence would suggest that Mrs. Addams was clear about the task in which she was engaging pupils, for in reporting the language that she heard in lessons, she focused on language dealing with socialization rather than content. Both Mrs. Addams and her pupils said that teacher questions served an instructional function, and Mrs. Addams saw pupil responses as serving an instructional function as well ("to let me know they know the answer"). It should be noted that this was the only classroom in which question cycles were spontaneously initiated by pupils on a regular basis. (Three other teachers structured some of their lessons so that they directed pupils to ask specific types of questions.) This type of pupil participation would be appropriate for the task of learning classroom procedures, for it would provide opportunities for pupils who were uncertain to ask for specific procedural information. Thus, even these types of pupil comments might serve an instructional function. Pupil patterns of attention were randomly distributed across status groups. Again, this might be seen as appropriate for a communication task focused on learning to follow classroom procedures.

The communication patterns in Mrs. Addams's classroom, then, showed that teacher communication skills defined the communication task clearly, that pupils of lower academic status had opportunities to participate, and that pupil patterns of participation and attention could have been appropriate to the communication task. The difficulty was that the communication task in which pupils were engaged was clearly not of a cognitive nature, yet Mrs. Addams's pupils were successful in showing high gains in final reading achievement. This finding is contradictory to those for the other five classrooms. How might this anomaly be explained?

At least two alternative explanations can be offered, both of which center on the fact that Mrs. Addams's class was the only second-grade class to participate in this study (see explanation in Chapter 2). One possibility is that learning how to "do school" is an essential requirement for successful learning (particularly for children of lower socioeconomic status, as all these pupils were), and that children at the second-grade level must accomplish this task before they can successfully achieve in learning the basic skills. If this were the case, then Mrs. Addams's emphasis on procedural matters in language arts lessons could have contributed an important ingredient to the education of children in her classroom. One ingredient of Mrs. Flood's success was apparently her ability to carry on class discussions that were similar to conversations at home; thus, she adapted classroom discourse to make it more like the informal discourse with which children were already familiar. Mrs. Addams moved in the opposite direction, by concentrating on teaching pupils to adapt to typical rules of classroom discourse. By her repetition of routines, she engaged pupils in "overlearning" classroom procedures. Although these were opposite approaches, in effect, they had similar consequences, for in each case the distance between children's "homegrown" communication skills and the skills required for participation in the lesson was shortened. In this way, the noncognitive communication task in which Mrs. Addams engaged her pupils could have been a positive rather than a negative factor in their final achievement.

The other possible explanation is that the high relative achievement of Mrs. Addams's class was a spurious finding. There were no other second-grade classes in this study to which Mrs. Addams's class could be compared. But there was a strong and continuing pattern of achievement differences between lower and middle elementary grades in this school. Typically, pupils in the first and second grades scored at or above national norms on standardized achievement tests of basic skills, whereas third-, fourth-, and fifth-grade pupils scored progressively lower. At least part of the difference in achievement of these second-grade pupils, then, could be attributable to this pervasive school pattern of achievement rather than to the particular procedures that Mrs. Addams used in instructing her class.

Both of these alternative explanations present viable reasons why the seemingly contradictory evidence provided by Mrs. Addams's class should not suffice to negate the evidence supplied by the other five classes. Certainly the identification of two classroom language factors that can contribute to pupil success in school through the mediating variables of pupil perceptions of classroom language and pupil participation in class discussions is a finding worthy of further testing. One means of such testing is to compare these findings with those of other studies already completed, and this is done in Chapter 8.

MAKING CONNECTIONS

This chapter has examined the ways in which pupil classroom status and classroom language factors were related to final achievement gains, both directly and indirectly through the mediating variables of pupil perceptions of classroom language and pupil participation in class discussion. Figure 6.1 illustrates the position of these variables within the framework of the study as a whole and demonstrates that important connections have been made.

Classroom status of pupils contributed directly to final achievement in that pupils high in entering reading achieved highly at the end of the year. Certainly, this was not an unexpected finding. Classroom status of pupils also contributed indirectly to success in school, however, because boys and pupils high in entering reading achievement and status with the teacher participated more frequently in class discussions, and pupils who participated more frequently scored higher in final reading achievement, even after controlling for entering reading achievement.

Classroom language factors contributed directly to final achievement, for there were significant classroom differences in final achievement after controlling for entering achievement. The classroom language factors that best distinguished among higher- and lower-achieving classrooms were teacher designation of a communication task that was cognitive in nature and teacher use of communication skills that were consonant with pupil beliefs that they could learn from class discussions. The latter factor was related to each of the two mediating variables. First, teacher use of these skills provided a close fit between pupil interpretations of classroom

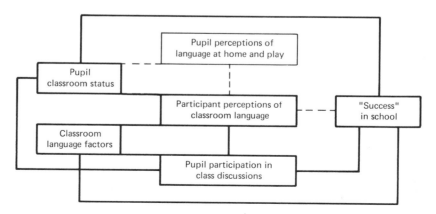

FIGURE 6.1   Final-phase variables located within the study.

language and teacher use of classroom language (or, to put it another way, both confirmed and acknowledged pupil understandings about the "rules" of classroom discourse). Second, one of the specific skills involved was teacher selection of pupils to participate who might be expected to provide accurate or useful information, so that other pupils could learn from these responses. Another classroom language factor that helped to distinguish between some higher- and lower-achieving classrooms was provision of opportunities for pupils of lower academic status (entering reading achievement, status with teacher) to contribute useful information to class discussions. This factor was associated with the mediating variable of pupil participation in class discussions, which was in turn associated with final achievement in reading.

Clearly, the original design of the study, which placed pupil perceptions of classroom language in a central position in the model that guided collection and analysis of data, was a productive design, because the pupil belief system about how to learn from class discussions provided an important connecting link between classroom language factors and eventual success in school. The original plan for the study would dictate that discussion of the findings should stop here, for important sociolinguistic factors related to student learning have been identified. However, as is often the case, the process of data collection and analysis in this study uncovered some additional findings of interest. These findings relate to patterns of pupil participation and attention in play-group conversations, and they may have additional implications for classroom teachers with regard to classroom language use. These findings are presented in Chapter 7.

7

Talking, Listening, and "Succeeding" in Play Settings

OPPORTUNITIES TO LEARN FROM PLAY

Child development specialists have long argued that children learn from play, and some instructional methods, such as the Montessori approach, have been built upon that assumption. Piaget (1955, 1962) demonstrated that researchers could also learn from children's play, and sociolinguists have been particularly interested in observing language in play settings. Stubbs (1976) admonished classroom researchers that the study of language in education "should be based primarily on naturalistic observations and recording of language in real social situations: mainly in the classroom itself, but also in the home, and in the peer group, which is the most powerful linguistic influence on children" (p. 112).

As the findings of this study unfolded, the idea that the peer group was the "most powerful linguistic influence on children" was more and more strongly reinforced. For example, when children were asked, "Who do you mostly talk with at home?" 57% answered "my brother" or "my sister," whereas only 31% said "my mother," and only 12% said "my father." Thus, pupil perceptions were that more time was spent in conversations with siblings (peers) than in conversations with parents (adults).

There was also evidence to suggest that status within the peer group was a factor in use of language among peers. When children were asked, "What do you say when you want to get your friend's attention [or "get your friend to do something"]?" and "What does your friend say when [he or she] wants to get your attention [or "get you to do something"]?" the sentences they generated showed that different forms of address were used, dependent upon the child's status in the group (see Chapter 3). For both language functions (getting attention and exerting influence), pupils low in status with their peers tended to attribute forms indicative of lower relative status to themselves, and forms indicative of higher relative status to their friends. Thus, they would report, "I say, do you want to ride bikes?" (a question form, or indirect way of exerting influence) and "My friend says, 'Give me the ball'" (a command form, or direct way of exerting influence). Pupils high in peer status tended to generate sentence forms for "getting someone to do something" that indicated their higher relative status, but used more nearly equal status forms for "getting someone's attention."

Perhaps most important of all was the evidence that the peer group, and status within the peer group, were important factors in pupil attention to classroom discourse (see Chapter 5). Although teacher talk predominated in lessons, pupils reported hearing the responses of other pupils proportionately more than teacher questions. In addition, there were peer status differences in patterns of attention. Pupils of higher peer status reported more pupil comments than pupils of low or middle status, and therefore reported more total information when asked what they heard anyone saying in a lesson.

While peer status was related to what pupils heard in classroom lessons, it was not related to who they heard or to patterns of pupil participation in lessons (see Chapter 5). Pupils high in peer status were no more apt to be heard or to contribute comments in class discussions than pupils low in peer status. This was in sharp contrast to most other classroom status variables. Entering reading achievement and status with teacher were both related to pupil patterns of attention and participation, with high-status pupils both participating more and being heard more (overall patterns). Gender was related to participation patterns, with boys participating more than girls. Thus, although peer status was apparently an important factor in pupil perceptions of classroom language, it did not operate in precisely the same way as other status variables.

There were also certain indications that patterns of language use among peers were quite different from patterns of discourse in lessons. For example, the question-response-react cycle identified so frequently in the literature on classroom interaction (Bellack et al., 1966; Mehan, Cazden, Coles, Fisher, & Maroules, 1976) clearly accounted for most of the language in the lessons examined in this study, yet when children described what kinds of things they did and said while playing with their friends at home and at school, 72% of them reported various forms of directives, or attempts to influence playmates, whereas only 4% reported asking for information, and only 6% reported giving information. Initial observations of the videotapes of play groups tended to corroborate the children's reports. Questions occurred very infrequently. Attempts to direct or influence others, and attempts to get the attention of others, occurred quite frequently.

All of these findings suggested that some valuable insights might be gained from further analysis of the data on conversations in play groups and comparison of these data to the data on classroom discussions. The findings reported in Chapter 6 showed that particular types of communication skills were associated with pupil success in classroom learning. If similar types of communication skills were associated with success in play groups, then skills developed in play settings might contribute to pupil success in school. If different types of communication skills were associated with success in play groups, then skills developed in play settings might contribute to pupil misinterpretation of classroom discourse and be detrimental to pupil success in school. The preliminary indications were that important differences might well exist.

The first questions to be answered dealt with similarities in language use and perceptions of language in the two settings. In particular, the following questions were identified as pertinent:

1. Because children's reports seemed to indicate that language events that predominated in play settings were different from those that predominated in lessons, would it follow that clear patterns of predominant language events in play settings could be identified by outside observers, and if so, would these patterns in reality be different from the patterns of classroom discourse?
2. Because the language events that predominated in lessons (e.g., teachers' opening moves) were not necessarily the events that were attended to most strongly by pupils, would the language events that predominated in play settings also be different from those that predominated in children's reports of what they heard being said?

Answers to these questions were sought in the belief that further understanding of the similarities and differences in language use and language meaning in classroom settings versus play settings could provide additional insight into possible reasons for pupil misinterpretations of classroom discourse. But comparing language use and language meaning in the two settings was not enough. It was also necessary to examine associations among pupil status variables, pupil communication skills, and pupil success in play settings to determine whether communication skills learned (practiced and reinforced) in play settings were skills that might interfere with successful communication in lessons.

Measuring "Success" in Play Settings

There is a good deal of agreement on what constitutes a useful measure of academic success, and achievement in basic skills as measured by performance on standardized achievement tests is the most frequently used operational definition of pupil learning in classroom studies of teaching effectiveness. What might be considered to constitute success in play settings is a question rarely, if ever, raised in research on teaching. In the absence of definitive guidelines from prior classroom research, three different measures of success in play settings were identified for use in this substudy.

Having attained high status within the peer group was regarded as one important measure of success. This measure was seen as akin to entering reading achievement as a measure of academic success (i.e., it indicated prior attainment of social skills in much the same way that entering reading achievement indicated prior attainment of academic skills). Peer status was identified through use of a sociometric measure (see Chapter 2), and relationships between peer status and participant patterns of attention to language in play settings were examined to determine what patterns of attention might be associated with success in play settings thus defined.

A second measure of success in play settings was identified as individual ability to become involved in and influence the flow of group activity. This type of success was measured by ratings of ten outside observers who were knowledgeable about child development and experienced in working with young children. Relationships among peer status, gender, and success in becoming involved in and influencing group activity were examined to determine how social status might be associated with this type of success in play settings.

A third measure of success in play settings was a group measure, which focused on ability of the play group to engage in cooperative, imaginative, and varied play activities. This type of success was also measured by ratings of ten outside observers. Group differences with regard to this type of play-group success were compared to group differences in patterns of classroom discourse to determine whether associations might exist between productive patterns of interaction in the two settings.

Observations of Language in Play Settings

Triangulation of data on language in play settings required coordination of data from three sets of observers, just as did the triangulation of data on language in classroom lessons. In this case, however, only one set of observers were actual participants in the setting.

Participants. Thirty-six pupils participated in the play settings, six in each of the six play groups. Each play group was composed of pupils from a single classroom. A play group consisted of three boys and three girls, and for each gender there was one pupil from each of the three peer status groups within the classroom (high status, middle status, and low status). As noted in Chapter 2, each play group was presented with a variety of construction toys and told they were free to play with these toys in any way. The 30-minute videotapes that resulted were edited to 12-minute tapes. Segments were selected on the basis of clarity of sound and inclusion of a variety of the activities in which the group engaged.

Reports of the participants about what they heard "anybody saying" after viewing these edited videotapes were analyzed in three ways. (See Chapter 2 for details of playback procedures.) First, for each pupil participant a measure of "information load" was obtained. This measure was determined by counting each separate report of actual language heard as one item of information, and adding one item of information for each report of the social context in which the language occurred (e.g., who said it, who it was said to, what was said in reply). Thus, if after viewing a "sword fight" held with Lincoln logs, a participant reported hearing the words "On guard!" it was counted as one item of information. If another participant reported that "Ray said 'On guard' to Gavino," it was counted as three items of information. (See Chapter 3 for more detail on this measure.)

Second, for each pupil participant a measure of the number of playmates cited as "sources" was obtained. This measure could range from zero to five, since each play group included six children. Citing oneself as a source of the language reported was not counted. Analysis of variance was used to determine whether either of these two measures varied by peer status or gender of the participants.

Third, for each pupil participant a frequency count was made of the number of language units reported that involved directive language, or language that functioned to influence the actions of other children in the play group. This measure was compared to a similar measure of the number of directive language units reported by the same pupils after viewing the third videotaped lesson in which they were participants and observers (i.e., the December or January lesson). Analysis of variance was used to determine whether this measure of directive language units reported as heard varied by peer status, gender, or setting in which the language occurred (lesson versus play).

In each of these three instances, a measure of attention to language in the play setting was compared to peer status of the participant to determine what patterns of attention were associated with "success" in play settings, as measured by prior attainment of status within the peer group.

Classmates. The second set of observers were the classmates of the pupils who participated in the play groups. Pupils from each classroom viewed the videotape of their own classmates at play and reported what they heard "anybody saying." A category system was developed to reflect the types of language that these children reported. The categories that emerged were then validated against a system developed to describe children's actual patterns of language in play groups (Wood, 1977) and were found to be quite similar. The following categories were included:

1. Word Play (e.g., "Monkey bars ... Monkey see, monkey do, I see a monkey ..."; "Any kind of an-i-mal, any kind of an-i-mal," said in sing-song intonation)
2. Attention Getting (e.g., "Lookit, it's a monkey bar"; "Look, Brian, a windmill"; "Look at me, I'm Superman.")
3. Information Seeking (e.g., "What is it?" "Did you see 'Heaven Can Wait'?" "Do you want a hat on the snake, Manny?")
4. Information Giving (e.g., "This is how worms are, but they aren't this color"; "When I went to catechism, a little boy got lost, and he was crying.")
5. Directing/Influencing (e.g., "Hey, you guys, let's knock Nacho's airplane down"; "Don't do that, Danny"; "Let's make a building.")
6. Teasing/Taunting (e.g., "The boys beat the girls"; "Kiss Christina"; "You're a *fat* Superman.")
7. Approving/Congratulating (e.g., "That's real tall!" "You got it, Delia!")

All instances of play-group language reported as heard by classmates and participants were coded independently by two separate coders using this category system. Intercoder agreement was .87 across all categories. When all pupil responses had been coded, the raw frequencies and proportional frequencies for each category were calculated by classroom. The Friedman two-way analysis of variance by ranks was used to determine whether the types of language reported most frequently were similar across the six classrooms (play groups). Patterns of pupil attention to particular language categories were then compared to patterns of language use as reported by the third set of observers.

Specialists. Ideally, the third set of observers should have been sociolinguists, who could have analyzed the play-group videotapes in detail, as was done with the classroom language tapes. However, even preparing transcripts of the play-group interaction would have been prohibitively time consuming, since several children were frequently talking at once, and much of the interaction was nonverbal. Since this was only a substudy, funds were not available for such a detailed analysis. Instead, ratings of language and interaction were obtained from ten independent outside observers, all of whom were experienced and knowledgeable observers of young children (four professors of human development, three classroom teachers of primary grade children, and three doctoral students in early childhood education).

These specialists first viewed the initial 3 to 5 minutes of a videotaped play session in order to get oriented to the play group and to identify the six children in the group by name. They then viewed the videotape in its entirety and were asked to "guess" the identities of the high- and low-peer-status boys and girls. They were also asked to identify the cues they used for purposes of identification. Cues reportedly used for identification of high-peer-status children included interaction with several other children, other children's acceptance of his or her suggestions or directions, and other children seeking his or her attention. Cues reportedly used for identification of low-peer-status children included playing alone, minimal verbal interaction with others, inability to get attention of others, and being teased by others. Thus, in making guesses about the identity of high- and low-peer-status children, these observers were in effect rating the individual children on their "success" in becoming involved in and influencing the flow of activity in the play-group setting. These ratings of individual success were compared to actual peer status, as measured by pupil responses to the sociometric task, to determine whether social status (both peer status and gender were examined) was associated with this measure of success in play-group settings.

After this rating, the videotape was again played in its entirety, and the specialist observers were asked to rate language use within the play group by ranking the seven language categories noted earlier (word play, attention getting, information seeking, information giving, directing/influencing, teasing/taunting, and approving/congratulating) according to the frequency with which they had occurred within that play setting. This ranking provided a measure of observed patterns of language use, which could then be compared to patterns of attention to language as reported by pupil observers.

Finally, the specialists rated the play group on a five-point scale on each of three dimensions related to "success" of the group in engaging in play activities. These dimensions were cooperative versus competitive play, imaginative versus unimaginative or routine use of materials, and variation versus repetitiveness of activities. Patterns of play measured in this way were compared to patterns of classroom interaction as described by sociolinguistic observers to determine whether patterns of interaction in the two settings were associated in any way.

When one play setting had been analyzed in this manner, the same sequence of procedures was repeated with another videotape. Over a two-day period, all six videotapes were observed and rated by the group of ten specialists. All ratings were done independently and without any group discussion of perceptions.

Each of these three sets of ratings from the specialist observers was placed in a ranked format, and the Kendall coefficient of concordance (Siegel, 1956) was used to analyze the rankings for agreement. The observers showed significant agreement on all three sets of observations, providing evidence of the reliability of these observations.

LANGUAGE USE AND LANGUAGE MEANING IN PLAY SETTINGS

The initial questions to be considered here have to do with similarities and differences in use of language and perceptions of language in the two different settings of classroom lessons and play-group activities. Data on use of language were derived from observations of specialists, whereas data on perceptions of language were derived from observations of pupils (play-group participants and their classmates).

Predominant Language Events

The ten experienced observers who viewed the videotapes of play groups showed clear agreement in their rankings of categories of language events by the frequency of their occurrence in each play setting. The Kendall coefficients of concordance for observations of each play group were as follows: Mrs. Addams's group, $W = .437$; Mrs. Brown's group, $W = .444$; Mrs. Case's group, $W = .629$; Miss DeLuca's group, $W = .285$; Mrs. Estes's group, $W = .929$; and Mrs. Flood's group, $W = .375$. Each of these coefficients was significant at $p < .01$.

As Siegel (1956) notes, it is suggested that "the best estimate of the 'true' ranking ... is provided, when W is significant, by the order of the various sums of ranks, R_j." Accordingly, R_j was used in determining whether the observed patterns of language events were consistent across classrooms. Table 7.1 presents transformed R_js, which have been used in a Friedman two-way analysis of variance by ranks. (The Kendall coefficient uses highest ranking as 1, whereas the Friedman two-way analysis of variance uses lowest ranking as 1, so a transformation was performed to yield reciprocal sums of ranks.) As noted in the table, x_r^2 was significant.

Not only did the specialist observers agree on the types of language events that were most and least frequent within each play setting, but across the six play settings there was significant agreement on the types of language events that predominated. The most frequently occurring language events, according to these observations, were information giving, attention getting, and directing/influencing. The least frequently occurring language events were approving/congratulating, word play, and information seeking. Thus, the observational evidence did corroborate children's reports pointing to attention getting and directing/influencing as frequent and potentially important language functions in play settings.

How different were these patterns from the patterns of classroom discourse? In these six classrooms, as in most, the predominant pattern in lessons was the following: the teacher asks a question (information seeking); children raise their hands (attention getting); a child answers the question (information giving); and the teacher does or does not react (possibly approving). Frequently, the teacher's opening move in this

TABLE 7.1. Observers' Rankings of Frequency of Language Events Observed in Play Groups (Transformed Sums of Rankings)[a]

Classroom Represented	Word play	Attention getting	Information seeking	Information giving	Directing/ influencing	Teasing	Approving
Mrs. Addams	49	51	17	52	49	42	20
Mrs. Brown	34	57	28	56	49	40	16
Mrs. Case	19	41	51	67	53	27	22
Miss DeLuca	38	42	29	46	46	58	21
Mrs. Estes	18	56	21	44	54	60	27
Mrs. Flood	37	42	45	65	41	20	30

[a] $\chi_r^2 = 23.19$; $df = 6$; $p < .001$.

question cycle involved several speech acts that are typically called managing (directing). (Chapters 4 and 6 provide details on how this general pattern was played out in these particular classrooms.) Clearly, attention getting, information giving, and directing/influencing were frequently occurring, important language functions in both classroom and play settings. But this is not to say that they operated similarly in both settings.

Attention getting was primarily nonverbal in classrooms. "Raise your hand" was the most universally understood rule of classroom discourse (see Chapter 3). Attention getting in these play groups was very verbal. The following were the most frequently used words and phrases: "Lookit"; "Hey, you guys"; "Kevin" (or calling another child by name); and "See what I'm making." These devices certainly did not guarantee the desired attention of playmates, and when attention was gained, it was fleeting. No one monitored the bids and distributed the attention among participants, as an effective teacher might. Each child dispensed his or her own attention to others, rarely in any equal fashion. The differences in attention getting in the two settings were clear. The similarity was that each child had to bid for attention in order to participate actively in either setting.

Information giving by pupils was largely reactive in classroom discourse; that is, it usually occurred in response to a teacher's question. One of the consequences of this was that pupil responses were not usually given in what teachers and grammarians call complete sentences. The information giving in these play groups was rarely in response to questions, for few questions were asked. Rather, children volunteered information that they wanted to share with others. It was interesting to note that most of these utterances *were* "complete sentences" (and were reported back as such by children who observed the videotape). For example:

> I'm gonna make a bridge.
> I'm finished.
> I'm building a trap for Bugs Bunny.
> I'm going to make a colored snake.
> This is the Lincoln log ride.
> This is how the log ride goes.
> It's my birthday tomorrow.
> "Jade" starts with a J.
> My mother's name isn't Karen.
> These pipe cleaners are good for making bracelets.
> It looks like a tower.
> It's so high I can't reach the top.

In addition, much of the information shared was in the form of "personal informatives"; that is, the speaker included himself or herself in the statement. This form of discourse contrasted to that used in these children's classrooms, where "nonpersonal informatives" (talking about objects, events, or concepts, without personal reference) predominated. Clearly information giving was enacted very differently in the two settings. However, in both settings pupils were providing information that could be useful to other pupils: information about the activities in the play setting and information about content (contained in pupil responses) in the lesson.

Directing/influencing was almost exclusively the teacher's prerogative during lessons in these six classrooms, as in most classroom discourse, but in the play setting everyone could get into the act. Children can get a good deal of practice in this language function while interacting with peers, and as Wilkinson & Dollaghan (1979) note, in peer-directed study groups, pupils can demonstrate skill in "softening" the forms of their directives and can also be skillful at indirect refusals to follow peer directives. Opportunity for pupils to use this communicative skill is not often present in teacher-directed lessons, however.

In sum, it would appear that although the *types* of language events that predominated in these play settings were also frequent events in the classroom discourse the children experienced, the carrying out of the associated language functions was quite different in the two settings. Even so, some of the communication skills that children practiced in the play setting were also exercised in the classroom lesson (e.g., bidding for attention, "learning" from other pupils).

It is also worth noting that observed differences in frequency of certain language events in the two settings did not necessarily indicate sharp differences in actual operation. For example, information seeking occurred infrequently in the play setting, but question asking occurred very frequently during classroom lessons. Despite this apparent difference, strong similarities did exist. To begin with, pupils rarely asked questions in lessons, so *their* use of this language category was actually infrequent in both settings. Secondly, the teacher questions to which pupils were asked to respond in lessons were known-information questions rather than "real" questions more than half of the time; thus, they were not information-seeking events in the same sense in which children's questions in the play setting were. For this reason, even information seeking (i.e., *real* information seeking) by teachers in lessons placed a poor third when compared in frequency to information giving and influencing/directing. In this instance, then, communication skills that were not practiced extensively by children in the play setting (i.e., information seeking and *responding* to information-seeking questions) were not practiced extensively by pupils in the classroom setting either. Thus, the classroom provided little opportunity for development of some important communication skills that were not practiced in play settings.

Predominant Patterns of Attention

The language events that pupils reported hearing after viewing videotape playbacks of play-group interaction were coded using the same categories as the experienced observers used in rating frequency of language events. For each classroom, proportions were derived by dividing the total number of responses in a particular category of language event by the total number of codable responses for that classroom. (Reports of single words out of sentence context could not be coded, e.g., ... footprints ..., ... cowboy ..., ... pancake ...). Table 7.2 presents information on total codable responses and mean responses per pupil for each classroom. Table 7.3 presents the proportions of responses for each type of language event by classroom. The Friedman two-way analysis of variance by ranks indicated that patterns of reporting language events as "heard" were consistent across classrooms.

The most frequently reported types of language events were directing/influencing and information giving, and the least frequently reported were approving and information seeking. There were certain obvious similarities and differences with regard to the predominance of language events that were observed and the predominance of language events that were reported. To begin with, information giving ranked first in observed language events and second in reported language events, whereas approving ranked last in both observed and reported events. In these cases, language events were attended to in rough proportion to the frequency of their occurrence.

This was not the case for directing/influencing, word play, or attention-getting events. Directing/influencing ranked third in observed language events, but it was a strong first in events reported by children. Word play ranked very low in observed events, but was clearly in the middle ranks of reported events. These types of language events were attended to by children somewhat more than they actually occurred. Attention getting, on the other hand, ranked second highest in observed events and fifth in reported events. It would seem that attention-getting behavior failed to command the attention of children who viewed videotapes of play groups, much as it often failed to command the attention of the peers toward whom it was directed during play activities. Perhaps reception skills that children

TABLE 7.2. Numbers of Codable Reports of Language Events (Totals and Means by Classroom)

Classroom	Number of pupils reporting	Total codable responses	Mean number of codable responses per pupil
Mrs. Addams	25	290	11.60
Mrs. Brown	24	250	10.42
Mrs. Case	27	254	9.41
Miss DeLuca	29	363	12.52
Mrs. Estes	24	308	12.83
Mrs. Flood	25	406	16.24

TABLE 7.3. Proportions of Language Events Reported[a]

Classroom	Word play	Attention getting	Information seeking	Information giving	Directing/ influencing	Teasing	Approving
Mrs. Addams	.141	.076	.048	.321	.397	.017	.000
Mrs. Brown	.184	.112	.024	.140	.268	.272	.000
Mrs. Case	.020	.094	.059	.319	.370	.138	.000
Miss DeLuca	.226	.041	.055	.215	.190	.267	.006
Mrs. Estes	.305	.097	.071	.127	.328	.068	.003
Mrs. Flood	.153	.102	.059	.227	.295	.159	.006

[a] $x_r^2 = 22.99$; $df = 6$; $p < .001$

learned and practiced in play settings included being particularly alert to attempts to influence them and screening out attempts to get their attention.

In any case, it was apparent that the selective attention exhibited by pupils in reporting the language of lessons was also exhibited in their reporting of the language of play groups. In classroom lessons, children tended to focus on pupil responses and screen out teacher questions and directives. In play settings, children tended to focus on directives and screen out attention-getting language. In both settings, skills of focusing attention on particular types of language events and ignoring or screening out other language events were clearly in use. However, the particular types of events to be focused on or ignored were very different in the two settings.

Of particular interest was the difference in attention to directives, or attempts to influence the behavior of others, for this particular language function might be associated quite differently with "success" in the two different settings. If ability to influence the flow of activities in a play setting is accepted as one measure of social success, then awareness of attempts to influence or direct the behavior of others would seem to be an important communication skill. The person attempting to direct the flow of activities would need to be aware of the directives issued by others, in order to counteract or amend them, thus maintaining control. Success in the play setting, then, might well be associated with an ability to *avoid* following the directives issued by playmates. In the classroom setting, however, academic success has been associated with pupil ability to *follow* the directives of the teacher (e.g., pupil "on-task" behavior has been shown to be significantly correlated with achievement gains). In this instance, a specific communication skill practiced and reinforced in the play setting could be detrimental to success in the classroom setting.

SUCCESSFUL PARTICIPATION IN PLAY SETTINGS

Such speculation is interesting, but solid evidence is more satisfying, and the results of this study did provide some clear relationships between success in play settings and success in the classroom. There were associations between group success at play and class academic achievement. There were also associations between individual success at play and individual social status in the classroom.

Group Differences in Success at Play

Group success at play was measured by ratings of the specialist observers on three dimensions of interaction: cooperative versus competitive play, imaginative versus routine use of materials, and varied versus repetitive

TABLE 7.4. Mean Ratings of Play Groups on Three Interactive Dimensions

Play group	Cooperative vs. competitive play	Imaginative vs. routine use of materials	Varied vs. repetitive activities
Mrs. Addams	3.2	3.9	3.3
Mrs. Brown	3.3	2.9	2.8
Mrs. Case	3.8	4.0	3.9
Miss DeLuca	2.8	3.4	3.1
Mrs. Estes	2.5	2.4	2.2
Mrs. Flood	4.2	3.7	3.2

activities. (Recall that videotapes of play groups had been edited to display as much variation of activities for each group as possible, but where little or no variation existed in the original tape, it could not be displayed in the edited tape.)

Each of these three dimensions was rated on a five-point scale. The Kendall coefficient of concordance was used to analyze these ratings (transformed to rankings). There was significant agreement among observers on ratings of the play groups on each of these interactive dimensions. The coefficients of concordance were as follows: cooperative versus competitive play, $W = .360$ ($p < .01$); imaginative versus routine use of materials, $W = .356$ ($p < .01$); and varied versus repetitive activities, $W = .242$ ($p < .05$).

Table 7.4 presents the mean ratings for each play group on each of these dimensions. (Competitive, unimaginative, and repetitive play were all at the lower end of the rating scale.) The lowest mean rating on all three of the interactive dimensions was accorded to Mrs. Estes's play group. This group focused on building block towers for 30 minutes, with the major variation being a contest between boys and girls to build the highest tower. They "stole" each other's blocks and knocked down each other's towers. The highest mean rating on cooperative play was given to Mrs. Flood's play group, which fell in the middle range of ratings on the other two dimensions. This group did some tower building, in which boys and girls worked together, and invented a catapult that sent blocks flying into the air.

These group differences in successful play were particularly interesting, for these were the two fourth-grade classes that differed significantly in final achievement gains.

Mrs. Estes's class, whose pupils were rated lowest on all three dimensions of play, showed significantly lower final reading achievement (entering reading controlled for) than Mrs. Flood's class, whose pupils were rated highest on cooperative play. Sociolinguists distinguished between these two classrooms as well, pointing out that Mrs. Flood conducted content-oriented lessons that were rather like natural conversations, with "real" questions being asked and children contributing information about their own experiences. Mrs. Estes, on the other hand, conducted lessons where the main task was to participate, tending to ask several children to respond to the same question, rarely identifying any response as best or most nearly accurate, and maintaining "iron-fisted control of the topic." (See Chapters 4 and 6 for more detailed descriptions of these classrooms.)

A reexamination of Table 7.1 may provide some clues about the type of verbal interaction occurring in these two play groups that led observers to make these ratings of the two groups. The sums of rankings show Mrs. Estes's group to be considerably higher than Mrs. Flood's group in relative frequency of teasing, whereas Mrs. Flood's group was markedly higher in information seeking, information giving, and word play. It seems possible that a more cooperative (or "natural") style of classroom conversation carried over into the play setting for children from Mrs. Flood's class, but a more competitive style of classroom interaction carried over into the play setting for children from Mrs. Estes's class. In any case, it is clear that, for these two classrooms at least, patterns of interaction that contributed to academic success were associated with patterns of interaction that contributed to success in group play activities, whereas patterns that contributed to lack of academic success were associated with patterns that contributed to lack of success in play activities.

The highest mean ratings on inventive and varied play activities went to Mrs. Case's play group, and this group was also highly rated on cooperative play. This group organized and ran a series of running, squatting, and crawling races. Mrs. Addams's play group was also high on imaginative and varied play and fell in the middle range on cooperative play. This group invented and played a game they called "Cat's Eye," but they also engaged in a good deal of individual play, a pattern not unexpected for second graders.

It is interesting to note that these two classrooms also stood out with regard to the data on classroom discourse. Mrs. Addams's and Mrs. Case's classrooms, whose pupils displayed the most inventive and varied play according to the specialist observers, were the classrooms whose discourse was described by one sociolinguistic analyst as the dullest and most routine of the six classrooms, with the "form of doing school" appearing to be more important to the teachers than any attempts to deal with content. (See Chapter 4 for further detail.) This result may be surprising to some, but it follows a pattern identified by Elkind, Deblinger, and Adler (1970), who found that children removed from uninteresting classrooms or activities were almost twice as "creative" on a variety of tests as children removed from interesting classrooms or activities.

This interpretation of these results is supported by the fact that Mrs. Brown's play group was rated fairly low on imaginative and varied play. This was the classroom that engaged in the most varied lessons, based on "models" of teaching (Joyce & Weil, 1972).

TABLE 7.5.   Rankings of Classrooms and Play Groups on Measures of Academic Success and Success at Cooperative Play

Classroom	Mean achievement gains	Rank in achievement gains	Rank in cooperative play
Mrs. Addams	18.8	1	4
Mrs. Brown	10.7	3	3
Mrs. Case	7.0	4	2
Miss DeLuca	6.9	5	5
Mrs. Estes	5.1	6	6
Mrs. Flood	11.6	2	1

These particular dimensions of success in play groups (imaginative and varied play) did appear, therefore, to be tied to patterns of classroom interaction, such that dull, routine classroom activities were associated with imaginative, varied play activities. However, these dimensions of success at play were not tied to classroom academic success, for Mrs. Case's class was not high in achievement gains, whereas Mrs. Brown's and Mrs. Addams's classes were. Thus, the dimension of cooperative versus competitive play, which was the dimension that distinguished most clearly between Mrs. Flood's and Mrs. Estes's play groups, was the dimension of success in play activities that was most clearly associated with classroom academic success. It is certainly worth noting that rankings of the six classrooms on final achievement gains were closely paralleled by rankings of the six play groups on cooperative versus competitive play. These rankings are displayed in Table 7.5.

Individual Differences in Success at Play

The data on individual differences in success at play also provided some interesting relationships. Individual success in the play group was measured by specialists' ratings of children's active involvement in group play and ability to direct the flow of activities. These ratings were expressed as "guesses" about the high or low status of pupils within the peer group.

Table 7.6 presents data on agreement among observers in identifying particular children as high or low in peer status (i.e., "successful" or "unsuccessful" within the play group). In all instances but one there was significant agreement. These ratings were compared to measures of peer status based on peer choices. In five out of six play groups the low-peer-status boy was clearly singled out and identified as unsuccessful by observers. In only one of the groups was the high-peer-status boy clearly singled out and identified as highly successful. In four out of six play groups the low-peer-status girl was clearly singled out and identified by observers as unsuccessful, whereas in three groups the high-peer-status girl was clearly singled out and identified as highly successful. In no instance was a

TABLE 7.6. Agreement among Observers in Identifying "Successful" and "Unsuccessful" Participants in Play Groups (Kendall Coefficient of Concordance)

	Mrs. Addams's play group	Mrs. Brown's play group	Mrs. Case's play group	Miss DeLuca's play group	Mrs. Estes's play group	Mrs. Flood's play group
Boys	.19	.49**	.49**	.48**	.52**	.84**
Girls	.37*	.31*	.67**	.31*	.49**	.52**

* $p < .05$.
** $p < .01$.

girl or boy of high peer status identified by observers as unsuccessful in the play setting. In one instance a girl of low peer status was identified by observers as very successful in the play setting. In several instances girls and boys of middle-level peer status were identified by observers as very successful participants in the play group; that is, they were seen as actively involved in play with others and as "in control," or able to direct the flow of play activities along the lines they suggested.

The possibilities for statistical analysis were somewhat limited here, given the ranked data and the low numbers of subjects. A 2×2 contingency table was formed, based on observers' ratings of children as successful versus unsuccessful in the play setting and peer ratings of children with regard to peer-group status (middle or high peer status versus low peer status). This table showed a strong significant relationship between peer-group status and success in the play setting ($x^2 = 20$, $df = 1$, $p < .001$, phi $= .746$). Children of low peer status were observed to be less successful in the play group. In particular, boys of low peer status were seen as isolated or excluded from the group activities. This was not so true for girls. Girls of low peer status tended to be included in the play activities of the girls. In most cases they were singled out by observers because they were teased by the middle- and high-status boys.

SUCCESS AND ATTENTION IN PLAY SETTINGS

The third measure of success in play settings was a measure of "prior achievement," and involved use of peer status ratings by classmates. Because pupils had been selected for participation in play groups based on their differences in peer status, it was relatively easy to determine whether this measure of success was related to patterns of attention to language within the play setting. Three aspects of attention were examined: attention to source of communications, attention to information contained within verbal utterances and information about the social context of the language (information load), and attention to use of directives.

Citing the Source

One way in which children might attain social success could be through special awareness of those with whom they interacted. One expression of such awareness could be particular attention to who was saying what in the course of group interaction. With this possibility in mind, an analysis was made of play participants' tendencies to "cite" other children in the group as sources of the language they reported (e.g., "Manny said, 'Here, this could be a big long boat going under the bridge.'"). This analysis involved simply noting how many other children in the play group were cited as sources one or more times.

TABLE 7.7. Participant Citations of Peers as Language Sources in Play Settings (Mean Number of Sources Cited by Sex and Peer Status)

	Low peer status (N = 12)	Middle peer status (N = 12)	High peer status (N = 12)
Females (N = 18)	2.67	2.50	3.50
Males (N = 18)	.67	2.33	1.67

TABLE 7.8. Analysis of Variance: Participant Citations of Peers as Language Sources in Play Settings

Source	SS	df	ms	F	P
Total	110.22	35			
Gender	16.00	1	16.00	5.84	<.05
Peer status	5.71	2	2.86	1.04	
Peer status × gender	6.19	2	3.10	1.13	
Error	82.32	30	2.74		

Table 7.7 presents mean numbers of sources cited for each subgroup of participants. Table 7.8 presents the analysis of variance data for these means. Gender contributed significantly to the variance in citing of peers as language sources, but peer status did not. Girls cited other pupils as language sources more frequently than boys. As Table 7.7 indicates, the gender differences were most marked for pupils of high and low peer status.

Socially successful children (i.e., children high in status with peers) were no more apt to cite other children as language sources than socially unsuccessful children, therefore, but socially unsuccessful girls (low peer status) did cite other children as language sources more than socially unsuccessful boys. It was also the case, as noted earlier, that low-peer-status girls were included in the play activities more than low-peer-status boys and thus were somewhat more "successful" in these particular play settings. The possibility remains, then, that particular awareness of language sources could be associated with success in a particular play situation, although it was not associated with the more general measure of success used in this substudy.

Acquiring Information

Another way in which children might attain social success could be through a heightened awareness of the totality of sociolinguistic information available within a social setting. "Information load" was a measure of acquisition of this type of information within this study. This measure counted a specific verbal utterance reported as one unit of information and each additional item of social context relative to that utterance (e.g., who said it, to whom it was said, what was said in reply) as another unit of information. The total number of units of information reported in response to the repeated question, "What did you hear anybody saying?" constituted the measure of information load.

In classroom lessons, peer status was related to variance in information load, with pupils low in peer status reporting back significantly less sociolinguistic information than pupils of middle or high peer status. Gender was not related to variance in information load. An examination of relationships between information load and peer status or gender in the play setting, then, made it possible to note ways in which attention to language might be related to social success and at the same time to check for similarities in attention patterns in the two settings of classroom lessons and play-group activities.

Table 7.9 presents data on the mean information load for each of the subgroups of participants in the play setting. Table 7.10 presents the analysis of variance data for these means. Peer status contributed significantly to the variance in information load, but gender did not. According to Duncan's Multiple-Range Test, children of higher peer status reported back significantly more total sociolinguistic information than children of low status ($p < .005$), but there were no significant differences between middle- and low-peer-status children or between high- and middle-peer-status children.

TABLE 7.9. Participant Reports of Sociolinguistic Information in Play Settings (Mean Information Load by Gender and Peer Status)

	Low peer status (N = 12)	Middle peer status (N = 12)	High peer status (N = 12)
Females (N = 18)	22.25	23.00	34.25
Males (N = 18)	14.08	23.33	30.92
Total subjects (N = 36)	18.25	23.17	32.58

TABLE 7.10. Analysis of Variance: Information Load in Play Settings

Source	SS	df	ms	F	P
Total	4194.81	35			
Gender	124.70	1	124.70	1.398	
Peer status	1016.05	2	508.03	5.697	< .01
Peer status × gender	379.06	2	189.53	2.125	
Error	2675.00	30	89.17		

Success at play, as measured by prior attainment of peer status, was associated with acquisition of sociolinguistic information within the play group situation, then. Furthermore, this pattern of attention to language was exhibited by socially successful children in both the play setting and the classroom setting. The fact that information load in classroom lessons did not vary significantly according to entering reading achievement (academic success) suggests that this is one indicator of a difference in communication skills associated with success in play settings as opposed to communication skills associated with success in classroom settings.

Attending to Directives

A third way in which children might attain success within the play setting could be by attending particularly to attempts to direct or influence the behavior of others, since ability to influence the flow of activities could be considered one measure of success within a play-group situation. Because in this study children as a whole focused their attention on language designed to influence or direct behavior (i.e., reported this type of language relatively more often than it actually occurred), it was decided to examine patterns of attention of the play-group participants to directive language in more detail.

Participants' reports of directive language in the play setting were compared to their reports of directive language in the December/January lesson, and relationships between these reports and peer status and gender were investigated. Table 7.11 shows mean units of language reported by each subgroup in each setting. Table 7.12 presents the analysis of variance data for these means. There were significant differences according to peer status and setting.

Participants of high peer status reported more units of directive language than participants of lower status. According to the F test for simple effects, high-peer-status participants were significantly different from participants of both middle and low peer status ($p < .001$), but participants of middle and low peer status did not differ significantly from each other. Participants as a whole reported significantly more units of

TABLE 7.11. Participant Attention to Directive Language in Play Groups and Lessons (Mean Number of Units Reported by Gender and Peer Status)

	Low peer status		Middle peer status		High peer status	
	Boys (n = 6)	Girls (n = 6)	Boys (n = 6)	Girls (n = 6)	Boys (n = 6)	Girls (n = 6)
Play group	4.00	4.33	3.83	3.50	5.67	5.67
January lesson	0.00	.33	1.50	1.33	2.33	1.50

TABLE 7.12.   Analysis of Variance: Participant Attention to Directive Language

Source	SS	df	ms	F	P
Total	448	71			
Between subjects	119	35			
Gender	.21	1	.21	< 1	
Peer status	34.70	2	17.35	6.36	<.005
Peer status × gender	2.12	2	1.06	< 1	
Error between	81.97	30	2.73		
Within subjects	329	36			
Setting	200	1	200	51.15	<.001
Setting × gender	.24	1	.24	< 1	
Setting × status	10.78	2	5.39	1.38	
Setting × status × gender	.64	2	.32	< 1	
Error within	117.34	30	3.91		

directive language in play settings than in classroom lessons. This latter finding demonstrated that directive language was perceived as particularly important in the play setting, for adult observers indicated that this type of language occurred frequently in both lessons and play groups, but children's attention to it was clearly much stronger in the play-group setting.

Since pupils of high peer status were more attentive to directive language than pupils of lower peer status, this pattern of attention was clearly associated with social success within the peer group. To determine whether this pattern of attention might also be associated with academic success, a further analysis was carried out.

For the 36 participants in the play-group activities, data were available on academic as well as social success. In this instance, the measure of academic success was frequency of participation in class discussions. This measure was an indication of pupil ability to exhibit the communication skills necessary for active involvement in the lesson, and it was also significantly related to final achievement in reading (after controlling for entering achievement); thus, in effect it could serve as a proxy measure of both short-term and long-term academic success. Participants in the play groups were not divided into exactly equal groups on the basis of frequency of participation in class discussions, but the groups were not drastically different in size.

Table 7.13 presents the mean units of directive language reported for each setting by play-group participants organized according to frequency of participation in class discussions. Table 7.14 shows the analysis of variance data for these means. The finding of significant differences by setting was of course reiterated in this analysis, but there was no evidence of significant differences according to frequency of participation in lessons. Attention to directive language was not associated with academic success, therefore.

TABLE 7.13. Attention to Directive Language in Play Groups and Lessons According to Academic Success (Mean Number of Units Reported by Frequency of Participation in Discussions)

	Low participation (n = 10)	Middle participation (n = 14)	High participation (n = 12)
Play group	4.30	4.29	6.33
January lesson	1.00	1.07	1.42

TABLE 7.14. Analysis of Variance: Attention to Directive Language and Academic Success

Source	SS	df	ms	F	P
Total	448	71			
Between subjects	119	35			
Participation in lessons	4	2	2	.57	
Error between	115	33	3.48		
Within subjects	329	36			
Setting	200	1	200	51.28	<.025
Setting × participation	.27	2	.14	.04	
Error within	128.73	33	3.90		

Thus, for pupils in this substudy, attention to directive language was related to social success but not to academic success. This pattern of attention suggests a second indicator of differences in communication skills associated with success in play settings as opposed to skills associated with success in classroom lessons.

COMMUNICATION SKILLS AT WORK AND PLAY

This special substudy was undertaken because of some intriguing findings from the main study indicating the importance of the peer group, and of status within the peer group, in relation to children's processing of information in classroom settings. Several findings from the main study also suggested that children perceived differences between conversations in play groups and discourse in classrooms. The findings presented here were based on a very limited sample of play groups, yet they provide interesting comparisons of use of communication skills relative to success in the two settings examined.

The finding that important language functions, such as attention getting, information giving, and directing/influencing, occurred frequently in both settings, but were carried out quite differently in classroom lessons as opposed to play settings was not very surprising. However, many prior studies that have compared children's language in these two settings have focused on minority culture groups, suggesting that the differences found resulted from differences between minority and dominant cultures and contributed singularly to the academic difficulties of minority-group children (e.g., Boggs, 1972; Dumont, 1972; Philips, 1972). These data suggest that a more pervasive difference may exist, the difference between the subculture of childhood and the dominant culture of adulthood. Most importantly for educators, perhaps, was the fact that many, but clearly not all, of the communication skills that these children were practicing and developing in play groups could also be used productively in the classroom setting.

Skills Practiced

Communication skills that were practiced in both play and classroom settings, and that were presumably useful in both settings, included selective attention, attention getting, information giving, and information getting. These skills were exercised differently in the two settings, but they were all clearly evident in both settings.

In play settings, children attended particularly to directive language and screened out attention-getting language. In lessons, children attended particularly to pupil responses to questions and screened out teacher questions and teacher directions. Interestingly enough, selective attention was associated with success in each of the two settings. Socially successful children (high peer status) paid more attention to directive language in both play groups and lessons than did less successful children. Academically successful children (high entering reading achievement) paid more attention to teacher questions and to the responses of other academically successful pupils in classroom lessons than did less successful children (see Chapter 5). Thus, selective attention was a communication skill that related to success in both "work" and play settings.

Another communication skill that was important in both settings was attention getting, and this skill was also related to success in both settings. In play settings, children's bids for attention were verbal ("Lookit!" Hey, you guys!"), and attention to the comments of others was "distributed" by each individual child. Children's bids for attention in lessons were non-verbal (raising hands), and attention (opportunity to talk) was distributed by the teacher. In both play groups and lessons, the less successful children were less adept at getting attention. Play-group children of low peer status, particularly boys of low status, were rated by observers as less able to get the attention of their playmates. In lessons, pupils of low entering reading achievement were called on less frequently by teachers (see Chapter 5). Thus, attention getting was a communication skill that was practiced in both settings, and inability to gain the attention of others was associated with lack of social success in play settings and with lack of academic success in classroom settings.

Information giving was a third communication skill that was practiced in both settings. In play groups, children initiated information-giving comments and presented information in the form of complete sentences. Most of the information shared included personal references (i.e., was categorized in this study as a "personal informative"). In classroom lessons, pupils provided information-giving comments in response to teacher questions and often presented information in the form of incomplete sentences (one- or two-word statements). Most of the information shared did not include personal references but dealt rather with abstractions (concepts) or impersonal facts (statements categorized as "nonpersonal informatives"). Despite these differences, information provided by other children was useful to participants in both settings and received the attention of children in both settings. In play groups, these comments informed others about the activities in which children were engaged. In classrooms, they provided information about the content with which the lesson dealt. Thus, the apparent belief of pupils that they could learn from the comments of other pupils in the lesson could have been operative in the play setting as well. Certainly, attention to the information-giving language of other children was a communication skill that was important in the classroom setting and that was exercised in the play setting as well.

Information getting was a fourth communication skill practiced in both play and lesson settings. In particular, this study examined children's acquisition of sociolinguistic information, as measured by "information load." Children acquired more sociolinguistic information in lessons than in informal settings of home and play conversations, and they acquired more information as the classroom became a more familiar social setting, from September to January (see Chapter 3), but they clearly were engaged in acquiring this type of information in both settings. Acquisition of sociolinguistic information was related to social success (peer status) in both play-group activities and classroom lessons. High-peer-status pupils acquired significantly more of such information in both settings than did lower-peer-status pupils. This type of information getting was not associated with academic success. Pupils high in entering reading achievement did not differ from lower-achieving pupils in their reporting of sociolinguistic information acquired during lessons.

As this summary shows, there were several ways in which communication skills important for success in the classroom could be practiced and developed by children in the play setting. In almost all instances, however, these skills were exercised differently in the two settings.

Skills Not Practiced

Two important communication skills were not practiced by these pupils in classroom lessons. Language that functioned to direct or influence the behavior of others was used fairly extensively by children in the play setting, but it was rarely used by children in lessons. In this instance, a skill that was very important to children in play groups (ability to influence the behavior of others was a measure of success in play activities) might have contributed to the variety of classroom interaction or might have been more effectively developed and refined as part of classroom learning, but neither of these possibilities was realized. If this were a skill only used by children in play groups, then such an avoidance in the classroom would be quite reasonable, but in fact it is a communication skill required for effective functioning in all adult roles as well as in children's play.

A second important communication skill was not practiced much by these children in either the play or the "work" setting, and that was the skill of information seeking, or question asking. Children initiated few questions in play groups and were provided relatively few opportunities to initiate questions during lessons (see Chapter 4). This is another instance of a communication skill required for effective adult functioning that might well contribute to variety of classroom interaction if more lessons were designed to develop such ability.

Since these skills were not practiced by pupils in this study during classroom lessons, no evidence was available from this study about the relationship of these skills to academic success. Some other studies have examined this question, however, and these will be discussed in Chapter 8.

Gender Differences

This study revealed some interesting gender differences in communication skills associated with success in play and lesson settings. In particular, there were differences with regard to active participation in the two settings.

In play groups, boys of low peer status stood out to specialist observers, because they interacted and were interacted with very differently. They stayed isolated from others, were ignored in their attempts to initiate interaction, and were frequently teased by others. Thus, boys who were *less* successful in the peer group participated *less* in the play-group activities than other children. (This was not true for girls of low peer status, who were included more in play activities and were identified by the outside observers because they were frequently teased by boys.)

In classroom lessons, on the other hand, girls of high academic status (entering reading) stood out to the outside observer (coder of interaction), because they interacted differently. They participated in class discussions significantly less frequently than high-achieving boys ($x^2 = 6.49$, $df = 2$, $p < .05$, $C = .34$). Thus, girls who were *more* successful in the academic group participated *less* in lesson activities.

These rather different patterns of relationships among success, gender, and participation in lesson and play-group settings would seem to deserve further investigation.

Classroom Differences

The findings presented here with regard to associations between patterns of classroom discourse and types of interaction exhibited in play settings were also intriguing and are probably deserving of further study. Doubtless no one would want to urge teachers to become more dull and routine in their lessons in an attempt to encourage more creative play among their pupils during free time. It would certainly be worth knowing, however, whether more content-oriented tasks and "natural" teacher language in lessons are consistently related to both increased academic learning and more cooperative play among children. Mrs. Flood's classroom demonstrated that such a relationship (desired by many) is at least possible. In addition, Mrs. Estes's classroom showed that classroom tasks focused on mere participation, and teacher use of "teacherese," can be related to both decreased academic learning and more competitive play. Further studies might provide useful additional information about the probability of such relationships occurring in other classrooms.

REITERATION

It would be inappropriate to conclude this chapter without clarifying the most important finding of this substudy on language in play settings. Although the question of factors associated with success in play settings was not a question that the major study was originally designed to address, the answers to this question, as reported here, do reinforce and reiterate the answers to the basic question that did drive the main study. In fact, Figure 6.1, which summarized Chapter 6, could be repeated here with very few changes as a summary of the associations reported in Chapter 7. This is illustrated in Figure 7.1.

By now the general outlines of this figure should be quite familiar to

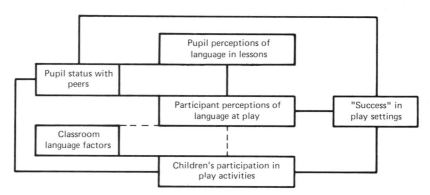

FIGURE 7.1   Associations among variables in the study of language at play.

the reader. Once again the dashed lines represent relationships not investigated in this particular piece of the study. Solid lines represent associations or relationships found in this substudy. Labels for the boxes denoting variables studied have been revised slightly to reflect the emphasis on language at play. However, a quick comparison between Figure 7.1 and Figure 6.1 will demonstrate a strong similarity in the types of associations found.

What this means is that the sociolinguist's basic premise about relationships among status, participation, and interpretation of language has been confirmed for two different types of social settings within this study. Furthermore, the classroom researcher's hunch that effects of pupil status and classroom interaction patterns on pupil success may be mediated by pupil perceptions of and participation in that interaction has been substantiated not only with regard to academic success, but also with regard to success in the more informal play-group settings.

Certainly these findings lend strength to Stubbs's (1976) statement that the peer group is "the most powerful linguistic influence on children." There has been much interest in recent years in comparing home and school settings in order to identify "discontinuities" that may exist and that may contribute to children's difficulties in learning to read. In fact, several of the seven sociolinguistic studies funded by the National Institute of Education in 1978, of which this was one, were designed to address that question. The findings of this substudy demonstrate that further investigation of this issue should not be limited to adult-child interactions in the out-of-school setting. Interactions among children in play groups can provide valuable information about how communication skills learned in informal settings may relate to communicative competence in the classroom. Such research could make it possible for more teachers to build classroom discussion processes on children's communicative competencies and to build children's communicative competencies through new forms of classroom discussion processes.

Part III

The Value of Meaning (and the Meaning of Value)

This study was begun with the expectation that information on pupil and teacher interpretations of classroom language could provide an important addition to our understanding of effective teaching. Part III reviews the findings of the study, identifies specific criteria to be used in determining the value of these findings for research and for teaching, and tests the findings against these criteria.

8

Potential Value for Research

The focus of this book has been on meaning. Part I emphasized the centrality of meaning in the framework of the research design. Part II described the construction of meaning, step by step, from the data collected. Part III examines the meaning that this study has within the context of current research on teaching and current practice in teaching, for no matter how interesting the findings in a general sense, if they have no connections to the field as a whole, they will have little practical value. This chapter explores the potential value of this study in relation to other research.

LIMITATION

The study reported here has some clear limitations, and these need to be stated before beginning a discussion of the study in relation to other research. The first and most important limitation is that this is a descriptive study. As such, it is not generalizable to any larger population. The findings indicate some of the possibilities that exist both with regard to variation in participation and interpretation of classroom language and with regard to the relationship of classroom communication patterns to pupil learning. This study, however, can provide no evidence about the probability that similar variations and relationships will occur in other classroom settings.

A second important limitation of this study has to do with the particular school setting. It is not unusual for a descriptive study to deal with a single school, and any given school will have certain unique aspects that set it apart from others and that need to be taken into account in interpreting research results. This study is no exception. The school in which this study took place had several unique characteristics that may have contributed to the specific findings in important ways, but this contribution cannot be carefully examined, because there was no comparison school involved. The only recourse is to carefully indicate these characteristics, with attendant warnings to the reader to keep them in mind when pondering the results of the study.

The first unique characteristic of the school setting has to do with the school community. It was a low socioeconomic, multiethnic community in an urban area, but it did not exhibit many additional characteristics that might typically be associated with these designations. This was a stable community, in that families remained there for many years, in that two-parent families predominated, and in that most fathers were employed, albeit in low-paying jobs. Furthermore, it was an integrated community, in that families of different cultural backgrounds lived side by side and interacted as friendly neighbors for the most part. In addition, most of the Mexican-American parents were bilingual, and children were fairly fluent in English. These characteristics may well have contributed to the fact that pupils generally followed the rules of classroom participation and exhibited few behavior problems. They may also have contributed to the findings of few differences in status, participation, or interpretation of classroom language related to cultural background of pupils. Apparently, the Mexican-American children in this study were not socially, culturally, or linguistically different enough from the other children in their school to perceive of or participate in classroom discourse in markedly different ways, or to be perceived by their teachers and peers as markedly different. Their evident deficit in entering reading achievement was not reinforced by concomitant deficits in status with teacher (teacher expectations) or participation in class discussions, and they did not fall significantly further behind in reading achievement as the school year progressed. This finding might not be replicated in different school/classroom settings (e.g., bilingual classes or a school community with a large population of migrant workers).

These findings do not necessarily contradict the prior research or assumptions on which this study was based (i.e., that the culturally different pupil may perceive classroom communication from a different perspective than the teacher and other pupils; that the teacher may have negative attitudes about the culturally different child's participation in classroom discourse; and that both of these factors may combine to lead to poor school achievement for the culturally different child). What they do demonstrate is that ethnic (cultural) difference, in and of itself, does not (need not) lead automatically to school failure. What they suggest is that we need to examine in much greater detail the interaction of cultural differences with socioeconomic and other differences in family background, as these relate to school achievement deficits. Thus, in this instance, a unique characteristic of the school setting that may have contributed to particular findings in this study points to important questions to be raised in further research.

A second unique characteristic of the school setting was the diversity of instructional practice. Many schools have a uniform curriculum within a given grade level and an articulated curriculum moving from one grade level to another. Such uniformity was not the rule at this school, despite the fact that teachers met together in grade-level teams periodically throughout the year. As an example of the diversity that existed, a study conducted two years earlier than this one showed that the three first-grade teachers used three totally different instructional systems to introduce reading to their pupils (Morine-Dershimer, 1979a), and pupils from these three different classes were mixed together when they were assigned to second-grade classrooms, so that each second-grade teacher was faced with pupils who had learned basic reading skills from three different approaches. This unique school characteristic of diversity in teaching may have contributed to both the findings of classroom differences in patterns of communication and the related findings of classroom differences in pupil perceptions of the functions of classroom question cycles. These findings might not be replicated in a school where a uniform curriculum was the norm.

These examples of limitations of the study make it clear why certain findings of this study are not readily generalizable to other school settings, and they raise the question of the practical value of any of the findings of the study. This question must be asked of all descriptive classroom research. It is a question that can be answered in at least two different ways. Findings of a descriptive study may be corroborated by one or more other studies, and this circumstance suggests that the findings are applicable in other settings to some degree. Findings of a descriptive study may also serve to explicate findings from experimental studies, and this can be a particularly valuable type of contribution to the field of research. In the case of this particular study, the findings are both corroborated by other research findings and explicative of other research findings; thus, there is clearly some practical value to be derived from the findings of the study. In addition, it can be argued that this study has made a practical contribution to the methodological tools available for research on teaching, as a result of the extensive testing of procedures associated with triangulation of data. Finally, this study raises some potentially productive questions for further research, which may be the ultimate test of practical value for many researchers. Each of these aspects of potential value for research is discussed in detail in the remainder of this chapter.

CORROBORATION

Findings of this study are corroborated by findings of a number of other studies, and these include studies from three different approaches to research on teaching. Sociolinguistic studies, studies of pupil processes, and studies of teacher information processing all provide findings supportive of and related to findings of this study. Each of these types of studies will be discussed in turn.

Sociolinguistic Studies

As noted in Chapter 1, this study was one of a series of sociolinguistic studies funded by the National Institute of Education in 1978. These studies, together with a few additional studies funded in 1979, have been extensively reviewed by Judith Green (1983a, 1983b; also Green & Smith, 1983). As part of her review, Green identified a set of constructs that she said helped to define the conceptual basis for the study of teaching as a linguistic process. She noted that these constructs both provided a framework for observation and collection of data and served as the products of the analysis of data (i.e., the findings). She provided a table that compared the 10 studies with regard to their use of 5 general and 26 specific constructs. That table is replicated here as Figure 8.1 so that the reader can see which other studies have used constructs similar to those used in this study. (Note that *use* refers to both employment of the construct in the design of the study and development of information relative to the construct in findings of the study.) Figure 8.1 serves to demonstrate that the study reported here had close connections conceptually with a number of other studies of teaching conducted according to the sociolinguistic tradition.

Since Green has provided a comprehensive review of these studies, it would be redundant to discuss them at length here. However, it is important to identify the general findings from the set of studies that relate most closely to the findings of this particular study. Not all of the studies did classroom comparisons, but those that did found clear classroom differences in the "linguistic environment" (Cook-Gumperz, Gumperz, & Simon, 1981; Erickson, Cazden, Carrasco, & Guzman, 1978–1981). The linguistic environment involved pupils in carrying out two simultaneous tasks. As the teacher was presenting content (an academic task), he or she was also presenting information about the requirements for participation in the lesson (Erickson, 1982; also Green & Harker, 1982; and Wallat & Green, 1982). Norms and expectations for behavior were signaled indirectly by the teacher in the way that he or she distributed turns to talk and acknowledged contributions of pupils, so that pupils had to infer the rules from the sequences of behavior (Erickson, 1982). Even within lessons teachers varied their use of language, particularly their use of praise and negative sanctions (Erickson et al., 1978–1981; also Cahir & Kovacs, 1981); thus, the signals about participation requirements could shift from one part of a lesson to another. Findings from each of the studies reviewed (Green, 1983a) indicated that classroom communication was rule governed, and that even though the teacher established routines for pupil participation in lessons, the specific requirements for participation shifted frequently within and across lessons (as well as across classrooms). For a pupil to participate appropriately in any particular lesson activity, he or she had to be engaged in actively interpreting the signals of the teacher with regard to the participation structure (who was chosen to participate and how responses were acknowledged) as well as actively tracking the development of the academic content of the lesson.

Associated findings of this study showed clear classroom differences in communication patterns (linguistic environment), and one of the interesting differences was in teacher emphasis on the academic (content) task versus the participation task. There were clear teacher differences in how opportunities to talk were distributed (in relation to pupils' academic status) and in use of praise and probing questions to acknowledge pupil contributions. Variation across lessons and within lessons was also found, particularly with regard to teacher reaction moves within the question cycle, and this kind of teacher signal about participation requirements was used by several teachers in ways that were potentially confusing for pupils (form-function complexities). All these communicative differences were associated to some degree with achievement differences, and the associations were most clearly demonstrated in the contrasts between the two fourth-grade teachers who differed significantly in final achievement. Mrs. Flood emphasized the academic task and provided clear signals to pupils about the participation structure by calling primarily on pupils of high academic status, by using moderate amounts of praise, and by avoiding form-function complexities in her reactions to pupil responses. Mrs. Estes emphasized the participation task, distributed turns to talk in a seemingly random fashion, and rarely provided either praise or negative sanctions in reaction to pupil contributions.

Findings with regard to pupil patterns of attention in this study suggested that students were attentive to teachers' signals with regard to participation structures of the lesson. Many pupils specifically named the pupils who were participating in class discussions, and pupils in general were more attentive to pupil comments that were acknowledged by the teacher through praise or extended questioning (conjunctive and embedded cycles). Classroom differences in pupil patterns of attention suggested that pupils had indeed inferred norms and expectations for behavior that were never explicitly stated by the teachers. For example, pupils in Mrs. Flood's class attended particularly to the comments of pupils of high academic status, pupils in Mrs. Estes's class attended particularly to the comments of pupils high in frequency of participation, and pupils in Mrs. Brown's class attended particularly to answers to divergent questions and to comments of pupils low in academic status. In each case, the predominant pattern of attention was appropriate to the communication task set by the teacher.

	Core NIE Studies										
Constructs	Borman, K.	Cole, Griffin, & Newman	Cook-Gumperz, Gumperz, & Simons	Cooper, Ayers-Lopez, & Marquis	DeStefano & Pepinsky	Erickson, Cazden, Carrasco, & Guzman	Hrybyk & Farnham-Diggory	Hymes	Merritt & Humphrey	Morine-Dershimer & Tenenberg	Totals
Focus of the Study											
Teacher-student interactions	X	X	X		X	X			X	X	7
Student-peer interactions	X	X	X	X				X		X	6
Classrooms Are Communicative Environments											
Differentiation of roles exists between teachers and students	X	X	X	X	X	X	X	X	X	X	10
Relationships between teachers and students are asymmetrical	X	X	X	X	X	X	X	X	X	X	10
Differential perceptions of events exist between teachers and students	X	X	X	X		X	X			X	7
Classrooms are differentiated communication environments		X	X			X		X		X	5
Lessons are differentiated communicative contexts		X	X			X		X		X	5
Communicative participation affects student achievement		X	X	X	X	X		X		X	7

Contexts Are Constructed During Interactions	X	X	X	X	X	X	X	X	X	X	10
Activities have participation structures		X	X			X		X	X		5
Contextualization cues signal meaning	X		X	X		X		X	X	X	7
Rules for participation are implicit	X	X	X		X	X		X	X	X	8
Behavior expectations are constructed as part of interactions	X	X	X		X	X	X	X	X		8
Meaning Is Context Specific											
All instances of a behavior are not equal	X	X	X	X	X	X	X	X	X	X	10
Meaning is signaled verbally and nonverbally	X	X	X	X	X	X	X	X	X	X	10
Contexts constrain meaning	X	X	X	X	X	X	X	X	X	X	10
Meaning is determined by and extracted from observed sequences of behavior	X	X	X	X	X	X	X	X	X	X	10
Communicative competence is reflected in appropriate behavior		X	X	X	X	X		X	X	X	8
Inferencing Is Required for Conversational Comprehension											
Frames of reference guide participation	X	X	X	X	X	X	X	X	X	X	10
Frame clashes result from differences in perception		X	X		X	X	X	X	X		7
Communication is a rule-governed activity		X	X	X	X	X		X	X	X	8
Frames of reference are developed over time	X	X	X		X	X	X	X			7
Form and function in speech used in conversations do not always match		X	X	X	X	X		X	X	X	8
Teachers Orchestrate Different Participation Levels											
Teachers evaluate student ability by observing performance during interactions		X	X		X	X		X			5
Demands for participation co-occur with academic demands		X	X			X					3
Teachers signal their theory or pedagogy by their behaviors (verbal and nonverbal)		X	X			X		X			4
Teachers' goals can be inferred from behaviors		X	X			X		X			4

FIGURE 8.1 Constructs extracted from core NIE studies on Teaching as a Linguistic Process. *Note:* The constructs presented above reflect those that were easily extracted from the studies. They do not reflect the entire theoretical orientation or history of the different researchers. From Judith Green and Deborah Smith, *Elementary School Journal* 1983, 8(94), pp. 354–91. Copyright © 1983 by The University of Chicago. Reprinted with permission.

Several of the studies reviewed by Green focused on interaction among peers, and some of these found that the resources (communication skills) that pupils had available to bring to classroom communication tasks were not being utilized in lessons (Carrasco, 1981; Cook-Gumperz & Worsley, 1981). Other studies showed that peer teaching/learning settings could provide productive opportunities for use and development of these skills (Cooper, Ayers-Lopez, & Marquis, 1981; Merritt & Humphrey, 1981). For example, in peer-teaching situations, pupils used both questions and attention-focusing statements to assist each other in learning, and use of these skills was associated with higher learning outcomes (Cooper et al., 1981).

Related findings from this study showed that children were using communication skills in play settings that they had no opportunity to use in classroom lessons (e.g., skill in directing or influencing the behavior of others). Furthermore, they rarely practiced the skill of question asking in either play or lesson settings. (It was suggested that this was a potentially productive skill that children might learn to advantage.) Attention getting was a skill that was practiced by children in both play and lesson settings, and it was associated with success in both settings. The Cooper et al. (1981) study relates to these findings and suggestions by showing that both question asking and attention getting can be associated with success in peer-teaching/learning settings. In another related study (a sociolinguistic study not included in Green's review), Wilkinson and Calculator (1982) examined communication in peer-directed reading groups. They also found that children in these settings practiced attention getting and question asking, and that success in getting questions answered by other pupils was associated with academic achievement.

As this brief overview indicates, the findings of the study reported here have been corroborated in a variety of ways by findings of other research in the set of sociolinguistic studies funded by the National Institute of Education in 1978–1979.

Studies of Pupil Processes

Research on cognitive and affective processes of pupils during classroom instruction has been increasing in recent years, and this line of research has been reviewed by Weinstein (1982, 1983). Findings from some of the studies on cognitive processes provide further corroboration for the results of the study under discussion here. Based on data collected using indirect interview procedures, this study concluded that pupils made active attempts to learn from class discussions, both by attending to responses of other pupils and by being alert to certain teacher signals or cues that served to mark certain responses (e.g., praise and extended questioning). In addition to classroom differences in attention patterns that pupils followed in these attempts to process classroom language, there were individual differences, with pupils of higher academic and social (peer) status exhibiting different patterns than pupils lower in status. In two other interesting studies, direct interview techniques were used to gather more explicit information from pupils about their attempts to learn from lessons.

Winne and Marx (1982) videotaped lessons and played them back for both teachers and pupils. Teachers were asked to indicate points in the lesson where they intended to elicit particular cognitive responses from pupils. Pupils were then questioned about their thinking at those points in the lesson, to determine how closely their interpretations of teacher intentions (learning task) matched the stated intentions. Although there was not always a close match between the specific teacher intention and the pupils' interpretation of the type of thinking desired, it was clear that students were involved in active attempts to process teacher cues or signals. In fact, students reported teacher intentions even for offhand remarks. When one teacher said, "Think hard now," pupils reported this as a warning that certain material would be included on a test. Furthermore, Winne and Marx found that pupils were more accurate in interpreting teacher intentions when the cognitive processes being called for and the signals being used were well practiced or familiar. Thus, students in this study were actively engaged in attempts to interpret teacher cues about the academic tasks with which they were confronted; they inferred teacher intentions from teacher comments, even when no particular intentions existed; they were frequently inaccurate in their inferences about teacher intentions; and they were more likely to be accurate when they were involved in routine (well-practiced) instructional activities.

Peterson and Swing (1982) interviewed pupils about their attention and thinking during math lessons. Students were clearly aware of both their levels of attention and their levels of understanding in these lessons, for self-reports of both these variables were positively related to their achievement (e.g., scores on seatwork during the lesson). Furthermore, students who identified specific cognitive strategies they were using (e.g., relating information being taught to prior knowledge) were higher in achievement than students who identified general cognitive strategies (e.g., "I was thinking" or "I was listening"). This study showed that there were individual differences in both the degree and type of mental participation by pupils in lessons, and that these differences were associated with academic success.

Findings from both of these studies substantiate the conclusion of the study under discussion here, to the effect that pupils were actively engaged in attempts to process information during lessons, although these studies focused on information provided by the teacher rather than other pupils. The Winne and Marx study showed that pupils did make inferences about how to learn, based on verbal cues of the teacher during the lesson. In the study reported here, teacher praise and probing questions were apparently interpreted by pupils as verbal cues signaling that particular pupil responses should be carefully attended to. The Winne and Marx study also showed that pupils were more apt to misinterpret teacher intentions when unfamiliar instructional routines were being followed. In the study reported here, Mrs. Brown repeatedly used instructional models that were new to her pupils, and pupils in this classroom had difficulty understanding (interpreting) the function of pupil responses in these lessons. The Peterson and Swing study showed that different pupils used different strategies in attending to information being imparted, and that these strategies were differentially effective with regard to pupil learning. In the study reported here, differential strategies in attending to classroom discourse were also related to classroom success. High-achieving pupils attended more to teacher questions and to the responses of other high-achieving pupils than did lower achievers. Pupils high in peer status attended more to the comments of their peers than did pupils lower in peer status. Thus, the studies conducted by Winne and Marx and by Peterson and Swing, using direct interview techniques with pupils, corroborated findings of this study, which used more indirect techniques.

Together these three studies provide important evidence that pupils in elementary classrooms are making active attempts to learn in interactive lessons. These studies also indicate that pupils are simultaneously engaged in processing information about subject matter content and in reading or interpreting teacher cues about which information they ought to be processing and how they ought to be processing that information. Furthermore, these studies demonstrate that these pupil attempts to learn may be differentially effective, depending on the strategies individual pupils use in focusing their attention, the familiarity of the instructional procedure in which they are engaged, and the skill with which the teacher provides cues about where to focus attention and what the instructional task involves. The duality of the learning task (and therefore the instructional task) that was emphasized by Green (1983) in her review of sociolinguistic studies is thus underscored by the findings of these studies of cognitive processes of pupils. Pupils must keep track of both the subject matter content and the participation requirements of the lesson in order to be actively and productively involved in learning.

Teacher Information-Processing Research

Studies of the information processing and decision making of teachers have been reviewed by Shavelson (1983). These studies are similar to both sociolinguistic and pupil process studies in that they use mainly descriptive methods. They are different in that they are much more teacher centered, focusing attention on the mental processes of the teacher before, during, and after instruction. All three types of studies deal with cognition in relation to action (i.e., teacher and/or pupil thinking about behavior in teaching-learning settings).

In all three of these approaches to research on teaching, some concern has been expressed about the effects of data collection procedures on the data collected. Sociolinguistic researchers have noted that because the social setting is a prime factor in determining appropriateness of language use, the "testing" situation, or data collection task, may itself create the particular kinds of responses obtained (e.g., Mehan, 1973). In similar fashion, researchers studying pupil and teacher cognitions have argued about the extent to which a particular interview procedure may "create" the thoughts that pupils and teachers report having about instruction. It would be reassuring to know that different data collection procedures lead to similar conclusions about the patterns of teacher or pupil cognitions. Findings of this study provide that type of corroboration.

One particular study of teacher information processing is of special interest with regard to corroboration of the findings of the sociolinguistic study described here. The "South Bay study" (McNair & Joyce, 1979a, 1979b; Morine-Dershimer, 1979a, 1979b) was conducted in the same school as this sociolinguistic study two years prior to data collection for this study. Two teachers, Mrs. Flood and Mrs. Case, participated in both studies. Thus, there was an opportunity to compare findings about the thinking and behavior of these two teachers, based on data collected at two different points in time, using two different methodological approaches. The resultant substudy (Morine-Dershimer, 1982) has been described as a "2 × 2 case study" (Schwarzer, 1982). Findings will be briefly reviewed here to demonstrate the corroborative nature of this substudy.

Mrs. Case.   As noted earlier (see Chapter 4), Mrs. Case relied heavily on the textbook as a source of classroom language, reading questions aloud from the teacher's guide. In reporting what she heard in lessons, she reported a good deal of textbook language. She rarely identified the specific source of pupil comments that she reported hearing. She thought that her questions served an instructional function, mistakenly identified pupil comments as comments of her own in one lesson, and noted that her positive feedback ("Okay") served on some occasions to indicate good answers and on other occasions to simply mark the end of the interchange. Pupils in this class had difficulty explaining the functions of teacher questions and pupil responses, and most of them did not think that praise served to mark good answers. This class was significantly lower than Mrs. Flood's class in final reading achievement, but it was not significantly different from the other third-grade classes.

In the information-processing study, Mrs. Case's planning, observations of pupils, and interactive decision making were examined, with the focus being on reading lessons. Both planning and interactive decisions were based largely on the teacher's guide of the basal reader. Observations of pupils emphasized their involvement in instruction, their peer relationships, and the instructional activities in which they were engaged during lessons (e.g., reading group versus seatwork). Interactive decisions were generally handled by routines, with little consideration of alternatives.

In one illustrative lesson, Mrs. Case was conducting a phonics lesson with the top reading group, and the exercise was reportedly being done at the board rather than as seatwork, so that she could provide more immediate corrective feedback to the pupils. The exercise involved creating "new" words from root words (*thank, child*) and endings (*-ly, -ful, -less*). Unfortunately, Mrs. Case was not always sure whether words created by the children were real words or not (e.g., *thankly, childly, thankless*). She reported following an instructional principle: to refrain from telling pupils that they were wrong. She decided to have the pupils use their words in sentences in the hope that the pupil would then be able to correct the word and/or the teacher would understand the meaning the pupil was attaching to the word. This technique did not lead to pupil self-correction, but it did provide Mrs. Case with some understanding of pupil meaning ("I saw a childly woman," "She was thankly that she was home," "Thankless—it means she doesn't have any manners"). Despite these types of pupil responses, most of which went uncorrected, and some of which were praised, Mrs. Case never mentioned any reconsideration of her decision to follow this particular principle of instruction.

Mrs. Case's goal for this lesson was to follow the procedures given in the teacher's guide, and these procedures were followed. She seemed unaware of any discrepancy between the instructional objectives for the phonics exercise stated in the teacher's guide and the reality of pupils' performance. Because she was uncertain as to which responses were right, she had no yardstick against which to measure pupil performance, and her observations about pupils tended to refer to prior information ("This is the top group, and they're usually pretty good readers ... they've already learned their phonics," "Stacy's from the Educationally Handicapped class, and I do believe he's bright, but he just can't get it together"). There was no indication that new information about pupils was being collected by the teacher in this lesson.

These two descriptions tended to reinforce each other. Mrs. Case was well-meaning but unsure of herself. She relied on the teacher's guide to plan her lessons and to frame her questions. She picked an instructional principle and followed it, no matter what. She heard what pupils said but seemed unaware of *who* said what. The language of the textbook was what really captured her attention. Above all, Mrs. Case had problems with providing feedback to pupils. She was unsure about the accuracy of some pupil responses. Perhaps her persistent use of *okay* to serve the dual, and frequently undifferentiated, functions of providing positive feedback and marking the end of an interactive sequence reflected that uncertainty. Clearly, the description of Mrs. Case based on data from the sociolinguistic study was corroborated by data from the information-processing study.

Mrs. Flood.　Mrs. Flood provided an interesting contrast to Mrs. Case. As noted earlier (Chapter 4), her lessons were strongly content oriented, but at the same time she maintained a "natural conversational style" and was particularly adept at "topic branching" (building on pupil responses to move the lesson along from topic to topic). In reporting what she heard being said in lessons, she focused strongly on pupil responses, regularly reporting who said what and organizing responses according to the type of thinking pupils were displaying. She identified both teacher questions and pupil responses as serving an informational function (she wanted to know what pupils thought, and they wanted to share their thinking), whereas praise served an instructional function (encouragement and positive reinforcement). Pupils had a similarly coordinated view of classroom question cycles, and they thought that questions at school were congruent with questions at home (i.e., were "real" questions). Mrs. Flood's pupils were significantly higher in final achievement than pupils in three of the other five classrooms (Mrs. Case, Miss DeLuca, and Mrs. Estes).

In the information-processing study, Mrs. Flood was observed teaching reading to a third-grade class. Her goals for this class focused on learning self-management as well as subject matter. Students had choices about the order in which they would complete assigned seatwork tasks, and task completions were recorded on a punch card that went home at the end of the week. In observations of pupils, Mrs. Flood focused on involvement in instruction and on pupil personality traits such as initiative and self-concept. Her interactive decisions were generally "fine-tuning" reactions to the responses of pupils during discussions.

In one illustrative lesson with a slow reading group, Mrs. Flood was observed introducing vocabulary words for a new story. It was clear from her interview that she had planned the lesson carefully and had certain expectations about what students would say in response to her questions. But when these expectations were not met, she did not view it as a pupil error but rather as a difference in interpretation of the meaning of the question. For example, at one point in the lesson Mrs. Flood said, "If you are in a car, you might be one of two places—where might you be?" A pupil responded, "The city." Mrs. Flood's later comment was

> That was sort of interesting because I was looking for "front" (seat) or "back" and Mark came up with "city." My thought was different from what I'd planned. I thought, maybe I can get him to see opposites using "city." And I said, "Well, if you're not in the city, where are you?" And he didn't come up with "country," he came up with "town." He was thinking same things, and I was thinking opposites.

In this lesson, Mrs. Flood did perceive some discrepancy between her plan and the reality of the lesson, in that pupils were not always responding in expected ways, but these discrepant answers were not seen as pupil errors for the most part. Mrs. Flood was very aware of the actual behavior of pupils in this lesson, and she reported many small decisions where she adjusted her questions and reactions to student responses, always keeping in mind her plan for the lesson (e.g., focusing attention on words that were opposites).

Evidence from both the information-processing study and the socio-linguistic study portrayed Mrs. Flood as a teacher with a strong sense of instructional goals. The goals of both pupil self-management and development of thinking skills focused on learning independence. Mrs. Flood showed high awareness of pupil behavior and pupil language during interactive lessons. In the information-processing study, she tracked pupil responses and used this information to make "fine-tuning" decisions. In the sociolinguistic study, she attended to the source of pupil comments and organized comments to reveal pupil thinking and learning. Her fine-tuning decisions were again evident in her careful topic branching. Her view of classroom questioning as a vehicle to gather information about pupil thinking was also evident in her analysis of Mark's interpretation of her question (thinking same things versus opposites).

Thus, in this instance as well, the description of a teacher's perceptions, derived from data collected by sociolinguistic techniques, was corroborated by data obtained by procedures typically used in information-processing studies. This type of corroboration can work two ways. It can promote confidence in the validity of the findings of the sociolinguistic study, and it can instill greater confidence that the findings from studies of teacher cognitions are not merely artifacts of the data collection procedures used.

The Value of Associations

The studies cited above are not the only instances in which findings from this study have been corroborated by results of other recent research. Differences between teacher intentions and pupil perceptions have been noted in other studies (e.g., Cooper & Good, 1983). Differences in verbal interaction patterns exhibited by mothers and teachers have been observed in other studies (e.g., Hess, Dickson, Price, & Leong, 1979). Classroom differences in patterns of interaction associated with differences in achievement have been documented in many other studies (e.g., Fisher, Berliner, Filby, Marliave, Cahen, & Dishaw, 1980). Good (1982) has discussed such classroom differences in relation to socialization in schools, and has even suggested that discontinuities in expectations for behavior may present as much of a problem for pupils in moving from class to class as in moving from home to school.

It is not the intent here to present an exhaustive review of all related research, however. The studies discussed here have been selected to demonstrate that, despite the limitations imposed by the descriptive nature of this study, the findings reported in the preceding chapters were not isolated findings. Not unexpectedly, this study has been shown to have connections with other sociolinguistic studies of teaching, including use of similar constructs and reporting of associated results. In addition, and perhaps more importantly, this study has been linked to studies based on other descriptive approaches to research on teaching. Corroboration of this nature not only serves to validate the findings of this study, but also strengthens confidence in the knowledge being developed by the field as a whole.

EXPLICATION

Linkages among studies can involve explication as well as corroboration, and these types of connections also demonstrate the practical value of a study. Findings of this study help to explicate findings from teacher-effectiveness studies based on the process-product approach to research on teaching. In particular, they provide possible explanations for the effectiveness of direct instruction as a general strategy and of teacher praise as a specific technique.

Direct Instruction

The effectiveness of direct instruction has been documented by a number of correlational studies (e.g., Brophy & Evertson, 1976; Stallings & Kaskowitz, 1974), and further experimental studies have demonstrated that student achievement can be improved when teachers are taught to use direct instructional procedures in their classrooms (e.g., Anderson, Evertson, & Brophy, 1979; Stallings, Needels, & Staybrook, 1979). In direct instruction, the teacher controls and directs a classroom dialogue that is focused on content and skills and that actively involves students in responding to primarily factual questions, which are pegged at a level of difficulty such that correct responses are given about 85% of the time. Students are reinforced for correct responses, and incorrect responses are followed by corrective feedback, probing questions, or redirecting questions. Although the term *direct instruction* has suggested pupil passivity to some educators, the effectiveness of this strategy is in fact associated with the very active participation of pupils.

How can sociolinguistic research results illuminate the phenomenon of direct instruction? To begin with, the communication patterns followed in direct instruction clearly delineate both the content task and the participation task confronting pupils, and they place an obvious emphasis on the content-learning task. When the participation task is clear and fairly well routinized, as in direct instruction, then pupils can concentrate on learning content rather than on trying to draw inferences about shifting requirements for participation. Furthermore, the direct-instruction strategy fits well with pupil beliefs about how to learn from class discussions. Because the factual questions being asked can be answered correctly by most pupils most of the time, most pupils will "know the answer" and can participate more frequently in class discussions. Also, pupils who are trying to learn by listening to the responses of their peers will be hearing correct answers most of the time. In addition, the teacher reactions used in direct instruction (praise, corrective feedback, probing questions) can provide signals to students about which answers they should attend to particularly, in their attempts to learn from the responses of others. Teacher reactions can also provide signals about what kinds of responses are appropriate to give, thus further delineating the participation task and encouraging more pupils to participate in the discussion. This active participation in the discussion in turn contributes to higher achievement.

In effect, direct instruction may be particularly effective because it is particularly responsive to pupil beliefs about the "rules" of classroom discourse, rules about how to talk and how to listen if you want to be a successful member of the group.

Praise

Early process-product studies focused particularly on teacher praise, suggesting that positive reinforcement was an important component of teaching effectiveness (e.g., Flanders, 1970). As studies accumulated, however, reviewers noted that praise was not a strong predictor of effectiveness (e.g., Rosenshine, 1971). Soar and Soar (1979) helped to clarify the issue by demonstrating a curvilinear relationship between teacher praise and pupil achievement. Brophy (1981) emphasized the difference between contingent and noncontingent use of praise and noted that less effective teachers used praise to serve a variety of functions other than reinforcement for good academic performance. For example, praise was given to lower-achieving pupils simply to acknowledge/encourage participation, regardless of accuracy of response. Based on his review of research, Brophy recommended 12 guidelines for effective praise, including the suggestions that praise should be contingent, specific, and spontaneous.

The patterns of pupil attention associated with praise in this study provide one possible explanation of how these types of praise may promote learning. The evidence here suggested that teacher praise signaled pupils that certain responses were important to remember, for comments praised by the teacher were reported as heard more than comments that were not praised. Furthermore, pupils high in academic status, who participated more in class discussions, reported that teacher praise was given because pupils gave good answers. Pupils low in academic status, who participated less in class discussions, reported that teacher praise served an instructional function (e.g., "to show us how to do it"). It would appear, then, that contingent praise can serve a dual purpose, providing reinforcement to pupils who are most often the recipients of that praise, and at the same time identifying the "best answers" for pupils who are the "audience" for the praise or the listeners in the discussion (see Morine-Dershimer, 1982, for fuller discussion). This dual function, which can be accomplished simultaneously, may help to explain why contingent praise is effective.

In addition, the signaling, or instructional, function of praise identified by pupils in this study helps to explain the curvilinear relationship of praise to achievement. Any signal loses its alerting value if it is used too frequently (remember the boy who cried, "Wolf!"). When praise is used in reaction to many pupil responses, it ceases to denote the best answers; thus, it fails to cue listeners as to what comments to remember, and it also fails to identify clearly the kind of response that is appropriate, so the participation task is not clearly defined. When praise is used rarely, the same lack of cuing occurs for the opposite reason. In effect, praise can only operate as an effective signal to pupils who are attempting to learn from class discussions when it is used in moderation.

Effective Linkages

Explanatory power is supposedly one of the strengths of qualitative research, so it is encouraging to note that findings of this study offer explanations for some of the findings of more quantitative studies. Although teaching effectiveness is a primary concern of the field of research on teaching, the effectiveness of the knowledge base being built must also be an important concern. Identifying links between studies using markedly different approaches for collection and analysis of data is an essential requirement in the process of building a strong knowledge base. The connections noted here provide a further indication of the practical value of the findings of this study.

TRIANGULATION

The methodological technique used in this study also has a certain practical value for the field of research on teaching. Triangulation is not a new technique. It has been used effectively in earlier descriptive studies to compare the perspectives of different observers of the same phenomenon (e.g., Adelman & Walker, 1975). It is an important technique because the validity of the information obtained, and of the interpretation of that information, is always a central issue in a descriptive study. When several sets of perceptions are used to test, corroborate, and elaborate each other, the validity of any conclusion is obviously enhanced. In addition, the final description is greatly enriched.

This study carried the use of triangulation to an extreme, and in doing so it demonstrated the versatility and adaptability of the technique. Three distinctly different kinds of triangulation were attempted, and each proved to be productive. They will be reviewed briefly here in order to emphasize the possibilities for application in further research.

Three Types

The first, and most typical, form of triangulation of data involved the coordination of perceptions of three different types of observers of the same event. Pupils, teachers, and outside observers all reported on their interpretations of the language of classroom lessons. Similarities in their perceptions helped to identify both explicit and implicit rules for participation in classroom discourse. Differences in their perceptions helped to clarify the ways in which status might affect interpretation of classroom discourse. Had any one of these sets of perceptions been used in isolation, the conclusions of the study would have been much more restricted.

A second, less typical, use of the triangulation technique involved coordination of pupil perceptions of language in three different types of settings. Each data collection task was used in conjunction with videotapes of interaction in classroom lessons, in family conversations, and in play-group activities. Similarities and differences in interaction across these settings helped to delineate the discontinuities that pupils faced in moving from setting to setting. Similarities and differences in perceptions helped to indicate the adjustments that pupils made in adapting to the expectations of the various settings, providing concrete demonstrations of communicative competence. Had the study examined only the classroom setting, the description of pupil perceptions of classroom language would be much more limited.

The third, and probably least typical, form of triangulation embarked on in this study involved coordination of descriptions of classroom language derived from three different observational systems. This was the most difficult to achieve, for it required that the same data set be used in all three analyses, and any student of classroom observation systems knows that different systems focus on different aspects of the classroom (e.g., verbal versus nonverbal behavior; inclusion versus exclusion of information on arrangements in space). Videotapes of the lessons were essential, but even a video camera must focus on some things and exclude others (e.g., should the camera follow the interaction, and move from speaker to speaker, or try to encompass the whole class at once?). The researchers who agreed to analyze these lessons had to be willing to work with data that had already been collected. They could not design the videotaping procedures to suit the requirements of their particular approach to analysis of language. Furthermore, they had to "surrender" their findings to what was in effect a meta-analysis. These were difficult conditions for the researchers who completed the substudies, but the benefits of this particular piece of triangulation to the study as a whole were enormous. Similarities in the three descriptions strengthened the credibility of the findings immensely, particularly when quantitative findings paralleled qualitative findings. Differences in the three descriptions provided useful information about the effects of analytic procedures on research findings and identified areas that needed to be investigated in more depth (see Green, Harker, & Wallat, in press, for fuller discussion). Had the study relied on a single sociolinguistic description of the classroom language, the findings on classroom differences would have been much less comprehensive.

Each of these three uses of the method of triangulation contributed to this study in important ways, improving both the breadth and the depth of the final conclusions. The study thus has provided a clear demonstration of the practical value of triangulation as a research tool.

Further Adaptations

The productive use of triangulation in this instance should provide some incentive for further adaptations in other studies. Such adaptations have already been tried in a study of teacher information processing conducted at the Austin Research and Development Center for Teacher Education. The study was designed to investigate teacher thinking about classroom management and discipline. Subjects were junior high school teachers who were studied over one full semester. Data collected included ethnographic descriptions of classroom interaction; stimulated recall interviews about interactive decisions made during videotaped lessons; and Kelly Repertory Grid interviews about views of teaching, perceptions of pupils, and beliefs about student misbehavior. Two triangulation procedures were used (Morine-Dershimer, 1983).

First, data from stimulated recall interviews were analyzed by three different systems. One focused on categorical content, one focused on complexity of thought, and one focused on imagery of language used to describe decisions (see also Morine-Dershimer, 1984). These three analyses were coordinated to form composite descriptions of teachers' decision-making characteristics. This method of triangulation was similar to that of the three different sociolinguistic analysis systems used in the study of participant perceptions of classroom language.

In addition, the Austin study compared the perspectives provided by three totally different methods for collecting data. The composite descriptions derived from analysis of the stimulated recall interviews were tested against and coordinated with data from the ethnographic observations and the Kelly Repertory Grid interviews. The descriptions were both confirmed and refined in this process, so that the final descriptions resulting from this two-step procedure were more carefully validated and more fully detailed.

The Austin study further illustrated the flexibility of the triangulation method and demonstrated the contribution it might make in studies of teacher information processing. It is reasonable to expect that it also could be a useful procedure in research using other approaches to the study of teaching. Thus, by testing this particular method in a variety of ways, the sociolinguistic study reported here has provided information of potential methodological value to the field.

EMBEDDED QUESTIONS

The final test of value has to do with questions raised for further research. Any productive program of research can be compared to a chain of embedded question cycles. As each question is answered, the response stimulates another question, aimed at further clarification of the topic under discussion (investigation). The conclusions of this study, therefore, ought to prompt additional questions for further research. A few of these questions will be raised briefly here, for purposes of illustration.

This study showed that there were clear discontinuities between patterns of appropriate language use at home and at school. Most pupils in this study seemed to understand the differences, and perceptions were not markedly different for pupils from Mexican-American homes. Furthermore, Mexican-American pupils were not lower in final achievement than other pupils, after entering reading achievement was controlled for, so individual differences with regard to degree of home-school discontinuity did not clearly contribute to academic success. However, classroom differences with regard to final achievement provided some interesting clues about alternative ways of compensating for home-school discontinuities. Mrs. Addams and Mrs. Flood were the two teachers whose classes scored highest in final achievement. Mrs. Addams strongly emphasized socialization to the rules of classroom discourse in her second-grade classroom. Mrs. Flood conducted fourth-grade class discussions that were somewhat reminiscent of conversations at home. Each procedure presumably served to make pupils better able to participate appropriately in class discussions. Further research should investigate this phenomenon, both to determine whether these two alternative procedures can be shown to be equally effective in other school settings and to learn whether these procedures are differentially effective at different grade levels.

Findings of this study also showed clear differences between language use in lessons and in play settings. An intriguing result here showed a possible relationship between successful interactions in the two settings. Mrs. Estes and Mrs. Flood were doubly contrasted in that Mrs. Estes's pupils scored significantly lower in final achievement, and they were clearly less successful in play-group activities with regard to both cooperative and inventive play. In general, there was a similarity in rankings of the six classrooms on the two variables of success in final reading achievement and success in cooperative play. Prior research on teacher effectiveness has been criticized for its seemingly narrow focus on academic success as measured by standardized achievement tests of basic skills. The results of this study suggest that observational data on other types of learning could be collected and analyzed with relative ease and minimal expense. Further studies should investigate more carefully the classroom interaction factors that contribute simultaneously to both desirable social learning and effective academic learning.

Findings of this study showed clear classroom differences in patterns of communication. If these differences are viewed as suggested by Good (1982), it is obvious that classroom discontinuities would exist for pupils in this school moving from grade level to grade level. Imagine, for example, the adjustments to be made by the pupil moving from Mrs. Addams's second grade to Mrs. Brown's third grade to Mrs. Flood's fourth grade. Each of these teachers was effective in promoting final achievement in reading, yet each presented very different communication tasks to pupils in their lessons. Having learned how to participate successfully in one classroom would not necessarily prepare a student to participate success-fully in the next classroom. In fact, it could be detrimental. The research on school effectiveness suggests that shared goals and values, curriculum articulation, and schoolwide staff development are all characteristics of the effective school (Purkey & Smith, 1983). All of these factors could help to minimize classroom discontinuities. To what degree would the effective-ness of any teacher be enhanced if students did not have to make large adjustments as they moved from grade to grade? To date, studies of teacher effectiveness have tended to examine each classroom as an isolated unit, without regard to the history of children's experiences in prior classes. Longitudinal studies should examine the factor of classroom discontinuity in relation to pupil achievement.

These questions, which are "embedded" in the findings of this study, serve as an additional demonstration of the practical value of the study, for they point to areas that may be productive for future research.

THE LARGER CONTEXT

Each of the earlier chapters has concluded with a figure that was designed to place a particular piece of this study into the framework of the study as a whole. Although each piece needed to be explicated in detail, no piece could be fully understood except in relation to the other pieces. In much the same way, this chapter has attempted to place the full study within the larger context of research on teaching. This context can be visualized as a series of expanding circles. First, linkages to other sociolinguistic studies were identified (the "inner circle"), then, linkages to other types of qualitative studies were examined, and finally, linkages to process-product studies were explored. The full set of circles thus encompasses the variety of approaches most commonly used in current research on teaching. Just as no single piece of a complex study can be fully understood in isolation, so no single study in a complex field of research can be fully understood in isolation. The potential value of any study lies in its connections to other research (Krathwohl, 1985). This study has potential value for the field of research on teaching because its findings are connected with other research, because its methodology can be useful in further research, and because its embedded questions can be productive of further research. Chapter 9 examines its potential value for teachers.

9

Potential Value for Teachers

The ultimate aim of any study of teaching is to provide information that can be helpful in the improvement of teaching. Since the knowledge derived from a descriptive study is not generalizable, there are certain limits with regard to appropriate use of the findings. At least two types of application are appropriate, however. The concepts developed for purposes of interpreting the data can be used productively in analyzing and understanding other classroom settings. In addition, teachers can test instructional procedures that have been found to be effective in other settings, to determine how well they apply in their own classrooms. This chapter reviews the concepts and instructional procedures identified in this study that have potential value for these types of application by teachers.

PLAYING THE GAME

The special form of communication that has characterized the classroom for years (Hoetker & Ahlbrandt, 1969) was called the classroom "language game" by Bellack (Bellack, Hyman, Smith, & Kliebard, 1966). The players in this game are the teacher and the pupils. These players take alternating turns as they play the game of question and answer. Most players know the basic "rules" of the game and follow them fairly well. The teacher asks the questions and decides the order in which pupils get a chance to take a turn at answering. The pupils must bid for their turns by raising their hands. If they try to join the game without bidding for a turn and being recognized as the next legitimate player, they may incur a penalty. The rules say that pupils should not bid for a turn unless they can accurately answer the question asked, so penalties may be given for responding incorrectly as well as for talking out of turn. The teacher acts as both player and referee, distributing turns and issuing both penalties and rewards.

The classroom language game is a complex game, but it has one distinct advantage over other interactive, competitive games. It is a game that need not have a limited number of winners. It is both possible and desirable for many players to win at the same time. Not only is it possible for the teacher as well as the pupils to win in this game, it is impossible for the teacher to win unless a fairly large number of pupils win, too. Furthermore, there are several different ways for pupils and teachers to win as they play the classroom language game. Some of these ways have been revealed in this study of classroom language.

Before some of the winning ways of pupils and teachers in this study are reviewed, some very basic requirements for winning should be noted. It is assumed that no one can win the game without playing. It is further assumed that people who decide to play want to be winners. In any given classroom there may be pupils who decide not to play the game, who refrain from participating in class discussions in any way. This study provides no information about such pupils. It can only indicate some ways in which pupils who wanted to participate in the communication game were able to succeed, and some ways in which teachers who wanted their pupils to succeed were able to play the game so that there were multiple winners.

WAYS FOR PUPILS TO WIN

Most studies of teaching have focused on one form of success to be achieved by pupils in the classroom communication game. Academic success of pupils, as measured by performance on standardized achievement tests (or in some instances criterion-referenced unit tests) of basic skills, has been the yardstick against which teaching effectiveness has been judged. This study has identified two additional forms of success that were enjoyed by pupils who chose to play the classroom communication game. Pupils could be successful by acquiring academic status (entering reading achievement or status with teacher), social status (status with peers), or communicative status (e.g., participation in class discussions) within the classroom. Some pupils in this study were particularly successful, for they were able to acquire all three types of status. Almost all pupils were successful to some degree, for only 11 children were found to be low on all four of the status measures noted above, and a total of 94 were recorded as high in status on at least one measure.

The measures of academic and social status used in this study were detailed in Chapter 3, but it might be well to reiterate here that status with teacher was a composite measure based on teacher predictions about probable pupil success in reading as well as teacher perceptions of pupil tendencies to listen attentively, participate actively, use standard English, and follow the "no talking" rules during lessons. Status with peers was a composite measure based on pupil judgments about best selections for a team for a television quiz show, a team for a sports contest, pupils who could take over in an emergency, and classmates they "hung around with" during play periods. Thus, in each case the status measure sampled various pupil characteristics that might be valued by the teacher and other pupils, and pupils who achieved high status on these measures could be seen as pupils who were succeeding in the classroom setting.

Communicative status was not one of the pupil status variables identified in the original design for the study. It was a concept that emerged from the results of the study, and it needs to be further explicated here (see also Morine-Dershimer, 1983, for more detailed discussion). Pupils who participated frequently in class discussions, and pupils whose comments were attended to particularly by other pupils, were the pupils who held high communicative status in these classrooms. This status was in accord with the pupil belief system that you could learn by listening to the comments of other pupils in class discussions. In general, pupils who participated most were those high in entering reading achievement and status with teacher, and pupils who were attended to most were those high in frequency of participation and those high in entering reading achievement; thus, pupils high in communicative status tended to be those high in academic status, and they were in fact the classmates from whom other pupils might be able to learn.

The general pattern was not followed completely in every classroom, however. As noted in Chapter 6, the communication task varied somewhat from classroom to classroom, and the types of pupils who participated most and were attended to most varied in accordance with the communication task. In Mrs. Estes's class, for example, the task was merely to participate. Participation was randomly distributed, and pupils high in frequency of participation and status with the teacher (who distributed turns to talk) were attended to most. In Mrs. Flood's class, the task was to report your own experiences and relate those experiences to material in the textbook. Pupils high in academic status participated most and were heard most, but pupils low in academic status were not ignored. They were given opportunities to participate and were also heard by others. In Mrs. Brown's class, the task was to produce good divergent ideas. Pupils who participated most were those high in academic status, but pupils who were heard most were those low in academic status (presumably pupils who were freer in voicing divergent ideas). Thus, in different classrooms different types of pupils were able to achieve high communicative status, and achieving this type of status was an additional way in which pupils might succeed in the classroom.

In these six classrooms, then, it was possible for a pupil to succeed in several different ways while playing the classroom communication game. A pupil could "win" the game by acquiring academic status (being high in reading achievement or status with teacher), social status (being high in status with peers), or communicative status (being high in frequency of participation or being attended to by other pupils). Various pupils displayed different patterns of success. Perhaps these can best be understood by viewing a few pupils in more detail.

Meet the Players

In general, pupils from Mrs. Flood's class were among the most successful pupils academically, for this class was higher in final achievement than three of the other five classrooms. However, not all pupils in this class were equally successful academically, and different pupils achieved different forms of success. Four pupils will be described here to illustrate these various patterns of success. In each case, examples of the pupil's reporting of classroom language will be given to show how patterns of attention were associated with ratings on other status variables.

Michael.   Michael was an Anglo boy who scored below the first quartile in entering reading achievement, who was low in status with the teacher and in frequency of participation in class discussions, and who scored in the middle range on status with peers. Thus, he was only moderately successful on one of the three types of success that he might have attained in Mrs. Flood's classroom. (Since he participated infrequently and was low on both measures of academic status, it is doubtful that he was attended to strongly by other pupils, but the analysis procedures used in this study revealed only the groups of pupils who received the attention of others, not the individual pupils who were heard most, so a definitive statement on this type of status cannot be made for individual pupils.)

In the November lesson on poetry interpretation, where pupils related their own embarrassing experiences to an experience described in poetic form, Michael reported hearing seven simple units of language and four compound units (both the content of the comment and the name of the person who made it were reported). Five of the units were comments of the teacher, and six were comments of other pupils. Three students were named as sources of language. Michael focused most of his attention on the segment of the lesson where pupils were reporting their own experiences, noting teacher questions and pupil responses as follows:

> Have you ever swallowed anything?
> How did you feel when you swallowed something?
> Have you ever felt embarrassed?
> ... somebody swallowed five bugs ...
> ... John hit a rock and dirt went inside his mouth ...

Steven said he was riding a dune buggy and going up this hill and a bunch of dust came up and he swallowed some.

Rachel said at her old school her dad would bring his guitar and Rachel would feel embarrassed.

Although Michael reported the actual language involved in the teacher's questions, he paraphrased all the comments of other pupils. The information that Michael was gaining in this lesson was mainly information about his peers, but although this was information that might help him to achieve a moderate degree of success in his interactions with peers, the amount of information that he collected was limited and lacked detail. This pattern of attention was very different from that exhibited by Shawn, a rather successful pupil.

Shawn. Shawn was an Anglo boy who scored above the third quartile in entering reading achievement, who was high in status with peers and frequency of participation, but who was low in status with the teacher. In reporting what he heard being said in the November lesson, Shawn identified one event (no actual language given), two simple units of language, two compound units, and four complex units (actual language plus two or more items placing the language in context). Eight of the units included language of the teacher, and four included responses of pupils. Three pupils, including himself, were named as sources. Three units dealt directly with the poem in the textbook, and four dealt with the related experiences reported by the pupils and the teacher. Six units contained information about the rules of participation being followed. Thus Shawn was gathering information about textbook content, about participation requirements, and about experiences of his peers during the course of this lesson. The examples that follow illustrate the latter two types of information.

Mrs. Flood said, "Shawn?" I said, "On a summer day, sometimes I swallow a bug because they go into my mouth."

"Have you ever been embarrassed before? Rachel?" "Sometimes when we go places my dad brings his guitar and plays in front of people and I really get embarrassed."

Mrs. Flood said, "Is there anybody else who hasn't spoke yet? Timmy?" Timmy said, "I saw this guy, and I thought I knew him . . . and he turned around and started laughing and I ran."

Anybody else who had any embarrassing experience? [pause] I guess not. I'll tell you one I had. When I was in the sixth grade we had a class picnic. I asked my mother if she would make a cake. My dad said, "So it will be fresh, I'll bring it over at 5:15." We got there and we played and we had a good time. We ate. And when it was dessert time, I looked up and saw my dad standing there. I thought he was going to say, "Get in the car and go home," but he didn't. I guess he understood we all make mistakes.

Shawn's reporting demonstrated his awareness of Mrs. Flood's tendency to ask a question, look for volunteers, then call on a pupil to respond, as well as his acknowledgment of her technique for making sure everyone had had a chance to participate. (Some pupils reported such things as, "Rachel raised her hand," in addition to these types of details about participation rules.) He reported actual comments of his peers with some accuracy, and note that he even included "quotes" for the characters in Mrs. Flood's little story about her own embarrassing experience. The type and amount of information that he was collecting could well be useful in helping him to achieve high status in all three areas (academic, social, and communicative).

Rachel. Another pattern of success was evident in Rachel, an Anglo girl who scored between the first and second quartiles in reading achievement (which placed her in the middle group of achievers in this classroom), was moderate in status with the teacher, low in status with peers, and high in communicative status. (Rachel's hand was always up, and she always commented at great length when she was called on.) In reporting on what she heard anyone saying in the November lesson, Rachel identified one simple unit of language, seven compound units, and one complex unit. Three units dealt with the poem in the textbook and four with pupil reports of their related experiences. Five units included teacher comments, and five included pupil comments. Three pupils were named as sources. Only one language unit identified by Rachel included an interchange between teacher and pupil, so she did not show a strong focus on language associated with selection of pupils to participate. She was aware of language used by the teacher to structure the communication task for the lesson, however. This can be seen in the following units:

> Mrs. Flood said, "We're not talking about trick or treating today, but let's talk about any other experience you have experienced."
> Mrs. Flood said, "I'm going to read you a poem and I want you to listen and see if you can tell an experience . . . ."
> Mrs. Flood said, "Who can tell us what he was doing?" and Bobby said, "He was explaining that he ate it."
> Mrs. Flood said, "What would you do if you swallowed a gnat?"
> Mrs. Flood said, "There are lots of things that people don't want to say because they're too embarrassing. [pause] Well, I'll share something that happened when I was a child in sixth grade. We were having a school picnic and in fact the whole school was going and we were going to do it at the junior school. And my mother was going to bake a cake and my dad said, 'I'll hurry home and change my clothes and bring the cake, so it will stay fresh, to the gate.' And he told me what gate. And so I went to the picnic and we played all day and we had games and then it was time to eat. And then someone said, 'Dessert,' and I'd forgot about the cake. So I looked over at the gate and there was my dad standing there, and I was so embarrassed."

These teacher signals about what experiences were appropriate for pupils to share in the lesson, especially her modeling of an appropriate story, were carefully noted by Rachel. She would need this information in order to participate actively and accurately in the manner that earned her a high communicative status. The information that Rachel collected about her peers was more limited, however. She reported hearing only comments made by high-achieving boys, as in the following examples:

> One day I was walking down the street and saw this person I thought I knew and said, Hi, and then the person started laughing and I ran. [This was Timmy's comment, but Rachel did not indicate who said it.]
>
> John said, "One day me and my mom were at the bank and I had money rolls—three dollars worth—and the lady said, Next, and I burped."
>
> Brian said, "My sister pinched me, and I said, Ouch, and bugs got in my mouth."

In this lesson Rachel was gathering some new information about other pupils in the class, but her strong attentiveness to high-achieving boys would probably not assist her in achieving higher peer status. Emilia provided an interesting contrast with regard to her attention to the comments of peers and teacher.

Emilia. Unlike Rachel, Emilia, a Mexican-American girl, was high in status with peers. She also scored between the first and second quartiles in reading achievement, but she was high in status with the teacher and only moderate in frequency of participation (a reversal of Rachel's pattern of success). In reporting on the November lesson, Emilia identified one event, one simple unit of language, nine compound units, and three complex units. Ten units included comments from pupils, and five included comments from the teacher. Seven pupils were named as sources (three were named twice). Only one unit referred to the poem in the textbook. Emilia's attention was strongly focused on information about the experience of other pupils, both boys and girls, as evidenced by these examples:

> Brian said, "My sister pinched me." And he said, "Ouch," and there were bugs all over and he swallowed five bugs.
>
> John said he was riding on a motorcycle on a hill and there was dust. He turned around so the bike wouldn't fall on him and he fell and swallowed some dust.
>
> Rachel said, "When I was at my old school my father always played the guitar at recess and I would just get so embarrassed."

Emilia was also aware of Mrs. Flood's use of probing questions to prompt more detailed information from pupils. In one instance she reported the pupil comments without the intervening teacher probe, and in two instances she reported the full interchange:

> Bobby said, "Me and my brother were playing on the swings and I swung

too high and fell off and got a rock in my ear. So my mom took me to the doctor, and I could of got it out myself."

Bobby said, "My mommy said I did have rocks in my head."

Shawn said, "I once swallowed a bug in the summer when I yawned." "What did you do?" "I ran to the faucet and drank some water."

Steven said, "I was riding on the dune buggy and there was a bunch of dust. It was terrible. And after, some got all over—in our mouths and face." "What kind of buggy?" "A dune or sand buggy."

This type of probing response can be a good strategy in informal conversation as well as in lessons, and could be a useful strategy in interacting with peers. Emilia reported using the strategy herself in a side conversation with another pupil that occurred during this lesson:

Steven said, "I once swallowed a marble." "A marble?" I said.

Emilia's reports of what she heard in this lesson indicated that she was gathering information about her peers and also about techniques for carrying on effective conversations. She tended to ignore the textbook content and information about teacher requirements for participation in the discussion. She acknowledged her own involvement in a side conversation. These patterns of attention could well be associated with her high peer status and her mid-level academic and communicative status.

Complexity and Concentration. Each of these four pupils participated in the same lesson, and each tracked the flow of interaction in a different way. There is a lesson to be learned here by teachers. Even in a seemingly simple lesson such as this one on interpreting a poem by relating it to one's own experiences, there was a great deal of complexity for pupils to deal with. Interpreting the discourse was probably much more difficult than interpreting the poem (the ostensible content of the lesson). Yet each of the three pupils who had achieved high status in some area paid particular attention to aspects of the discussion that might contribute to acquisition or maintenance of that status. Emilia, who was successful in status with peers, apparently concentrated on learning more about her classmates and about conversational techniques. Rachel, who was successful in communicative status, seemed to concentrate on learning about the participation structure for the lesson. Shawn, who was successful in academic status, peer status, and communicative status, gathered information about textbook content, about his classmates, and about the participation structure. Michael, who was not highly successful in any area, gathered very limited information from this lesson, but what he did learn was associated with experiences of his peers, and status with peers was the only area where he enjoyed even moderate success.

Clearly, these pupils had their own agendas as they participated in this lesson, and their agendas did not always coincide completely with the teacher's agenda. But note also that the structure of the lesson was such that each of these pupils could act on his or her own agenda while still participating in the lesson. More importantly, perhaps, Mrs. Flood legitimized each of the three agendas that pupils might be pursuing in order to be successful in the various status systems present in the classroom. The procedures that she used to manage this feat are worth reviewing here.

The academic task, the communication task, and the social learning opportunities were all denoted by Mrs. Flood in her introduction to the lesson, as she said:

> There's a poem I want to share with you from our language book, and I'm going to read it to you. Then what I'm going to ask you to do is (*Communication Task*) *think of an experience you've had that's similar to the poem* that (*Social Learning Opportunity*) *you might like to share with us.* This particular poem is called "Accidentally." That's the name of the poem. Now you (*Academic Task*) *see if you can figure out what happened to the person in the poem.*

Throughout the lesson Mrs. Flood continued to provide cues that helped to legitimize and define these various learning opportunities and that encouraged pupils to engage in them. Here are some examples of her comments relative to the academic task (interpreting the meaning of the poem):

> You think that's a funny poem? Would it be funny if you were the one that ate the gnat?
> What was happening to this person?
> How do you think you'd feel if you swallowed a bug and you went to tell somebody about it? What would you be feeling? Would you be bragging about it?

Here are some examples of her comments relative to the communication task (reporting on relevant personal experiences):

> Have you ever accidentally swallowed anything? ... Tell us about it.
> Who else has ever accidentally swallowed anything?
> Can you think of anything else that's happened to you—besides swallowing—where you felt embarrassed—something that happened to you and you felt silly or embarrassed by it?
> Anybody else that we haven't heard from this morning?

Here are some examples of comments relative to social learning opportunities (indicating that it can be interesting to learn about the experiences of others, that certain feelings may be common to all, and that these feelings are to be honored):

> [After John's report that "I swallowed some dirt."] How did you do that?
> [After Steven's report that "Last night I swallowed some dust and it was terrible! We were going in this buggy, and we were going up this one hill, and the dust was coming up and then it goes all over us, and it was all over our faces and we couldn't see a thing."] What kind of buggy was this?

[After Rachel's report that "Where I used to go to school, my daddy used to always bring his guitar and play for us outside, you know, and everybody would gather all around and start singing and I'd get embarrassed."] Would the rest of you be embarrassed if that happened?

Is there anybody in here who's never been embarrassed about anything? ... Gee, most people have been, then. Then I guess it's something we can accept as being part of living.

Anybody else that's been embarrassed, that's willing to share it? Sometimes they're so embarrassing you don't want to share it.

All of these are simple procedures, but they could carry a powerful message to children—the message that there are a variety of things to be learned in the lesson and that each of the agendas that pupils may have can be legitimately pursued. The fact that Mrs. Flood provided these multiple opportunities for learning made it possible for Shawn, Rachel, and Emilia all to be actively engaged in processing different types of information within this lesson, and benefitting thereby. Michael was not so well served, and neither were the high-achieving girls in this class, who tended in this lesson, as in others, to refrain from adding their comments and ideas to the discussion. Perhaps for these types of pupils other kinds of opportunities could have been provided, such as pairing of pupils for brief discussions where they could share relevant experiences with each other rather than the whole class, or small peer-directed study groups where they could read and interpret a poem together, or peer tutoring sessions where they could instruct each other in activities where they had exhibited some skill and knowledge.

What counted as "winning" in the communication game varied from pupil to pupil in this classroom. It is doubtful that any one lesson could provide the optimum opportunity for every pupil to win, but this lesson did provide an important variety of types of opportunities, and pupils who were winners in this classroom were apparently taking advantage of those opportunities.

WHO'S COUNTING?

Similarly, what counts as "winning" for teachers can vary according to who is doing the counting. Research on teacher effectiveness has emphasized winning through academic achievement (Medley, 1979), and political forays into the education arena have also stressed academic achievement of pupils as the measure of teacher success (see, e.g., National Commission on Excellence in Education, 1983). Research on teacher thinking, on the other hand, suggests that teachers themselves tend to judge their effectiveness by how well they sustain the flow of a lesson and by how involved and interested their students are (Clark & Yinger, 1979). Thus, teachers emphasize winning through communicative accomplishments of pupils.

This is not necessarily in opposition to winning through pupil achievement, for results of the Beginning Teacher Evaluation Study (B.T.E.S.) in California suggested that pupil on-task behavior (involvement) could be a useful proxy measure for ongoing pupil achievement (Marliave, 1980).

At least one study of pupil processes suggests that what counts most for pupils in the middle elementary grades is acquiring a recognized place in the peer-group social system (Morine-Dershimer, 1985). Thus, pupils may judge teacher effectiveness in terms of pupil ability to interact comfortably with their classmates. This path to teacher success is not necessarily in opposition to winning through academic achievement either. Pupils who are unable to find their place in the peer group may also be unable to concentrate on academic learning.

WAYS FOR TEACHERS TO WIN

Clearly, there is more than one way for teachers, as well as pupils, to win when they play the classroom communication game. Teachers can win by helping their pupils achieve academically, by helping them develop useful social skills, or by helping them become adept in use of communication skills. But no teacher can win unless he or she is providing opportunities for pupils to be successful in some area, and the most effective teachers try to provide opportunities for pupils to experience success in all these areas. Several of the teachers in this study were able to provide these multiple opportunities within a single lesson. A few examples will illustrate the possibilities.

Building Mental Pictures

The first week in December, Miss DeLuca's class had a lesson on building mental pictures. This was one of a series of lessons on giving good descriptions. Selected segments from the lesson transcript give a flavor of the interaction.

MISS DELUCA: Here's what we're going to do. We're going to build mental pictures in our heads. Can you tell me what a mental picture is? Ysa, what is a mental picture?

YSA: Something that you see—put in your mind.

MISS DELUCA: Something that you put in your mind. Okay. We're going to see mental pictures . . . to use your imagination . . . everybody's pictures will probably be different. Close your eyes to see it, to see the thing in your head. And then, when you're picturing in your mind, you can ask—what do you see? What do you feel? What do you hear? Tell us about what you saw at that moment .... Now, after I do about three with you, I'm going to let you be the teacher, and you're going to get to come up and ask about it—ask the class to build a mental picture .... Okay? Let's try one. Let's start with something really easy. Close your eyes and concentrate ... after you build your picture, then Miss DeLuca's going to ask you to open your eyes up and tell us what you see, and we'll try to take turns and will try to get to everybody. Okay? I see something that is red and running. Do you see something that is red and running in your mind? Try to picture it so you can tell us about it. Okay? Open up your eyes. Who would like to tell us about what they saw? Ray?

RAY: A red fox running.

MISS DELUCA: A red fox running. Robert?

ROBERT: I had my hand up, like that, and I saw first like red bricks, and when I moved my eyes, it made them move.

MISS DELUCA: Wow! Everyone will have different answers, won't they? Mark?

MARK: I saw a roadrunner.

CHRIS: I seen a red rabbit.

MISS DELUCA: Chris saw a red rabbit. All of these are very good. Ysa?

YSA: A red clown.

MISS DELUCA: A red clown. What was he doing? Was his face red, too? Did he have a red suit on, or what?

YSA: He had red all over him, and red buttons, and he was juggling.

TONY: I saw a red horse running around 'cause a cowboy was chasing him.

MISS DELUCA: That's good. Mike.

MIKE: I seen this guy carrying a red rectangle and there was blood coming off of it.

MISS DELUCA: A red rectangle with blood coming off of it.

GAVINO: I saw a red dog and his tail was going up and down.

MISS DELUCA: Maybe like an Irish setter, or something. Was everybody's picture different from just about everybody else's?—They were, huh? And they were all good.

MISS DELUCA: I'll give you one more quick one. Close your eyes—and go for a walk in the woods. That's your picture, you're walking in the woods, and all of a

	sudden, this monster comes out. [laughter] So see him, see what you do, how you feel, he might be saying something, I don't know. Okay. Open your eyes. Rick.
RICK:	I saw like a cave, with a dragon in it. It had two tongues, and two things were popping out at me.
MISS DELUCA:	Good.
BOBBY:	I was walking through the woods and as soon as this monster jumped out of the trees, my eyes popped out like springs.
MISS DELUCA:	And what did he look like?
BOBBY:	He had two fangs, and was big and hairy, and he had an ape face on.
MISS DELUCA:	An ape face. Okay. James.
JAMES:	While I was walking through the woods I seen this monster and the monster had a head that was like from a person and it had a horse body.
MISS DELUCA:	A head from a person and a horse's body. Okay. Let's stop here, and I'm going to ask someone to come up and play this game with us. [At this point a student leader took over and followed the pattern set by Miss DeLuca.]

In this lesson, Miss DeLuca provided opportunities for pupils to "win" by practicing their academic skills, their social skills, and their communication skills. In the academic area they were practicing use of descriptive language. Miss DeLuca periodically gave feedback that corrected language usage (I seen—Chris saw). She asked probing questions that encouraged pupils to expand on their descriptions. She used contingent praise to mark responses that were more imaginative or more extensive. As the lesson progressed, the descriptions did become more imaginative and detailed. (Eliminating "I seen" would take more than periodic feedback.)

In the area of social skills, pupils could learn which of their classmates had good imaginations, and what kinds of things they liked to imagine (e.g., who had gory ideas about blood dripping off things). As one sociolinguist pointed out, they were also practicing a useful conversational skill, known as one-upping, as they tried to give more imaginative and detailed responses than those already offered. Miss DeLuca encouraged this by noting that everyone's ideas would be different.

Since imaginative, divergent responses were called for in this lesson, Miss DeLuca was particularly careful to provide plenty of information about the participation structure of the lesson, to insure that pupils could practice communication skills by participating actively. She explained the process they would go through, she emphasized the fact that variation in responses was expected, and she noted that everyone would have a turn. She did in fact give every pupil a chance to participate, but the communication task clearly involved more than mere participation. Her probing questions and praise served simultaneously to delineate the participation structure (indicate what kind of responses were appropriate) and to reinforce the practice of academic skills (giving imaginative and detailed descriptions). Furthermore, after giving pupils a chance to learn the "format" of the exercise, Miss DeLuca turned the lesson over to some student leaders, giving a few volunteers the opportunity to practice asking questions and leading the discussion of the class. (This technique was used in several of her lessons, so that over time, many pupils had an opportunity for this type of practice.)

In this lesson, then, all pupils had the opportunity to practice academic skills, social skills, and communication skills, and different pupils might focus their attention on different aspects of the lesson, building on their own particular strengths and gathering the information that was most important to them.

Asking Good Questions

In early December, Mrs. Brown taught a lesson using an "Inquiry Training Model" (Joyce & Weil, 1972). This strategy was designed to help students learn to ask questions that would gradually limit the field of search and zero in on the target (the thing the teacher had in mind). Only questions that could be answered by "yes" or "no" were permissible. The students asked the questions and the teacher answered "yes" or "no." This was the first time Mrs. Brown's pupils had tried this strategy, so she was helping them learn the rules and procedures in this lesson. Two segments of the lesson will illustrate the process.

MRS. BROWN:	Mrs. Brown is thinking about a teacher at this school, and I want you to ask me some good questions that will help lead you to the answer. Now, don't just guess, don't just say, "Is it Mrs. Hart?" I don't want that kind of question. I want you to ask some good questions that will lead to the answer. Darren.
DARREN:	Is it a third-grade teacher?
MRS. BROWN:	Is it a third grade teacher? No, it is not. Good question, though. Good question. Now you can eliminate third-grade teachers. All right, Madeline.
MADELINE:	Is her hair blonde?
MRS. BROWN:	No, her hair is not blonde. Good question.
ARTHUR:	Is she pretty?

MRS. BROWN:	Yes. Yes.
MELANIE:	Is it Miss DeLuca?
MRS. BROWN:	Do you have enough information to ask that question? What color is Miss DeLuca's hair?
AMANI:	Blonde.
MRS. BROWN:	And what did Madeline ask me? Madeline, what did you ask me before?
MADELINE:	If her hair was blonde.
MRS. BROWN:	And what did I say?
KEVIN:	No.
MRS. BROWN:	So you also have to be a very good listener in this game. A very good listener. Frank.
FRANK:	Is her hair brown?
MRS. BROWN:	Yes.
CHORUS OF PUPILS:	Oh, I know. OH! OH! I know, I know!
MRS. BROWN:	David.
DAVID:	Is it you?
MRS. BROWN:	Is it me? Thank you, but no. Have you figured out what grade this teacher is in yet? Alexandra.
ALEXANDRA:	Is it a fourth-grade teacher?
MRS. BROWN:	No. ... Arthur.
ARTHUR:	Is she a fifth grader?
MRS. BROWN:	She's a fifth-grade teacher, not a fifth grader. She's a fifth-grade teacher. What do we know about this teacher so far now? Fifth grade, and what else?
JADE:	She's pretty.
MRS. BROWN:	She's pretty, and what else? What else do we know about her?
SEVERAL PUPILS:	Brown. Brown hair.
MRS. BROWN:	That's right. Do you think you have enough information? ... Melanie.
MELANIE:	Is it Mrs. Jackson?
MRS. BROWN:	Yes. It is Mrs. Jackson. Fifth grade, pretty, and her hair is brown. Yes. All right. How many of you like this kind of game?
ARTHUR:	How about a hard one?
MRS. BROWN:	I thought I was asking hard ones, Arthur. All right, let's do one more, since you're enjoying this so much. I'm thinking about a particular animal.
	...
MIKE:	A whale?
MRS. BROWN:	Yes. It's a whale. You had enough information to figure that out, didn't you?

KEVIN:	One of us should have said, does it swim in the ocean.
MRS. BROWN:	What were some gray animals that you were thinking about that you eliminated? When we found out it wasn't furry, what did you eliminate? What animal, Kevin?
KEVIN:	Uh—rabbit, bear.
MRS. BROWN:	Okay, Kevin was thinking about some other things, but when he heard it wasn't furry, he immediately eliminated those out of his mind, set them aside. Yes.
FRANK:	An elephant.
MRS. BROWN:	You were thinking of an elephant. All right. An elephant isn't really hairy, is it? Kind of smooth. What made you think it was the whale over the elephant? They're both gray, they're both big. What made you think it was the whale over the elephant? What does an elephant have that we said this animal didn't have?
MIKE:	A big nose.
MRS. BROWN:	A big nose. Good. So you eliminated the elephant. Well, that was very good, boys and girls, for the first time you played that game this year.

In this lesson, pupils also had opportunities to practice academic, social, and communication skills. Since this lesson was based on an instructional strategy that was new to the children, the initial part of the lesson (presented above) focused mainly on the communication skills involved. Mrs. Brown explained the general task rather briefly, but she used several techniques designed to clarify the participation structure as the lesson progressed. For example, the first few times she said "no" in response to a pupil's question, she followed immediately with "good question." This served to indicate that in this lesson, a "no" from the teacher did not signal an incorrect response. At the first inappropriate question asked by a pupil, she reacted with a series of questions reviewing "known" information, then stated directly, "you have to be a very good listener." This indicated the importance of careful listening and of building new questions on information already revealed. A little later, she led pupils to review what they knew so far, showing them how to determine when they had enough information to ask a culminating question. Through praise and probing questions (corrective feedback), therefore, she gradually defined the participation requirements for this new communication game. By calling on a wide variety of students, she provided many pupils with the chance to practice the new skills involved. These same techniques were used throughout the lesson.

In this lesson, as in many language arts lessons, the academic skill being learned was also a communication skill: how to ask good questions. Good questions in this strategy were those that worked through a general characteristic (e.g., grade level taught) until a specific characteristic of the "object" under investigation had been identified, then moved to a new general characteristic and pursued that to a similar end. In effect, children were practicing simple deductive thinking, using familiar categories to locate an example that fit in the intersection of several sets (fifth-grade teachers, pretty teachers, teachers with brown hair). Mrs. Brown was very careful to begin with a problem that presented a fairly narrow field of search (teachers at this school), and that enabled pupils to draw on information from concrete experience. This minimized the academic difficulties of the task, enabling pupils to concentrate initially on understanding the new participation requirements. The second problem was more difficult, for it broadened the area of search considerably (any animal, not even farm animals, or wild animals), and required pupils to draw on more abstract knowledge (few of these children had seen elephants or whales face to face). Thus, as the communication task became more familiar, the academic task increased in difficulty.

A second academic skill in this lesson involved using the information derived from questioning to solve a problem. Mrs. Brown ended the lesson by having pupils reflect on their thinking, reporting on the possibilities they were considering and the way they used information to eliminate possibilities. This sharing of information served to explicate productive mental processes for other pupils and could make them more aware of the processes they themselves were using.

Pupils in this lesson, therefore, had an opportunity to learn more about the thinking of their classmates, by listening to the kinds of questions they asked and by hearing their reports of how they used information to eliminate certain possibilities. They could also practice the social skill of cooperative inquiry as they built on the information revealed by their classmates' questions. In fact, academic, social, and communicative skills were closely intertwined in this lesson. Although pupils might focus on one type of skill, they could hardly avoid practice of all three as they participated in the inquiry game.

Changing Statements to Commands

In late November Mrs. Flood taught a lesson on changing statements to commands. A series of segments illustrate the development of tasks in this lesson.

MRS. FLOOD:	In the morning when you get up, what are all the things you do? What's one of the things that you do? Mike?
MIKE:	Eat breakfast.
MRS. FLOOD:	You eat breakfast. Kim.
KIM:	Make my bed.
MRS. FLOOD:	All right. Rachel.
RACHEL:	I put my clothes on my bunk bed, and I get dressed on my bunk.
MRS. FLOOD:	All right. Johnny, what's the first thing you do when you get up?
JOHNNY:	Eat breakfast.
MRS. FLOOD:	That's first. Is there anybody who does something before they eat breakfast? Steven?
STEVEN:	Get out of bed.
MRS. FLOOD:	I think that's got to be the all time—I don't think there's anything before that. I like that Steve, 'cause I think that's what comes first. Now, I put a few sentences up on the board this morning and—Brandon, can you see them? Okay. Would you read the very first sentence for us?
BRANDON:	You will brush your teeth.
MRS. FLOOD:	All right. The next one, Karen?
KAREN:	You will put on your clothes.
MRS. FLOOD:	Arlene.
ARLENE:	You will eat your breakfast.
MRS. FLOOD:	And the last one, Yvonne?
YVONNE:	You will go to school.
MRS. FLOOD:	Now, I didn't put those in any specific order. I don't know if that's the way you do it or not. That's not the order that I do it. How would you change the order to fit you? Which one would you do first? Arlene?
ARLENE:	I would—put on my clothes.
MRS. FLOOD:	You put on your clothes first. Okay. Who has something different that they do first? Rachel.
RACHEL:	Eat breakfast.
MRS. FLOOD:	You have your breakfast before you put your clothes on. Okay. I do, too, come to think of it. I do, too. Shawn?
SHAWN:	Brush my teeth.
MRS. FLOOD:	All right. Does anybody do the last one first?
SEVERAL PUPILS:	No. Huh uh. I don't. You wouldn't be ready.
MRS. FLOOD:	You're not going to be ready. Now I'd like you to look at those four sentences and see what you can

	see about them that's the same. See anything that's the same? Nina.
NINA:	"You will . . . ."
MRS. FLOOD:	Okay. I wonder if—let's see who's nice and tall—Kris, do you think you could come over, and reach up and erase those two words that she just mentioned [Kris does so]—'cause we're just going to throw those two words away. Now those were statements that were up on the board, and now let's see what's left. Would you read one for us, Kendra?
KENDRA:	Brush your teeth.
MRS. FLOOD:	All right. Steven.
STEVEN:	Put on your clothes.

. . .

MRS. FLOOD:	How are those different from the four that were up there before? How would you think they're different, Shawn?
SHAWN:	They're demands.
MRS. FLOOD:	They're demands. And we call them commands. They're demands that you do something . . . . Do you see the difference between a statement and a command? Let's see if you can change some for me. "You will go out to recess today if it doesn't rain." Can you make that a command? Nina.
NINA:	Go out to recess if it doesn't rain.
MRS. FLOOD:	Let's try another one. "You will eat your turkey." Can you make that a command for us? Pam.
PAM:	Eat your turkey.
MRS. FLOOD:	Let's see if we can change a few [in your textbook]. The very first one on the top of the page says, "You will feed the rabbit a carrot." Kendra.
KENDRA:	Feed the rabbit a carrot.
MRS. FLOOD:	Good. "You will erase the blackboard." Kim.
KIM:	Erase the blackboard.
MRS. FLOOD:	Good for you.
MRS. FLOOD:	Can you think of a command that fits this? Now, this is something that you might actually see happen. A dog is running after a ball out in the street, and there's a car coming. What command might you say? Think about it for a minute. A dog is running out into the street after a ball and there's a car coming. What could you say? John?
JOHN:	Get back here.

MRS. FLOOD:	Get back here. What were you thinking about, Don?
DON:	Get out of the street.
MRS. FLOOD:	Fine. Another command?
BOB:	Don't go in the street.
MRS. FLOOD:	Okay.
RACHEL:	Don't go yet. There's a car.
MRS. FLOOD:	It's fun to try to do those. Next time you hear a command, would you stop and think about it, "Ah, that's a command I could change into a statement." And once in a while when you hear a statement, see if you can change it into a command. Sometimes it's fun to do that. Can you close up your books and put them away?

While the focus of this lesson is on the academic task, pupils also had opportunities to practice communication skills and to learn more about their classmates. The academic tasks that pupils faced gradually increased in difficulty as the lesson went along, moving from reporting on their own early-morning habits, to identifying similarities in sentences, to transforming given statements into commands, to generating commands appropriate for a specific situation. The shift in level of difficulty was marked by a change in Mrs. Flood's patterns of reaction. In the early stages she used simple acceptance ("All right," "Okay"), but in the later stages she used more positive feedback ("Good," "Good for you," "Fine"). This served to mark the later responses as more important, or to signal pupils that what she wanted them to remember was how to form commands, not what their classmates did when they got up in the morning. The gradual shift in difficulty encouraged the less academically able pupils to participate by building their confidence early in the lesson, and by providing practice in simple tasks, reinforcing the skills needed to accomplish the later tasks. Pupils at all levels of academic ability did respond, and respond correctly, throughout the lesson.

The participation structure of this lesson was a very familiar one to these pupils, and this also encouraged wide participation in the discussion. The lesson opened with "real" questions, and the conversational tone was furthered by Mrs. Flood's volunteering of information about her own early-morning habits. After moving to more structured, "known-information" questions, taken from the textbook, the lesson ended with real questions based on a situation familiar to these pupils (playing in the street). Thus, pupils in this lesson had opportunities to practice answering both conversational questions and "school" questions.

Finally, pupils who wished to could learn more about the home life of their classmates. Although this information was not marked as important to remember by Mrs. Flood's use of praise, it did serve to introduce the lesson, and it helped pupils to be recognized as individuals by their peers.

Winning Combinations

In each of these three illustrative lessons, teachers were winning as they played the classroom communication game. In each case, they were winning because they were providing opportunities for pupils to win the game, too, in a variety of ways. In each lesson, pupils had opportunities to practice academic skills, communication skills, and social skills. Different pupils could focus on learning different things within the same lesson. The most successful pupils probably practiced all three types of skills to some degree, but everyone had an opportunity to gather information that he or she considered important.

These lessons also illustrated other types of "winning combinations," or opportunities for pupils to use different types of skills within the same lesson. In each lesson, both subject matter content and thinking processes were important. Mrs. Flood's lesson focused on learning content (characteristics of commands), but thinking skills were practiced, too (applying a transformation rule to new examples). Miss DeLuca's lesson focused on learning thinking skills (imagination), but subject matter content was also included (characteristics of good descriptions). Mrs. Brown's lesson focused equally on content (characteristics of good questions) and thinking skills (use of simple deduction in problem solving). In each case, pupils were simultaneously accumulating information and learning to process information.

In each case, also, pupils were learning that they themselves could be valuable sources of information, that their ideas and experiences were useful. This reinforced pupil beliefs that they could learn from the comments of their peers, but it also encouraged pupils to believe that they had an important role in the communication game. They were certainly accurate in this belief, for in fact the classroom communication game could never be played without the participation of pupils. The most important winning combination was the combination of teacher and pupil, helping each other to win, for neither one could ever win all alone.

THE FINAL DECISION

None of the lessons presented here was a perfect lesson. None of the techniques practiced by these teachers was applied successfully in all instances. None of the attention strategies followed by the pupils described here guaranteed totally effective results. None of the findings of this study can predict what might happen in other lessons, with other teachers and pupils, in other classrooms and school settings. But there is information here that has potential value for teachers.

Specifically, there are concepts and findings that can be useful to teachers in thinking about the way the communication game gets played in their own lessons. These include the following:

1. Pupil beliefs that they can learn from class discussions by listening to the comments of their classmates;
2. Pupil patterns of attending to different aspects of a lesson, in accordance with their acquisition of different types of classroom status;
3. Teacher ability, through skillful use of reactions to pupil comments, to provide signals that guide pupils' attention and provide information about the participation structure of the lesson;
4. Teacher ability to construct lessons that enable pupils to simultaneously practice academic skills, communication skills, and social skills, so that different pupils can succeed by learning different things within the same lesson;
5. Teacher ability to construct lessons that enable pupils to both acquire information and practice processing information within the same lesson;
6. Teacher ability to construct lessons in which pupil ideas and experiences are viewed as important contributions in the development of knowledge; and
7. Teacher ability to construct lessons in which they can be winners in the classroom communication game because they provide varied opportunities for many pupils to participate and win as well.

It is only as these ideas are applied by individual teachers and found to be useful that their practical value can be demonstrated. Until that occurs, what exists within these pages will remain merely a description of what happened once in one small corner of the educational world. The final decision about the value of this research for teachers must be made by teachers who test these findings by trying to recreate one or more of them in their own small corner of the world.

Notes

1. An alternative explanation would be that pupils were learning to perform the reporting task in more detail as they became more practiced in the task. This explanation was tested. In May, when the reporting task was thoroughly familiar to pupils, half of the subjects in each classroom were shown a videotape of a lesson in an unfamiliar classroom. The teacher in the lesson was an adult they had seen in school, and the lesson topic was familiar to all. It involved a discussion of children's favorite television programs. When patterns of reporting on what was heard in this lesson were compared to patterns in the September and December/January lessons in pupils' own classrooms, pupils' responses to the unfamiliar classroom were found to be most similar to their responses to their own classrooms at the beginning of the school year. Number of events mentioned, information load, and degree of complexity were all compared across the three settings, using analysis of variance and Scheffe's contrasts. There were significant differences across settings in all three cases. Scheffe's contrasts for information load and degree of complexity were significant ($p < .01$) for differences between the unfamiliar classroom and the mid-winter lesson in the familiar classroom, but not significant for differences between the unfamiliar classroom and the September lesson in the newly assigned class-room. It was concluded that differences over time in pupil responses to this task were not simply a result of learning to perform the task.

2. The measure of conjunctive development was calculated as follows:

$$\frac{\text{Number of questions that initiate a conjunctive series}}{\text{Number of questions contained in the vertical sequence}} \times \frac{\text{Average number of questions}}{\text{in a conjunctive sequence}}$$

3. The measure of embedded development was calculated as follows:

$$\frac{\text{Number of question cycles that include an embedded cycle within them}}{\text{Total number of question cycles in lesson, including conjunctive cycles}} \times \text{Average number of embedded cycles within main questions}$$

4. A pupil did not need to be *named* by a classmate as the source of a comment to be counted as "heard" by another pupil. Each comment reported was located on the lesson transcript, so the source could be identified by the transcript regardless of identification by the pupil reporting.

5. It was probably not the case that all pupils in these classrooms believed that it was desirable to respond to teacher questions, and certainly there may be classrooms where the norm is for pupils to avoid participating whenever possible, but the evidence in this study suggested that most pupils in these classrooms expected that any pupil who knew the answer would volunteer to participate.

6. The reader is reminded that there was only one second-grade classroom in this study; thus, developmental comparisons were somewhat restricted by the uneven numbers of pupils at the different grade levels. Further investigation of grade-level shifts is needed.

7. Some educators will raise questions about this practice. The teacher expectation literature (e.g., Cooper & Good, 1983) indicates the problems associated with teacher behavior that sustains differences in pupil behavior. Thus a teacher who directs only experiential questions to lower-achieving pupils, and reserves analytical questions for higher-achieving pupils, may be preventing lower achievers from developing skills required to move them to higher levels of achievement. In this instance, both types of questions were addressed to the whole class, all pupils were free to volunteer, and the teacher called on both high and low achievers to respond to both types of questions. The point is that lower achievers had more opportunities to respond to questions where they could be sure of knowing "the answer" than they might have had if only concept-application questions were being asked. Thus, they could participate more actively in the lesson.

Sample Protocols
for Two Pupils

Excerpts of the protocols for two pupils are presented here as examples of the type of information provided by individual pupils, and to provide a clearer sense of the way in which interviews were conducted. Both of these pupils were in Miss DeLuca's third grade. Manuel was a participant in the play session for his classroom. Lori was a participant in the videotape of family conversations. Real names of these pupils are not used here.

MANUEL

Manuel was a Mexican-American boy. He was high in peer status, high in status with the teacher, and high in frequency of participation in class discussions. He scored between the second and third quartiles in entering reading achievement, which placed him in the middle range of achievers in his classroom.

Rules of Discourse Interview, September 11

INTERVIEWER: How are kids expected to talk in your classroom? When do they talk and what kinds of things do they say?

MANUEL: We're supposed to talk properly—the right way. Whoever says bad words, they're gonna get their mouth washed out with soap.

INTERVIEWER: What else can you tell me about how kids are expected to talk in your room?

MANUEL: You're supposed to raise your hand in the classroom when you're gonna say something.

INTERVIEWER: Anything else?

MANUEL: You should not shout out.

INTERVIEWER: What else?

MANUEL: The only time you can speak out without raising your hand is when it's free time or you're on the playground.

INTERVIEWER: Okay. How can you expect the teacher to talk in your classroom? When does she talk, and what kinds of things does she say?

MANUEL: She talks when she's in the middle of the room.

INTERVIEWER: What else can you tell me about when the teacher talks, or what kinds of things she says?

MANUEL: If she said a bad word, you shouldn't say it just because she did. If you did, she'd probably blow her top.

INTERVIEWER: Anything else you can tell me about how or when the teacher talks?

MANUEL: She talks when she has to—so we can learn.

Rules of Discourse Interview, October 13

INTERVIEWER: Suppose there was a new boy in your classroom, and you wanted to help him get to know about the class. What would you tell him about how kids talk in your classroom?

MANUEL: They should raise up their hand.

INTERVIEWER: What else would you tell a new boy about how kids talk in your class?

MANUEL: When we have free time, we can't talk loud, because other people might be doing their work.

INTERVIEWER: Anything else?

MANUEL: She likes her classroom nice and neat, and when she puts up decorations she doesn't like no one knocking them down.

INTERVIEWER: What else would you tell a new boy about how kids talk in your classroom?

MANUEL: She doesn't like people to talk out when she's doing things like writing on the board.

INTERVIEWER: What would you tell a new boy about how the teacher talks in your classroom? When does she talk, and what kinds of things does she say?

MANUEL: She talks when she's trying to get everybody's attention.

INTERVIEWER: Anything else?

MANUEL: She talks when she's trying to teach us something.

INTERVIEWER: What else?

MANUEL: She says things to tell us what to do and when to do it.

Rules of Discourse, Sentence-Completion Task, November 29

INTERVIEWER: I'm going to read some unfinished sentences, and I want you to finish them so they'll tell me about how people talk in your classroom.

1. When the teacher wants us to get quiet, she ... rings the bell.
2. When I want to ask the teacher something, I ... raise up my hand.
3. If I know the answer to a question I ... raise up my hand.
4. If I don't know the answer to a question I ... say so.
5. If I need help I ... tell her.
6. I talk quietly when ... she's doing work.

7. When the teacher talks, I ... listen.
8. I don't talk when ... she's talking.
9. The teacher doesn't talk when ... we're talking.
10. At recess I talk to ... my friends.
11. When I finish my work, I talk to ... James.
12. During a lesson, I talk to ... nobody.
13. I ask a question when ... I raise up my hand, or when it's my turn to talk.
14. The teacher asks a question when ... she's in front of the room.
15. Before we begin to work, the teacher says ... how to do the work.
16. After we finish our work, the teacher says ... you may go out for recess.
17. The teacher says "good" when ... our work's correct.

Units and Features of Language Identified in September Lesson

A partial transcript of the lesson is presented here to give the reader a sense of the relationship between what was said and what Manuel reported that he heard.

MISS DELUCA:	We're going to be playing a little game this morning, and I want to see if you can help me. I'm going to show you a group of words that's up here on the board. You see these words? Let's all read the words I'm pointing to.
PUPILS AND TEACHER:	Snowman, coming, cowboy, sing.
MISS DELUCA:	Now, I'm looking for a special group of words, and I'm going to give you some clues. Every word that belongs to what I'm looking for, I'm going to put a "yes" by it, so watch carefully. This word [*snowman*] would be a "yes." It fits into my game of what I'm looking for. This word [*coming*] would be a "no." It would not fit what I'm looking for. This word [*cowboy*] fits into my game—a special kind of word that I'm looking for. It is a "yes." Now see if you can look at the "yeses" and discover how those words are alike. This word [*sing*] does not fit into my idea. Would you like me to give you another one?
PUPILS:	Yes. [Nods.]
MISS DELUCA:	This one [writes *doorbell* on board] will fit into the group of words that I'm looking for. It's going to be a "yes." Now keep studying the "yeses" and see if you can tell what I'm looking for. Oh, some people are starting to get it. Okay, this one will be a "no". [Writes *tricking* on board.] Raise your hand if you think you know what I'm looking for. Okay. We've got about seven, eight, ... nine, ten, eleven, twelve. Okay, put your hands down. I'll give you a couple more.
MISS DELUCA:	[Writes *goldfish* on board] What do you think? Is this going to be a "yes" or "no"?
SEVERAL PUPILS:	Yes.
MISS DELUCA:	This is going to be a yes. What am I looking for?
ROBERT:	Compound words.
MISS DELUCA:	Compound words. James, what is a compound word?

JAMES:	Two words together.
MISS DeLUCA:	Two words put together. Okay. As we look at the "yeses," tell me the two little words that are in each word. What's in this word?
PUPILS:	Snow and man.
MISS DeLUCA:	How about this one?
PUPILS:	Cow and boy.
MISS DeLUCA:	When did you get the idea of compound word? When did you know what I was looking for? How far down did you go? James?
JAMES:	Down to cowboy.
MISS DeLUCA:	Down to cowboy, and then you knew it. When did you know it, Bob?
BOB:	Goldfish.
MISS DeLUCA:	When we got to goldfish. And when did you know it, Rena?
RENA:	By doorbell.
MISS DeLUCA:	And how did you get it? How'd your mind start knowing what I was looking for?
RENA:	I saw two little words in each word.
MISS DeLUCA:	Okay. There were always two little words in my "yes" words. Can someone notice something about all the "no" words? Linda, what can you notice?
LINDA:	They're not a compound word.
MISS DeLUCA:	Can you notice anything else about all the "no" words? Mark?
MARK:	They all have -*ing* at the end.
MISS DeLUCA:	Okay. We're going to finish playing our game. I have a bunch of words up here and they're all mixed up on the felt board. You're gonna come up and try to make up compound words for me. Look at the ones on this side and see if you can match them to ones on the other side. Okay, Manuel. Let's see what Manuel makes.
MANUEL:	[constructs word on felt board]
MISS DeLUCA:	Cowboy. That's a good one. Okay. Come on up, Bill. Let's see what Billy makes.
MISS DeLUCA:	You can see over on the board I have a chart, and it says, "Two words make a compound word." Let's read the words on the chart.
PUPILS:	Milk, man, milkman. Side, walk, sidewalk. Air, plane, airplane. . . .
MISS DeLUCA:	Very good. Now, if Miss DeLuca asked you tomorrow what a compound word is, could you tell us? Cheryl. What would you tell us a compound word is?
CHERYL:	Two little words put together to make one big word.
MISS DeLUCA:	Would you agree with that, class?
PUPILS:	Yes.
MISS DeLUCA:	I would too. You did a really nice job on that.
[End of videotape]	

INTERVIEWER: Manuel, what did you hear anybody saying in the part of the lesson we just saw [on the television]?

Manuel reported hearing the following units of language. (They are presented here in the order in which they were said in the lesson. This is not necessarily the order in which he reported them. No record was kept of that order.)

> Boys and girls, we're going to play a game now.
> I have a whole bunch of little words up here.
> (*She put yes and no on the board.*)
> (*One girl raised up her hand.*)
> ... a "yes" word.
> I'll put another one on the board.
> How many know what I'm looking for?
> We have about 8, 9, 10, 11, 12 people that know what I'm talking about.
> Do you want me to put another one on the board?
> I'll give you another one.
> James, what's a compound word?
> A compound word is two little words put together.
> Who else knows what a compound word is?
> James, when did you get to know what I was thinking?
> Manuel, come up, and let's see what he can make.
> Bill. Let's see what Bill can make.
> Is fishhook a word? Have you ever heard fish and hook?
> Robert made mousetrap, and that's a fun game too.
> There's some compound words on the board over here. Read them with me.
> Who knows what a compound word is?
> If I ask you what a compound word is tomorrow, will you know it?
> Cheryl.
> > A compound word is two little words put together.

INTERVIEWER: [arranging unit cards in random array on the rug in front of Manuel] Manuel, these are all the things you heard being said in the lesson. Some of these things are sort of like each other because people were saying the same kinds of things. Can you show me some cards that belong together because people were saying the same kinds of things?

Manuel formed the following groups of unit cards, and gave the following reasons in explaining why they went together, or how they were alike.

These all have "compound" in them.
> Cheryl.
> > A compound word is two little words put together.
> A compound word is two little words put together.
> Who knows what a compound word is?
> Who else knows what a compound word is?
> There's some compound words over here. Read them with me.
> If I ask you what a compound word is tomorrow, will you know it?

These all begin with a capital I.
> I have a whole bunch of little words up here.
> I'll give you another one.
> I'll put another one on the board.
> Is fishhook a word? Have you ever heard fish and hook?

Here she's asking us if we want another one on the board.
> Do you want me to put another one on the board?
> I'll give you another one.

These people went up to make some words.
Robert made mousetrap and that's a fun game too.
Bill. Let's see what Bill can make.
Manuel, come up, and let's see what he can make.
Cheryl.
A compound word is two little words put together.

(*Note:* Cheryl was one of the pupils who went to the board to form a compound word, although Manuel did not report that. Here he uses a unit card that identifies another contribution that she made to the lesson to include her in the group of pupils who formed words on the felt board.)

Units and Features of Language Identified in Late November Lesson

(Topic was Building Mental Pictures—Transcript in Chapter 9)

What is a mental picture?
(*Ysa raises her hand.*)
A picture that you see in your head.
You say, what do you see, and ... (She said)
Take out your crayons and pencils. (She said)
There's a piece of paper in front of you. You might want to draw a picture. (She said)
After I do three, then we'll let some of the kids do some. (She said)
Close your eyes and think of a mental picture. Think of something red and running. (Miss DeLuca said)
What did you see in your mental picture? (She said)
(*She called on Mark.*) A road runner.
(*She called on Ysa.*) I seen a. ...
(*She called on Robert T.*) I imagined a red ball bouncing in the desert and the ball was chasing something.
(*She called on Eloisa.*) A boy was chasing a strawberry and the strawberry was running from the boy.
(*She called on Tony.*) I imagined a red horse running from a cowboy because the cowboy was chasing it.
(*She called on Ricky.*) I imagined a big ball of goop running down the table.
I imagined a stream of blood. That wasn't a very good idea. (Miss DeLuca said)
(*She called on Robert T.*) I seen a hairy monster with two fangs. When I seen the monster my tongue went way down and my eyes popped out.
(*She called on James.*) I seen a monster with a human's head and a horse body.
(*She called on Ysa.*) I seen a Jawa.
(*She called on Mark.*) I seen a hairy monster and he was going to eat me.
What did he look like?
He looked like a bat.
(*She called on me.*) I seen a monster with a long head. He was walking around me with his hands behind his back.
What did he look like?

INTERVIEWER: Manuel, these are all the things you heard people saying in the lesson. Which things go together because people were saying the same kinds of things?

Manuel formed the following groups for the following reasons.

Here she's telling them about describing.

What did you see in your mental picture? (She said)
What is a mental picture?
(*Ysa raises her hand.*)
A picture that you see in your head.

These all have something with red.
Close your eyes and think of a mental picture. Think of something red and running. (Miss DeLuca said)
(*She called on Tony.*) I imagined a red horse running from a cowboy because the cowboy was chasing it.

Units and Features Identified in the Family Conversations Videotape

(*Dawn's little brother kept on shouting out.*)
(*The older sister was telling Dawn the spelling words.*)
(*Dawn was trying to spell Chinese, but she kept on getting it wrong.*)
How was Dawn doing on her spelling words? (The mother said)
She messed up on Chinese. (The older sister said)
Did you guys clean your room? (The mother said)
Come straight home from school and don't let no kids in the house and don't be fighting. (The mother said)
(*Lori's sister was laughing.*)
(*The brother kept shouting out.*)
Mother. You know what? (Lori said)
What? (Mother said)
I know how to spell language.
(*She spelled language.*)
Very good.
Mama. You know what? (Lori said)
What? (Mother said)
You know that old house around the corner—the one by the blue house?
Well, the tree there, it was falling over.
The branch is going to break off. (The sister said)
I had this dream last night, and when I woke up, I kept on trying to remember, but I couldn't. (Lori said)
Elias and Bobby—they were doing something and they broke the window.
Manuel and somebody were throwing the ball, and they blamed it on us, and Miss DeLuca ripped us up, and then she taped it back together. (*Lori said, when she was telling about her dream.*)
I'm purple. (*Ray said*)
No, I am. (*His mother said*)
I am! (*Ray said*)
Look what you could have done. (Ray said)
(*He jumped her man or something and he started clapping.*)
Ma, I want that Super Jock Football. (Ray said)
(*The TV was talking about something at the airport.*)
Shhh.
(*Mother wanted them to be quiet so she could listen.*)
Yesterday they were practicing to . . . (Mother said)
(*They started speaking Spanish, which I couldn't understand.*)

INTERVIEWER: Manuel, these are all things you heard people saying. Which cards do you think belong together because people were saying the same kinds of things?

Manuel formed the following groups and gave the following reasons.

These go together because Dawn's and Lori's brothers kept on shouting out.
(*Dawn's little brother kept on shouting out.*)
(*The brother kept shouting out.*)

This is all in Lori's dream.
I had this dream last night, and when I woke up, I kept on trying to remember, but I couldn't. (Lori said)
Elias and Bobby—they were doing something and they broke the window. Manuel and somebody were throwing the ball, and they blamed it on us, and Miss DeLuca ripped us up, and then she taped it back together. (*Lori said, about her dream.*)
(*Note:* Actually, in the last segment, Lori had been reporting on a real incident in school, one in which Manuel was involved, and apparently "in the wrong." In reporting what Lori said to her mother, Manuel said that this was part of Lori's dream.)

Dawn and Lori were both doing something in spelling.
Mother. You know what? (Lori said)
What? (Mother)
I know how to spell language.
(*She spelled language.*)
Very good.
(*The older sister was telling Dawn the spelling words.*)
(*Dawn was trying to spell Chinese, but she kept on getting it wrong.*)
How was Dawn doing on her spelling words? (Mother)
She messed up on Chinese. (Older sister)

Units and Features Identified in Play Session

(*I heard Amy's feet stomping on the floor, when she was using the jump rope.*)
(*Raymond and I were building the Empire State Building.*)
We're almost done. (Amy said)
Well we are done. (I said)
We're finished with the Empire State Building.
Let's build something on the box. (Ray said)
Let's put the box on it. (I said)
Let's put a fence around it. (I said)
(*Bobby wrecked mine and Raymond's building.*)
I'm gonna murder you. (I said)
(*Raymond was gonna build Superman.*)
Why don't you build Spiderman? He's the one who climbs walls. (Amy said)
Well, he doesn't fly. (Ray said)
There's a flat building on the floor, and that's how Spiderman climbs up walls. (Ray said)
(*When they were building that block thing*)
Amy, I'm gonna knock down your building. (Ray said)
I'm gonna tell your mom, Amy. (Raymond said)
You don't even know my mom's name. (Amy said)
Your mom's name's Karen. (Ray said)
Huh uh. 'Cause that's my sister's name and if her name was the same as my mom's name then Karen would be named after my mom. (Amy said)
What's your mom's name? (Raymond said)
None of your beeswax. (Amy said)

That's all Amy can say is "none of your beeswax." (I said)
Here's your lipstick, Bobby. (Ysa said)
(*Bobby got mad and threw it.*)
This is a neat color for braces. (Ray said)
(*I put one on.*)
(*Amy started laughing.*)
Wow! (I said)

INTERVIEWER: Manuel, these are all the things you heard people saying in the play group. Which cards do you think belong together because people were saying the same kinds of things?

Manuel put the following unit cards together for the following reasons.

Because they wrecked down buildings in these.
(*When they were building that block thing.*)
Amy, I'm gonna knock down your building. (Ray)
(*Bobby knocked down mine and Raymond's building.*)
I'm gonna murder you. (I said)

These all have to do with the building. First we finished it, then we built a fence around it, then Bobby wrecked it.
We're finished with the building.
Let's build something on the box. (Ray)
Let's put the box on it. (I said)
Let's put a fence around it. (I said)
(*Bobby wrecked mine and Raymond's building.*)
I'm gonna murder you. (I said)

Appropriate Forms of Language Identified in May

INTERVIEWER: Which of these things [indicating random array of examples] might your mother or father say when they want to get your attention?

Manuel selected the following cards from the examples provided.

Come here a minute.
What happened in school today?

INTERVIEWER: Which of these things might your teacher say when she wants to get your attention?

Manuel selected the following cards.

(*Rings the bell.*)
Manuel.
(*Turns out the lights.*)

INTERVIEWER: Which of these things might your friend say when he wants to get your attention?

Manuel selected the following cards.

Look it.
You know what?

INTERVIEWER: Can you think of some other things, that aren't on these cards, that your mother or father might say or do to get your attention?

MANUEL: Did you have a nice day at school?

INTERVIEWER: Do they say that kind of thing very often?

MANUEL: All the time.

INTERVIEWER: What do you say or do when you want to get your mother's or father's attention?

MANUEL: Ma.

INTERVIEWER: Can you think of some other things, not on these cards, that your *teacher* might say or do to get your attention?

MANUEL: She would come up to me and talk to me.

INTERVIEWER: Does she do that very often?

MANUEL: When the class is noisy—not very often.

INTERVIEWER: What do you say or do when you want to get your teacher's attention?

MANUEL: I raise my hand.

INTERVIEWER: Can you think of some other things your *friend* might say or do to get your attention when you're playing?

MANUEL: He would hit me on the back.

INTERVIEWER: Does he do that very often?

MANUEL: Mostly, when I play with him.

INTERVIEWER: What do you say or do to get your friend's attention?

MANUEL: I hit him on the back.

INTERVIEWER: Which of these things [indicating set of examples on 3 × 5 cards] might your mother or father say to you if they wanted to get you to do something?

Manuel selected the following cards.

Do you want to go to the store?
Feed the dog.
Follow me.
Did you clean your room?

INTERVIEWER: Which of these things might your teacher say, if she wanted to get you to do something?

Manuel selected the following cards.

Study your spelling words.
Get me the scissors.

INTERVIEWER: Which of these things might your friend say to you if he wanted to get you to do something?

Manuel selected the following cards.

Throw me the ball.
Do you want to go to the store?

INTERVIEWER: Can you think of some other things, not on these cards, that your mother or father might say when they want to get you to do something?

MANUEL: Junior, go mow the lawn.

INTERVIEWER:	Do they say that kind of thing very often?
MANUEL:	Once in a while.
INTERVIEWER:	What do you say or do when you want to get your mother or father to do something?
MANUEL:	Mom, could you please take me to the store?
INTERVIEWER:	Can you think of some other things, not on the cards, that your *teacher* might say or do when she wants to get you to do something?
MANUEL:	She could ring the bell. Or she could say, clean up your desk.
INTERVIEWER:	Does she say that kind of thing very often?
MANUEL:	Mostly all the time.
INTERVIEWER:	What do you say when you want to get your teacher to do something?
MANUEL:	I raise my hand, or I go up to her, or I say, Miss DeLuca, can you get me a pencil?
INTERVIEWER:	Can you think of some other things your *friend* might say if he wanted to get you to do something?
MANUEL:	Can you play?
INTERVIEWER:	Does he say that kind of thing very often?
MANUEL:	When he's got all his work done.
INTERVIEWER:	What do you say to your friend when you want to get him to do something?
MANUEL:	Let's go over to the school.

LORI

Lori was a black girl. She was high in status with the teacher, mid-level in peer status, and low in frequency of participation in class discussions. She scored above the third quartile in entering reading achievement, which put her among the high achievers in this classroom.

Rules of Discourse Interview, September 11

INTERVIEWER:	How are kids expected to talk in your classroom? When do they talk and what kinds of things do they say?
LORI:	They ask the teacher if they can go up to the desk.
INTERVIEWER:	How do they ask the teacher?
LORI:	By raising their hands.
INTERVIEWER:	What else can you tell me about how kids talk in your classroom?
LORI:	They talk quietly.
INTERVIEWER:	When do they talk?
LORI:	At free time.
INTERVIEWER:	How does the teacher talk in your classroom? When does she talk and what kinds of things does she say?
LORI:	She tells us what to do.
INTERVIEWER:	What else can you tell me about how she talks?
LORI:	First she rings the bell and then she tells us what she wants us to do.
INTERVIEWER:	Why do you think she rings the bell?
LORI:	To get our attention.

Rules of Discourse Interview, October 13

INTERVIEWER:	Suppose there were a new girl in your classroom, and you wanted to help her get to know about the class. What would you tell her about how kids talk in your classroom?
LORI:	They talk quietly.
INTERVIEWER:	When do kids talk, and what kinds of things do they say?
LORI:	They talk at free time.
INTERVIEWER:	What else?
LORI:	They talk when they ask somebody how to do the paper if they didn't hear the teacher correctly.
INTERVIEWER:	Anything else you would tell a new girl about how kids talk in your room?
LORI:	They raise their hand before they talk.
INTERVIEWER:	What would you tell a new girl about how the teacher talks in your room? When does she talk and what kinds of things does she say?
LORI:	She tells us how to do our papers.
INTERVIEWER:	When does she talk?
LORI:	If we ask her a question, she talks.
INTERVIEWER:	Anything else you would tell a new girl about how or when the teacher talks?
LORI:	She talks all the time.

Rules of Discourse, Sentence-Completion Task, November 29

INTERVIEWER: I'm going to read some unfinished sentences, and I want you to finish them so they'll tell me about how people talk in your classroom.

1. When the teacher wants us to get quiet, she . . . rings the bell.
2. When I want to ask the teacher something, I . . . raise my hand.
3. If I know the answer to a question I . . . raise my hand.
4. If I don't know the answer to a question I . . . don't answer it.
5. If I need help I . . . raise my hand.
6. I talk quietly when . . . I'm in class.
7. When the teacher talks, I . . . be quiet and let her talk.
8. I don't talk when . . . I'm in class.
9. The teacher doesn't talk when . . . she's not teaching a lesson.
10. At recess I talk to . . . my friends.
11. When I finish my work, I talk to . . . my friends.
12. During a lesson I talk to . . . nobody.
13. I ask a question when . . . I want to know something, or I need help.
14. The teacher asks a question when . . . she's teaching us math.
15. Before we begin to work, the teacher says . . . put everything in the corner of our desk.
16. After we finish our work, the teacher says . . . get ready for the next thing.
17. The teacher says "good" when . . . we have good printing on our papers.

Units and Features of Language Identified in September Lesson

(The transcript for this lesson is included in Manuel's protocol.)

> INTERVIEWER: Lori, what did you hear anybody saying in the part of the lesson we just saw?

Lori reported hearing the following units of language, not necessarily in the order they are presented here.

> Okay now, let's play this little game.
> Say the words. (She said)
> This is a "yes" word.
> How many people have already figured out what the problem was?
> Please raise your hand.
> I'll put another word on the board so that other people can have a chance.
> Do you know what kind of words I'm looking for?
> Now we need some more.
> Who can think of one?
> Can you think of any other words?
> Lori, could you think of one?
> Bedroom. (I said)
> Judy, when did you know it was a compound word?
> What word did you go down to when you discovered that it was a compound word?
> Now, see the compound words over on the wall. Now let's read them.
> Tomorrow if I asked you what the compound word was, what would you say, Cheryl?

> INTERVIEWER: [*Arranging unit cards in random array on the rug in front of Lori*] Lori, these are all the things you heard people saying in the lesson, and some of them are sort of like each other because people were saying the same kinds of things. Can you show me some cards that sort of go together because people were saying the same kinds of things?

Lori formed the following groups and gave the following explanations of why they belonged together.

All these things were said together.
> Now we need some more.
> Who can think of one?
> Bedroom. (I said)

See, she called on me and then I said "bedroom."
> Lori, could you think of one?
> Bedroom. (I said)

Because she was asking people when they discovered they were compound words.
> What word did you go down to when you discovered that it was a compound word?
> Judy, when did you know it was a compound word?
> How many people have already figured out what the problem was?
> Do you know what kind of words I'm looking for?
> I'll put another word on the board so that other people can have a chance.

Units and Features of Language Identified in Late November Lesson

(Topic was Building Mental Pictures—Transcript in Chapter 9)
>Who can tell me what mental pictures are? (Miss DeLuca)
>>(*She asked Ysa.*)
>>It's something that you see in your mind. (Ysa)
>When I tell you to close your eyes, then I'm going to tell you to think of something in your mind.
>You'll need your crayons and your pencil. (Miss DeLuca)
>If you can't describe what's in your head, that's what the piece of paper is for, to draw a picture. It's much easier.
>I'm just going to give you about three things to think up in your mind. Then I'm going to let the rest of you be the teacher and ask the questions.
>>(*She called on Rena to tell her what she saw in her mind.*)
>>I saw a boy running with all sorts of red powder around him. (Rena said)
>Were the stories good things or bad things? (Miss DeLuca)
>>Good things. (Everyone said)
>>When I was thinking, I was thinking in my head of a big stream of blood running down. That wasn't a very good one. (Miss DeLuca)
>Now close your eyes, and I'm going to tell you something to think about. I want you to imagine about a monster. Now everybody close your eyes.—Now open your eyes.
>>(*She called on Bobby T.*) I saw a monster and he was coming after me and my eyes popped out like springs.
>>(*She called on James.*) I saw a monster with a face like ours and a horse's body.
>>(*She called on Rena.*) A monster came after me. I was close by a tree and I hurried up and climbed it.

>INTERVIEWER: Lori, these are all the things you heard people saying in the lesson. Which things go together because people were saying the same kinds of things?

Lori formed the following groups for the following reasons.

'Cause in all of these she was asking questions and she was calling on people to describe what they saw in their mind.
>Who can tell me what mental pictures are? (Miss DeLuca)
>>(*She asked Ysa.*)
>>It's something you see in your mind.
>>(*She called on James.*) I saw a monster with a face like ours and a horse's body.
>>(*She called on Rena.*) A monster came after me. I was close by a tree and I hurried and climbed up it.
>>(*She called on Bobby T.*) I saw a monster and he was coming after me and my eyes popped out like springs.

These were all the ones that she was talking about when she was telling us to describe a monster.
>Now close your eyes and I'm going to tell you something to think about. I want you to imagine about a monster. Now everybody close your eyes.—Now open your eyes.
>>(*She called on James.*) ...
>>(*She called on Rena.*) ...
>>(*She called on Bobby T.*) ...

Because she said both of those at the same time.
>You'll need your crayons and your pencil. (Miss DeLuca)

If you can't describe what's in your head, that's what the piece of paper is for, to draw a picture. It's much easier.

Units and Features Identified in the Family Conversations Videotape

> (*Her baby brother was talking.*)
> Just tell her if the words are wrong.
> I can't hear you. (Jewel—Dawn's older sister)
> I can't hear you either. (Dawn's mother)
> Dawn doesn't know how to spell Chinese good.
> Study your lesson. (Mom)
> Put the baby down.
> Let me get the baby dressed. (Mother)
> I know how to spell language. (I said)
> Bobby and Manuel broke Eli's glasses.
> Did they get busted? (My sister said)
> No, but you know how Miss DeLuca gets mad as a bear.
> Here, do you want some? (My mom)
> No, the bread has too much butter on it.
> Come on, Christopher, let's get down.
> No, I'm purple!
> Mom, there's this Super Jock I want.
> Dad! Dad!

> INTERVIEWER: Lori, these are all the things you heard people saying. Which cards do you think belong together because people were saying the same kinds of things?

Lori formed the following groups and gave the following reasons.

Because we were both spelling words.
> Dawn doesn't know how to spell Chinese good.
> I know how to spell language. (I said)

Because Dawn's mom said, "Study your lesson," and when her mom said to Jewel, "Just tell her if the words are wrong," Dawn was studying her lesson.
> Study your lesson. (Mom)
> Just tell her if the words are wrong.

Because Jewel said, "I can't hear you," and Dawn started talking again, and her mother said, "I can't hear you either."
> I can't hear you. (Jewel)
> I can't hear you either. (Dawn's mother)

Units and Features Identified in Play Session

> I need the rest.
> No, I don't.
> Look, there's no more.
> We're almost finished.
> You are finished.
> We're done with the Empire State Building.
> That's not so tall.
> Hey, let's build a fence around it.
> Look at that fence.

Look at my windmill.
It's gonna fall.
Oh, please! Don't fall down!
Darn it!
I'm gonna murder you.
Superman.
It does look like Superman.
You ought to build Spiderman.
I'll tell your mom, Amy.
You don't even know my mom.
Yes, I do. Her name is Karen.
Karen would be named after my mother if my mother's name was Karen.
What's your name?
None of your beeswax.
You silly!
Have you ever heard your voice?
No.
Amy, here it comes. Amy!
Help, Manuel!
Happy birthday!

INTERVIEWER: [*Arranging unit cards in random array*] Lori, these are all the things you heard people saying in the play group. Which of these cards do you think might belong together because people were saying the same kinds of things?

Lori put the following cards together for the following reasons.

Because Raymond said this and then Amy said that.
We're done with the Empire State Building.
That's not so tall.

Because when they knocked down the Empire State Building, Manuel said this and then he said that.
Darn it!
I'm gonna murder you.

Because he said, "It does look like Superman," and then he said, "S-u-u-perman."
It does look like Superman.
Superman.

Because somebody asked Amy this and she answered that.
What's your name?
None of your beeswax.

Because these were all at the same time.
I'll tell your mom, Amy.
You don't even know my mom.
Yes, I do. Her name's Karen.
Karen would be named after my mother if my mother's name was Karen.

Appropriate Forms of Language Identified in May

INTERVIEWER: Which of these things might your mother or father say if they wanted to get your attention?

Lori selected the following cards from the random array of possible examples.
>Lori.
>Did you hear me?

INTERVIEWER: Which of these things might your teacher say if she wanted to get your attention?

Lori selected the following examples.
>All right.
>Be quiet.
>(*Rings the bell*)

INTERVIEWER: Which of these things might your friend say if she wanted to get your attention?

Lori selected the following examples.
>Look it.
>You know what?
>Come here a minute.
>Hey, you guys.

INTERVIEWER: Can you think of some other things, not on these cards, that your mother or father might say if they wanted to get your attention?
LORI: Nope.
INTERVIEWER: Do your mother and father say these kinds of things very often?
LORI: Every day.
INTERVIEWER: What do you say or do when you want to get your mother or father's attention?
LORI: Nothin'.
INTERVIEWER: Can you think of some other things, not on these cards, that your *teacher* might say when she wants to get your attention?
LORI: Sit down.
INTERVIEWER: Does she say these kinds of things very often?
LORI: Every minute.
INTERVIEWER: What do you say or do when you want to get your teacher's attention?
LORI: Miss DeLuca.
INTERVIEWER: Can you think of some other things your *friend* might say if she wants to get your attention while you're playing?
LORI: Nope.
INTERVIEWER: What do you say if you want to get your friend's attention?
LORI: Hey, Cindy.

INTERVIEWER: Which of these things [indicating new set of examples] might your mother or father say to you if they wanted to get you to do something?

Lori selected the following cards.
>Feed the dog.
>Study your spelling words.
>Be quiet.

INTERVIEWER: Which of these things might your teacher say to you if she wanted to get you to do something?

Lori selected the following examples.
Get me the scissors.
Be quiet.
Did you finish your work?
Read this story.
Open your book.

INTERVIEWER: Which of these things might your friend say to you if she wanted to get you to do something?

Lori selected the following examples.
Throw me the ball.
Do you want to go to the store?

INTERVIEWER: Can you think of some other things, not on these cards, that your mother or father might say to you if they wanted to get you to do something?
LORI: Dress the baby.
INTERVIEWER: Do they say these kinds of things to you very often?
LORI: Every day.
INTERVIEWER: What do you say or do when you want to get your mother or father to do something?
LORI: Nothin'.
INTERVIEWER: Can you think of some other things that your *teacher* might say when she wants to get you to do something?
LORI: Scrub and bubble your desk.
INTERVIEWER: Does she say that kind of thing very often?
LORI: About every two weeks.
INTERVIEWER: What do you say or do when you want to get the teacher to do something?
LORI: I don't know.
INTERVIEWER: Can you think of some other things your *friend* might say if she wants to get you to do something?
LORI: Nothing.
INTERVIEWER: What do you say to your friend if you want to get her to do something?
LORI: I just answer her.

References

Adelman, C., & Walker, R. (1975). Developing pictures for other frames: Action research and case study. In G. Chanan & S. Delamont (Eds.), *Frontiers of classroom research*. Slough, England: National Foundation for Educational Research.

Almy, M., & Chittenden, E. (1966). *Young children's thinking*. New York: Teachers College Press.

Anderson, L., Evertson, C., & Brophy, J. (1979). An experimental study of effective teaching in first-grade reading groups. *Elementary School Journal, 79*, 193–223.

Atkinson, P. (1975). In cold blood: Bedside teaching in a medical school. In J. Chanan & S. Delamont (Eds.), *Frontiers of classroom research*. Slough, England: National Foundation for Educational Research.

Ausubel, D. P. (1963). *The psychology of meaningful verbal learning*. New York: Grune & Stratton.

Barnes, D., & Todd, F. (1975). *Communication and learning in small groups* (Report to Social Science Research Council). London, England.

Beez, W. (1968). *Influence of biased psychological reports on teacher behavior and pupil performance*. Paper presented at the American Psychological Association meetings.

Bellack, A. (1973). *Studies in the classroom language*. New York: Teachers College Press.

Bellack, A., Hyman, R. T., Smith, F. L., & Kliebard, H. M. (1966). *The language of the classroom*. New York: Teachers College Press.

Berko, J. (1958). The child's learning of English morphology. *Word, 14*, 150–177.

Berliner, D. C., & Rosenshine, B. (1976). *The acquisition of knowledge in the classroom*. Beginning Teacher Evaluation Study (Technical Report Series). San Francisco: Far West Laboratory.

Bernstein, B. (Ed.) (1971). *Class, codes and control* (Vol. 1). London: Routledge & Kegan Paul.

Bernstein, B. (1972). A critique of the concept "compulsory education." In C. B. Cazden, D. Hymes, & V. John (Eds.), *Functions of language in the classroom*. New York: Teachers College Press.

Bloom, J. P., & Gumperz, J. (1972). Social meaning of linguistic structures: Code switching in Norway. In J. Gumperz & D. Hymes (Eds.), *Directions in sociolinguistics: The ethnography of communication*. New York: Holt, Rinehart and Winston.

Boggs, S. T. (1972). The meaning of questions and narratives to Hawaiian children. In C. Cazden, D. Hymes, & V. John (Eds.), *Functions of language in the classroom*. New York: Teachers College Press.

Borman, K., Piazza, S., Barrett, D., & Sheoran, P. (1981a). *The ecology of children's play* (Final report NIE G-79-0123). Washington, D.C.: National Institute of Education.

Borman, K., Piazza, S., Barrett, D., & Sheoran, P. (1981b). *Children's interpersonal relationships, playground games, and social-cognitive skills* (Final report NIE G-79-0123). Washington, D.C.: National Institute of Education.

Brandis, W., & Henderson, D. (1970). *Social class, language and communication*. Beverly Hills, CA: Sage.

Brophy, J. E. (1981). Teacher praise: A functional analysis. *Review of Educational Research, 51*(1), 5–32

Brophy, J. E. (1983a). Classroom organization and management. *Elementary School Journal, 83*, 265–286.

Brophy, J. E. (1983b). Classroom organization and management. In D.C. Smith (Ed.), *Essential knowledge for beginning educators*. Washington, D.C.: American Association of Colleges for Teacher Education.

Brophy, J., & Evertson, C. (1976). *Learning from teaching: A developmental perspective*. Boston: Allyn & Bacon.

Brophy, J., & Good, T. (1969). *Teachers' communication of differential expectations for children's classroom performance: Some behavioral data* (Texas Research and Development Center for Teacher Education, Report No. 25). Austin: University of Texas.

Brophy, J., & Good, T. (1974). *Teacher-student relationships: Causes and consequences*. New York: Holt, Rinehart and Winston.

Brown, R., & Bellugi, U. (1964). Three processes in the child's acquisition of syntax. *Harvard Educational Review, 34*, 133–151.

Brown, R., & Berko, J. (1960). Word association and the acquisition of grammar. *Child Development, 31*, 1–14.

Bruner, J. S., Goodnow, J. J., & Austin, G. A. (1956). *A study of thinking*. New York: Wiley.

Bugenthal, D., Love, L., & Gianetto, R. (1971). Perfidious feminine faces. *Journal of Personality and Social Psychology, 17*, 314–318.

Burnham, J. (1968). Effects of experimenters' expectancies on children's ability to learn how to swim. Unpublished master's thesis, Purdue University, West Lafayette, IN.

Bussis, A. M., Chittenden, E. A., & Amarel, M. (1976). *Beyond surface curriculum*. Boulder, CO: Westview Press.

Cahir, S. R., & Kovacs, C. (1981). *Exploring functional language*. Washington, D.C.: Center for Applied Linguistics.

Carlson, P., & Anisfeld, M. (1969). Some observations on the linguistic competence of a two-year-old child. *Child Development, 40*, 569–575.

Carrasco, R. (1981). Expanded awareness of student performance: A case study in applied ethnographic monitoring in a bilingual classroom. In H. T. Trueba, G. T. Guthrie, & K. Au (Eds.), *Culture and the bilingual classroom: Studies in classroom ethnography*. Rowley, MA: Newbury.

Cazden, C. (1970). The situation: A neglected source of difference in language use. *The Journal of Social Issues*, 26, 35–60.

Cazden, C. (1972). *Child language and education*. New York: Holt, Rinehart and Winston.

Cazden, C. (1974). *Teaching as a linguistic process in a cultural setting* (Report of Panel 5, NIE Conference on Studies in Teaching). Washington, D.C.: National Institute of Education.

Chomsky, C. (1969). *The acquisition of syntax in children 5 to 10*. Cambridge: Massachusetts Institute of Technology.

Cicirelli, V. (1969). *The impact of Head Start: An evaluation of the effects of Head Start on children's cognitive and affective development* (Vols. I and II). Bladensburg, MD: Westinghouse Learning Corporation.

Clark, E. (1971). On the acquisition of the meaning of "before" and "after." *Journal of Verbal Learning and Verbal Behavior*, 10, 266–275.

Clark, E. (1972). On the acquisition of antonyms in two semantic fields. *Journal of Verbal Learning and Verbal Behavior*, 11, 750–758.

Clark, C., & Yinger, R. (1979). Teachers' thinking. In P. L. Peterson & H. J. Walberg (Eds.), *Research on teaching: Concepts, findings, and implications*. Berkeley, CA: McCutchan.

Cole, M., & Bruner, J. (1971). Cultural differences and inferences about psychological processes. *American Psychologist*, 26, 867–876.

Cole, M., Griffin, P., & Newman, D. (1978–81). *The effect of different classroom organizations on the learning of classroom discourse rules and cognitive content* (Mid-quarter report NIE G-78-0159). Washington, D.C.: National Institute of Education.

Cole, M., Griffin, P., & Newman D. (1979). *They're all the same in their own way* (Mid-quarter report NIE G-78-1059). Washington, D.C.: National Institute of Education.

Cook-Gumperz, J., Gumperz, J., & Simons, H. D. (Eds.) (1981). *School-home ethnography project* (Final report NIE-G-78-0082). Washington, D.C.: National Institute of Education.

Cook-Gumperz, J., & Worsley, L. (1981). Report on the narrative discourse study. In J. Cook-Gumperz, J. Gumperz, & H. D. Simons (Eds.), *School-home ethnography project* (Final report NIE G-78-0082). Washington, D.C.: National Institute of Education.

Cooper, C., Ayers-Lopez, S., & Marquis, A. (1981). *Children's discourse in cooperative and didactic interaction: Developmental patterns in effective learning* (Final report NIE G-78-0098). Washington, D.C.: National Institute of Education.

Cooper, H. M., & Good, T. L. (1983). *Pygmalion grows up*. New York: Longman.

Cronbach, L. J., & Furby, L. (1970). How we should measure "change"—or should we? *Psychological Bulletin*, 74(1), 68–80.

DeStafano, J., & Pepinsky, H. (1981). *The learning of discourse rules of culturally different children in first-grade literacy instruction* (Final report NIE G-79-0032). Washington, D.C.: National Institute of Education.

Dimitrovsky, L. (1964). The ability to identify the emotional meaning of vocal expression at successive age levels. In J. R. Davitz, *The communication of emotional meaning*. New York: McGraw-Hill.

Donaldson, M., & Wales, R. (1970). On the acquisition of some relational terms. In J. Hayes (Ed.), *Cognition and the development of language*. New York: Wiley.

Dumont, R. V. (1972). Learning English and how to be silent: Studies in Sioux and Cherokee classrooms. In C. Cazden, D. Hymes, & V. John (Eds.), *Functions of language in the classroom*. New York: Teachers College Press.

Elkind, D., Deblinger, J., & Adler, D. (1970). Motivation and creativity: The context effect. *American Educational Research Journal, 7*(3), 351–357.

Erickson, F. (1982). Classroom discourse as improvisation: Relationships between academic task structure and social participation structure in lessons. In L. C. Wilkinson (Ed.), *Communicating in the classroom*. New York: Academic Press.

Erickson, F., Cazden, C., Carrasco, R., & Guzman, A. (1978–1981). *Social and cultural organization of interaction in classrooms of bilingual children* (Midquarter report NIE G-78-0099). Washington, D.C.: National Institute of Education.

Ervin, S. (1965). Imitation and structural change in children's language. In E. Lenneberg (Ed.), *New directions in the study of language*. Cambridge: M.I.T. Press.

Fenster, A., & Goldstein, A. M. (1971). The emotional world of children "vis à vis" the emotional world of adults: An examination of vocal communication. *The Journal of Communication, 21*, 353–362.

Fisher, C. W., Berliner, D.C., Filby, N. N., Marliave, R., Cahen, L. S., & Dishaw, M. M. (1980). Teaching behavior, academic learning time, and student achievement: An overview. In C. Denham & A. Lieberman (Eds.), *Time to learn*. Washington, D.C.: Department of Education.

Flanders, N. A. (1970). *Analyzing teaching behavior*. Reading, MA: Addison-Wesley.

Formanek, R., & Morine, G. (1968). Categorizing in young children: Two views. *Teachers College Record, 69*, 409–420.

Glucksberg, S., Krauss, R. M., & Weisberg, R. (1966). Referential communication in nursery school children: Method and some preliminary findings. *Journal of Experimental Child Psychology, 3*, 333–342.

Good, T. (1982). *Classroom research: What we know and what we need to know*. Austin: Research and Development Center for Teacher Education, University of Texas.

Green, J. L. (1983a). Research on teaching as a linguistic process: A state of the art. *Review of Research in Education, 10*, 151–252.

Green, J. L. (1983b). Exploring classroom discourse: Linguistic perspectives on teaching-learning processes. *Educational Psychologist, 18*, 180–199.

Green, J. L., & Harker, J. O. (1982). Gaining access to learning: Conversational, social, and cognitive demands of group participation. In L. C. Wilkinson (Ed.), *Communicating in the classroom*. New York: Academic Press.

Green, J. L., Harker, J. O., & Wallat, C. (Eds.) (in press). *Multiple analysis of classroom discourse processes*. Norwood, NJ: Ablex.

Green, J. L., & Smith, D. (1983). Teaching and learning: A linguistic perspective. *The Elementary School Journal, 83*, 353–391.

Gumperz, J. (1971). *Language in social groups*. Stanford, CA: Stanford University Press.

Gumperz, J. J., & Herasimchuk, E. (1972). The conversational analysis of social meaning: A study of classroom interaction. In R. Shuy (Ed.), *Sociolinguistics* (Georgetown Monograph Series on Language and Linguistics), *25*.

Gumperz, J. J., & Hernandez, E. (1972). Bilingualism, bidialectalism and classroom interaction. In C. Cazden, D. Hymes, & V. John (Eds.), *The Functions of language in the classroom*. New York: Teachers College Press.

Hammersley, M. (1974). The organization of pupil participation. *Sociological Review*, *22*(3), 355–368.

Hawkins, P. R. (1969). Social class, the nominal group and reference. *Language and Speech*, *12*, 125–135.

Heider, E. R. (1971). Style and accuracy of verbal communication within and between social classes. *Journal of Personality and Social Psychology*, *18*, 33–47.

Heider, E. R., Cazden, C. B., & Brown, R. (1968). *Social class differences in the effectiveness and style of children's coding ability* (Project Literacy Reports, No. 9). Ithaca, NY: Cornell University.

Hess, R., Dickson, W., Price, G., & Leong, D. (1979). Some contrasts between mothers and preschool teachers in interactions with four-year-old children. *American Educational Research Journal*, *16*(3), 307–316.

Hoetker, J., & Ahlbrandt, P. A. (1969). The persistence of recitation. *American Educational Research Journal*, *6*, 2.

Horner, V. M. (1968). *The verbal world of the lower-class three-year-old: A pilot study in linguistic ecology*. Unpublished doctoral dissertation, University of Rochester, Rochester, NY.

Houston, S. H. (1970). A reexamination of some assumptions about the language of the disadvantaged child. *Child Development*, *41*, 947–963.

Hrybyk, M., & Farnham-Diggory, S. (1981). *Children's groups in school: A developmental case study* (Final report NIE G-79-0124). Washington, D.C.: National Institute of Education.

Hymes, D. (1971). Competence and performance in linguistic theory. In R. Huxley & E. Ingram (Eds.), *Language acquisition: Models and methods*. New York: Academic Press.

Hymes, D. (1972). Introduction. In C. Cazden, D. Hymes, & V. John (Eds.), *Functions of language in the classroom*. New York: Teachers College Press.

Inhelder, B., & Piaget, J. (1964). *The early growth of logic in the child*. New York: Harper & Row.

Jackson, P. W. (1968). *Life in classrooms*. New York: Holt, Rinehart and Winston.

Johnson, M. C. (1979). *Discussion dynamics*. Series in sociolinguistics. Rowley, MA: Newbury.

Jones, S., & Aiello, J. (1973). Proxemic behavior of black and white first-, second-, third-, and fifth-grade children. *Journal of Personality and Social Psychology*, *25*, 21–27.

Joyce, B. (1975). *Variables, designs, and instruments in the search for teacher effectiveness*. San Francisco: Far West Laboratory for Educational Research and Development.

Joyce, B., & Weil, M. (1972). *Models of teaching*. Englewood Cliffs, NJ: Prentice-Hall.

Juskin, J. T. (1970). The social perception of language variations: Black and white teachers' attitudes toward speakers from different racial and social class backgrounds. Unpublished doctoral dissertation, University of Michigan, Ann Arbor.

Kagan, L. (1964). Acquisition and significance of sex typing and sex role identity. In M. Hoffman & L. Hoffman (Eds.), *Review of child development research.* New York: Russell Sage Foundation.

Keddie, N. (1973). *The myth of cultural deprivation.* Harmondsworth, England: Penguin.

Krathwohl, D. (1985). *Basic concepts of behavioral science research.* San Francisco: Jossey-Bass.

Krauss, R. M., & Glucksberg, S. (1969). The development of communication: Competence as a function of age. *Child Development, 40,* 255–266.

Labov, W. (1970). The logic of nonstandard English. In F. Williams (Ed.), *Language and poverty: Perspectives on a theme.* Chicago: Markham.

Labov, W. (1972). *Language in the inner city: Studies in the Black English vernacular.* Philadelphia: University of Pennsylvania Press.

Labov, W., Cohen, P., Robins, C., & Lewis, J. (1968). *A study of the non-standard English of Negro and Puerto Rican speakers in New York City* (Vols. 1 and 2) (Final Report of Cooperative Research Project No. 3288). New York: Columbia University.

Leiter, K. (1974). Ad-hocing in the schools: A study of placement practices in the kindergartens of two schools. In A. Cicourel (Ed.), *Language use and school performance.* New York: Academic Press.

Lenneberg, E. (1969). *Biological foundations of language.* New York: Wiley.

Marliave, R. (1980). *Beyond engaged time: Approximations of task appropriateness as a component of ongoing student learning.* Paper presented at American Educational Research Association meeting, Boston, MA.

Marx, R. W. (1983). Student perception in classrooms. *Educational Psychologist, 18,* 145–163.

McDermott, R. (1974). Achieving school failure: An anthropological approach to illiteracy and social stratification. In G. D. Spindler (Ed.), *Education and cultural process: Toward an anthropology of education.* New York: Holt, Rinehart and Winston.

McNair, K., & Joyce, B. (1979a). *Teaching styles at South Bay school: The South Bay Study, Part 1.* East Lansing: Institute for Research on Teaching.

McNair, K., & Joyce, B. (1979b). *Teachers' thoughts while teaching: The South Bay Study, Part II.* East Lansing: Institute for Research on Teaching.

McNeill, D. (1970). *The acquisition of language: The study of developmental psycholinguistics.* New York: Harper & Row.

Medley, D. M. (1979). The effectiveness of teachers. In P. L. Peterson & H. J. Walberg (Eds.), *Research on teaching: Concepts, findings and implications.* Berkeley, CA: McCutchan.

Mehan, H. (1973). Assessing children's school performance. In H. P. Dreitzel (Ed.), *Childhood and socialization. Recent sociology, 5.* London: Macmillan.

Mehan, H. (1974). Accomplishing classroom lessons. In A. Cicourel (Ed.), *Language use and school performance.* New York: Academic Press.

Mehan, H., Cazden, C. B., Coles, L., Fisher, S., & Maroules, N. (1976). *The social organization of classroom lessons* (CHIP Report 67). LaJolla, CA:

University of California, San Diego, Center for Human Information Processing.

Menyuk, P. (1969). *Sentences children use.* Cambridge: M.I.T. Press.

Menyuk, P. (1971). *The acquisition and development of language.* Englewood Cliffs, NJ: Prentice-Hall.

Merritt, M., & Humphrey, F. (1981). *Service-like events during individual work time and their contribution to the nature of communication in primary classrooms* (Final report NIE G-78-0159). Washington, D.C.: National Institute of Education.

Metropolitan Achievement Tests. (1970). New York: Harcourt Brace Jovanovich.

Michael, G., & Willis, F. (1968). The development of gestures as a function of social class, education, and sex. *The Psychological Record, 18,* 515–519.

Morine, G. (1975). Interaction analysis in the classroom: Alternative applications. In R. A. Weinberg & F. Wood (Eds.), *Observation of pupils and teachers in mainstream and special education settings: Alternative strategies.* Minneapolis: University of Minnesota.

Morine, G., & Vallance, E. (1975). *A study of teacher and pupil perceptions of classroom interaction* (Beginning Teacher Evaluation Study Technical Report). San Francisco: Far West Laboratory for Educational Research and Development.

Morine, H., & Morine, G. (1973). *Discovery: A challenge to teachers.* Englewood Cliffs, NJ: Prentice-Hall.

Morine-Dershimer, G. (1976). *Teacher judgements and pupil observations: Beauty in the eye of the beholder.* Paper presented at American Education Research Association Meeting, San Francisco.

Morine-Dershimer, G. (1979a). *Teachers' conceptions of pupils—An outgrowth of instructional context: The South Bay Study, Part III.* East Lansing: Institute for Research on Teaching.

Morine-Dershimer, G. (1979b). *Teacher plan and classroom reality: The South Bay Study, Part IV.* East Lansing: Institute for Research on Teaching.

Morine-Dershimer, G. (1982). Pupil perceptions of teacher praise. *Elementary School Journal, 82,* 421–434.

Morine-Dershimer, G. (1983). Instructional strategy and the "creation" of classroom status. *American Educational Research Journal, 20,* 645–661.

Morine-Dershimer, G. (1984). *Complexity and imagery in teacher thought: Alternative analyses of stimulated recall data.* Paper presented at American Educational Research Association meetings, New Orleans, LA.

Morine-Dershimer, G. (1985). Gender, classroom organization and grade level as factors in pupil perceptions of the classroom interaction of peers. In L. C. Wilkinson & C. B. Marrett (Eds.), *Gender-related differences in the classroom.* San Francisco: Academic Press.

Morine-Dershimer, G., & Tenenberg, M. (1977). *Participant perspectives of classroom discourse* (Proposal to the National Institute of Education). Hayward, CA: University of California at Hayward.

Morine-Dershimer, G., & Tenenberg, M. (1981). *Participant perspectives of classroom discourse* (Final report NIE G-78-0161). Washington, D.C.: National Institute of Education.

Morine-Dershimer, G., Weil, M., & Vallance, E. (1976). *Responsive teaching: The concept formation model.* Instructor's manual. Tampa, FL: National Resource

Dissemination Center.

Mueller, E. C. (1971). *An analysis of children's communications in free play*. Unpublished doctoral dissertation, Cornell University, Ithaca, NY.

National Commission on Excellence in Education. (1983). *A nation at risk: The imperative for educational reform*. A report to the nation and the Secretary of Education. U.S. Department of Education.

Nelson, K. (1973). Structure and strategy in learning to talk. *Monograph of the Society for Research in Child Development, 38* (No. 149).

Parsons, T. (1968). *Guided self-analysis system for professional development*. Berkeley, CA: Professional Development Systems.

Peterson, P., & Swing, S. (1982). Beyond time on task: Students' reports of their thought processes during direct instruction. *Elementary School Journal, 82*, 481–491.

Philips, S. U. (1972). Participation structures and communicative competence: Warm Springs children in community and classroom. In C. Cazden, D. Hymes, & V. John (Eds.), *Functions of language in the classroom*. New York: Teachers College Press.

Piaget, Jean. (1955). *The construction of reality in the child*. New York: Basic Books.

Piaget, Jean. (1962). *Play, dreams, and imitation in childhood*. New York: Norton.

Postman, N., Morine, H., & Morine, G. (1963). *Discovering your language*. New York: Holt, Rinehart and Winston.

Pride, J. B. (1970). Sociolinguistics. In J. Lyons (Ed.), *New horizons in linguistics*. Harmondsworth, England: Penguin.

Psathas, G. (1968). Comment. *American Psychologist, 23*, 135–137.

Purkey, S. C., & Smith, M. S. (1983). Effective schools: A review. *The Elementary School Journal, 83*(4), 427–452.

Rainey, M. (1969). *Style switching in a Head Start class*. University of California at Berkeley, Language and Behavior Research Laboratory, Working Paper No. 16.

Ramirez, A. (1979). *Discourse patterns during composition lessons: The sequence of speech acts*. Paper presented at American Educational Research Association meeting, San Francisco, CA.

Rist, R. (1970). Student social class and teacher self-fulfilling prophecy in ghetto education. *Harvard Educational Review, 40*, 411–450.

Roberts, P. (1966). *The Roberts English Series: A linguistic program*. New York: Harcourt Brace Jovanovich.

Robinson, W. P. (1968). *Restricted codes in sociolinguistics and the sociology of education*. Paper presented at Ninth International Seminar, University College, Dar es Salaam (December).

Rosenshine, B. (1971). *Teaching behaviours and student achievement*. Slough, England: National Foundation for Educational Research in England and Wales.

Rosenshine, B. (1977). *Primary grades instruction and student achievement gain*. Paper presented at American Educational Research Association meetings, New York.

Rowe, M. (1969). Science, silence, and sanctions. *Science and Children, 6*, 11–13.

Schlegoff, E. (1968). Sequencing in conversational opening. *American Anthropologist, 70*(6), 1075–1095.

Schrank, W. (1968). The labeling effect of ability grouping. *Journal of Educational Research, 62*, 51–52.

Schwarzer, R. (1982). *Critique of papers in symposium on "Teacher cognitions: Research and theory from multiple perspectives."* Comments presented at American Educational Research Association meetings, New York.

Shamo, G. W. (1970). *The psychological correlates of speech characteristics: On sounding "disadvantaged," a southern replication.* Paper presented at American Educational Research Association meetings, Minneapolis.

Shavelson, R. J. (1983). Review of research on teachers' pedagogical judgments, plans and decisions. *Elementary School Journal, 83*, 392–413.

Shavelson, R. J., & Stern, P. (1981). Research on teachers' pedagogical thoughts, judgments, decisions, and behavior. *Review of Educational Research, 51*, 455–498.

Shulman, L. (1974). *Teaching as clinical information processing* (Report of Panel 6, NIE Conference on Studies in Teaching). Washington, D.C.: National Institute of Education.

Siegel, S. (1956). *Nonparametric statistics for the behavioral sciences.* New York: McGraw-Hill.

Sinclair, J. M. (1973). English for effect. *Commonwealth Education Liaison Committee Newsletter, 3*, 11.

Sinclair, J. M., & Coulthard, R. M. (1974). *Toward an analysis of discourse: The English used by teachers and pupils.* London: Oxford University Press.

Slobin, D. (1967). Imitation and grammatical development in children. In N. S. Endler, L. R. Boulter, & H. Osser (Eds.), *Contemporary issues in developmental psychology.* New York: Holt, Rinehart and Winston.

Slobin, D. (1971). *Psycholinguistics.* Glenview, IL: Scott, Foresman.

Snyder, B. (1971). *The hidden curriculum.* New York: Knopf.

Soar, R. S., & Soar, R. M. (1979). Emotional climate and management. In P. L. Peterson & H. J. Walberg (Eds.), *Research on teaching: Concepts, findings and implications.* Berkeley, CA: McCutchan.

Stallings, J. A., & Kaskowitz, D. H. (1974). *Follow-through classroom observation evaluation, 1972–73.* Menlo Park, CA: Standford Research Institute.

Stallings, J., Needels, M., & Stayrook, N. (1979). *How to change the process of teaching basic reading skills in secondary schools.* Menlo Park, CA: SRI International.

Strandberg, T. E., & Griffith, J. (1968). *A study of the effects of training in visual literacy on verbal language behavior.* Charleston: Eastern Illinois University.

Stubbs, M. (1975). Teaching and talking: A sociolinguistic approach to classroom interaction. In G. Chanan & S. Delamont (Eds.), *Frontiers of classroom research.* Slough, England: National Foundation for Educational Research.

Stubbs, M. (1976). *Language, schools and classrooms.* London: Methuen.

Taba, H. (1967). *Teachers' handbook for elementary social studies.* Reading, MA: Addison-Wesley.

Tikunoff, W. J., & Ward, B. A. (1976). *Some selected findings from three studies* (Effective Teacher Education Program Report). San Francisco: Far West Laboratory.

Torode, B. (1974). *Constituting the classroom context* [Mimeo]. Dublin: Trinity College.

Turner, V. (1969). *The ritual process: Structure and anti-structure.* Chicago:

Aldine-Atherton.

Walker, R., & Adelman, C. (1972). *Toward a sociography of the classroom* (Report to Social Science Research Council). London, England.

Walker, R., & Adelman, C. (1975). *A guide to classroom observation.* London: Methuen.

Walker, R., & Adelman, C. (1976). Strawberries. In M. Stubbs & S. Delamont (Eds.), *Explorations in classroom observation.* London: Wiley.

Wallat, C., & Green, J. L. (1982). Construction of social norms. In K. Borman (Ed.), *Social life of children in a changing society.* Hillsdale, NJ: Erlbaum.

Weeks, T. E. (1970). Speech registers in young children. In *Papers and Reports on Child Language Development* (No. 1). Stanford, CA: Stanford University Committee on Linguistics (March).

Weinstein, R. (1982). *Expectations in the classroom: The student perspective.* Paper presented at American Educational Research Association meetings, New York.

Weinstein, R. (1983). Student perceptions of schooling. *Elementary School Journal, 83,* 287–312.

Wight, J. (1971). Dialect in school. *Educational Review, 24,* 1.

Wight, J. (1975). Language through the looking glass. *Ideas,* Curriculum Magazine, *31.* Goldsmiths College, London.

Wight, J., & Norris, R. (1970). *Teaching English to West Indian children* (Schools Council Working Paper 29). London: Methuen.

Wilkinson, L. C., & Calculator, S. (1982). Requests and responses in peer-directed reading groups. *American Educational Research Journal, 19,* 107–120.

Wilkinson, L. C., & Dollaghan, C. (1979). Peer communication in first grade reading groups. *Theory into Practice, 18*(4), 267–274.

Winne, P. H., & Marx, R. W. (1982). Students' and teachers' views of thinking processes involved in classroom learning. *Elementary School Journal, 82,* 493–518.

Wood, B. S. (Ed.) (1977). *Development of functional communication competencies: Pre-K–grade 6.* Urbana, IL: ERIC Clearinghouse on Reading and Communication Skills.

Woods, P. (1975). "Showing them up" in secondary school. In G. Chanan & S. Delamont (Eds.), *Frontiers of classroom research.* Slough, England: National Foundation for Educational Research.

Index

(Series page continued from p. *ii*)

BARBARA LARRIVEE, *Effective Teaching for Successful Mainstreaming*

GRETA MORINE-DERSHIMER, *Talking, Listening, and Learning in Elementary Classrooms*

FORTHCOMING

DEE ANN SPENCER, *Contemporary Women Teachers: Balancing School and Home*